Ants, Galileo, and Gandhi

Designing the Future of Business through Nature, Genius, and Compassion

Edited by Sissel Waage

Ants, Galileo, & Gandhi

Designing the Future of Business through Nature, Genius, and Compassion

Greenleaf
PUBLISHING
2 0 0 3

© 2003 Greenleaf Publishing Limited
(excepting chapters 2,5 and 9, printed with permission)

Published by Greenleaf Publishing Limited
Aizlewood's Mill
Nursery Street
Sheffield S3 8GG
UK

Printed on paper made from at least 75% post-consumer waste
using TCF and ECF bleaching.
Printed and bound by The Cromwell Press, UK.
Cover by Utter.

British Library Cataloguing in Publication Data:
 A catalogue record for this book is available from the British Library.

 Hardback: ISBN 1 874719 76 4
 Paperback: ISBN 1 874719 71 3

Contents

Acknowledgments

This book is truly the result of many people's work. The seeds can be traced back to Sweden and the work of Karl-Henrik Robèrt, John Holmberg and other scientists, too numerous to list here, who developed first The Natural Step Framework and principles of sustainability. Their ongoing efforts continue to expand and inspire innovations in businesses, government agencies, non-profit organizations, communities, and universities. The proliferation of initiatives inspired by The Natural Step has enabled ongoing refinements in the development of a framework for addressing sustainability issues.

Concurrently, a number of other sustainability-focused efforts have emerged in the past 15 years that have built the sustainability field. All the contributors in this volume, and the organizations with which they are affiliated, represent this work. Many other theorists and practitioners are also working on sustainability, but, owing to space constraints, are not represented in this book. The sustainability field is in the fortunate position of having innovation and forward progress outstripping the ability to capture examples in writing. However, the full range of ongoing efforts informs many of the chapters in this book.

The book is the direct outgrowth from The Natural Step's 2002 conference on sustainability, held in San Francisco, CA. The title is the brainchild of Catherine Gray and George Basile, developed for Catherine's speech at the conference. (It was adopted following input from Chris Green and Eric Olson.) An amazing set of speakers was assembled at the conference thanks to the tireless efforts of Catherine Gray, George Basile, Ruth Rominger and Jill Rosenblum, as well as the entire US team of The Natural Step: Amanda Dates, Sahra Girshick, Ann Grodnik, John Hagen, Caroline McDowell, Sara Mossman, Chris Pemberton, and Rajesh Shah. The conference production was flawlessly managed by Christie Basile. The Natural Step US Board of Directors was extremely supportive, attending and speaking at the event. Our sincere thanks go to Ray Anderson, Anthony Cortese, Diane Dillon-

Ridgley, Matt Klein, Dane Nichols, Salley Ranney, Sarah Severn, Edward Skloot, Mike Wick, and Jin Zidell. In addition, board members and staff from The Natural Step International offices—including Australia, Canada, England, Israel, Japan, New Zealand, South Africa, and Sweden—participated and ensured that the event was a rich dialog in moving toward global sustainability. Thank you, Limor Alouf, David Cook, Magnus Huss, Brian Nattrass, Mary Altomare Nattrass, Karl-Henrik Robèrt, Lin Roberts, Jimmy Sjöblom, Sachiko Takami, Chris Tipler, and Peter Willis.

Most of the contributors to this volume were speakers at the conference. I would like to thank each of you for taking the time to develop your speeches into chapters. Several of the chapters, however, were written by people who did not speak at the conference but who are undertaking work that is important for moving toward sustainability. Enormous thanks to each of you for developing chapters, some on relatively quick time-lines. And to all the contributors, I would like to express my sincere appreciation for your good humor and dedication in the numerous rounds of edits and rewrites. You have all made this project an enjoyable process.

I would also like to thank Island Press for granting us permission to reprint a version of the prolog to Gretchen Daily's and Katherine Ellison's *The New Economy of Nature*. The World Economic Forum and Yale University kindly granted us permission to reprint an adapted version of Alois Flatz's chapter. Ecotrust allowed us to reprint the coastal temperate rainforest map. We are grateful for these permissions allowing us to draw on past work.

In the editing process, Ruth Rominger, Jill Rosenblum, Mike Smith, and Heather Sarantis provided extremely useful input on refining and finalizing the manuscript. Your input has immeasurably improved the work. Karl-Henrik Robèrt and Magnus Huss, of The Natural Step, Stockholm, Sweden, also read early drafts and provided thoughtful comments. Many thanks for your time and recommendations for strengthening the manuscript. In addition, I would like to offer my immense thanks to Maya Porter, John Maybury, Candice Chase, and Dave Reed for serving as voluntary proofreaders for chapters of the book.

Sincere thanks also go to John Stuart and Dean Bargh, of Greenleaf Publishing, for all of their work on this project. I, and the entire US team of The Natural Step, are impressed with your work on publishing leading titles on sustainability and business.

There is not sufficient space to thank all the donors and supporters who make our work possible. As a non-profit organization, The Natural Step has been extremely fortunate to receive support from a number of amazing philanthropic foundations and public agencies—including the Surdna Foundation, Garfield Foundation, Compton Foundation, Roy A. Hunt Foundation, Conrad N. Hilton Foundation, Overbrook Foundation, Kwijibo Charitable Foundation, Arntz Family Foundation, Fred Gellert Family Foundation, V. Kann Ramussen Foundation, National Endowment for the Arts, Silicon Valley Social Venture Fund, Interface Foundation, Arthur M. Blank Family Foundation, Community Foundation for the National Capital Region, Rockefeller Financial Services, and the Jin and Linda Zidell Fund of the Marin Community Foundation. In addition, there are numerous individuals who act as our angels, including the members of Eleanor's Circle and the Sustainable Society, Michael Baldwin, Chrissie and Charlie Bascom, Danielle Blank, Nina Brown, Bina and Brian Garfield, Mats Lederhausen, Jennie McCann, Mark Parnes,

Jonathan Roseman, Vicki and Roger Sant, Candace Skarlatos, and Eleanor Wasson. We are grateful for your support.

Finally, I would also like to thank Steven, with whom I have the immense joy of travelling through life. Thank you for sharing your excitement and knowledge, for reading drafts and for fielding numerous questions with patience and an endless good humor. *Hjertlig takk, min kjeare venn.*

The extensive group of people who have contributed to the development of this book illustrate what is needed to address the global challenges that we all face. The pathways forward will continue to emerge as increasing numbers of organizations and individuals address sustainability concerns. It is my hope that this book will both further ongoing change and inspire new efforts.

Sissel Waage
The Natural Step
San Francisco, CA
February 2003

Preface

Galileo illustrated the power and politics of changing our perspective on the world. His work, building on Copernicus's theories, ultimately enabled people to understand that the Earth orbits the Sun. No longer was the Earth seen as the center of the Universe. Instead, it became possible to see a broader system in a new way.

Similarly, we need a new vantage point on modern business. Such a shift would highlight interrelationships between specific companies and the broader economic, social, and ecological systems in which we all live.

The current view on businesses tightly circumscribes the "system" within which a firm operates. Often, customers and the supply chain are the immediate focus. Business decisions seldom consider that healthy ecological systems provide critical resources, which may be both limited and unable to absorb our industrial waste. Corporate decision-makers also tend to overlook the destabilizing effects of disparities in wealth and the inability of many people to access basic resources and address their fundamental needs.

However, a Galileo type of alternative perspective on businesses is emerging. It is informed by an understanding of the basic dynamics between ecological, social, and economic systems. The chapters in this book reveal early signs of efforts to operationalize this new perspective within enterprises. The cases show the enormous opportunities for innovation and demonstrate that change is already occurring.

Why ants, Galileo, and Gandhi?

The grouping of ants, Galileo, and Gandhi offers a metaphor for generating a new perspective on the dynamics of business. Ants symbolize the lessons to be learned from Nature and the dependence of individual beings on broader, complex systems.

Galileo embodies brilliance in perceiving and proving that the current paradigm is flawed. Gandhi exemplifies brilliant compassion and determination in fighting for fundamental change. All of these attributes are increasingly relevant in a world where, globally, we are experiencing both a steady decline in life-supporting resources and a rise in demands. Disparities between rich and poor are increasing, and essentials such as clean air, safe water, and productive topsoil are becoming rare. Poverty and inadequate access to water, food, healthcare, and education affect the context in which companies operate. Limited water quantity, air quality, and soil productivity also shape the opportunities available to businesses, and people, around the world.

Recognition of these challenges is sparking innovation within the private sector, where the first glimmers of change can be seen. What are emerging are 21st-century enterprises that recognize their reliance on broad social and ecological systems ("ants"), incorporate sparks of genius rooted in rigorous analyses ("Galileo"), and acknowledge the importance of compassion and determination within any endeavor ("Gandhi"). Today, many efforts at integrating sustainability into businesses are nascent and vary in scope and focus. Yet pioneering companies show that new opportunities emerge from recognizing the broader systems on which all businesses rely. Efforts to work *with* the ecological and social dynamics of vibrancy and resilience offer a new space for innovation. Companies are stepping into this space and exploring innovative approaches to developing sustainability-focused products, operations, and strategies.

These sustainability-inspired business efforts are considering new ways to address human needs and desires. The most promising approaches are based on systems thinking and recognition of the links between "upstream" and "down-stream" effects of actions. That is, understanding the undesired "downstream" impacts of a firm's practices draws attention "upstream" (to the sources of problems). This assessment highlights the most expedient approach—to design these impacts out of enterprises from the very start.

These efforts pivot on the broadened perspective. It is a perspective rooted in the understanding that all companies accrue an array of returns at all times—assessed in terms of financial, ecological, and social measures. All of these parameters will become increasingly relevant to companies, as they are held responsible for their full "footprint" resulting from the actions and practices both within firms as well as throughout their supply chains. In this changing context, the expanded perspective of sustainability thinking offers a powerful approach to creating far more responsive and aware business models.

Concurrent with these developments, however, a growing number of people—including activists, analysts, consumers, and members of the general public—are asking critical questions about both the responsibilities of businesses as well as the sincerity and results of corporate sustainability initiatives. Are current efforts reflective of fundamental change? Or are they merely superficial distractions from core problems? Can large, complex organizations be retrofitted and reinvented into new sustainability-focused models and enterprises? Are measurable environmental and social performance improvements under way? Are the theories and tools of sustainability-focused businesses actually being applied and having an impact?

Although sustainability efforts in business are still a work in progress, it is increasingly clear that key elements of this new generation of enterprises will be radically different from those of our contemporary modern industrial economy. The core distinctions between what currently exists and what is being created can best be communicated through a combination of the characteristics of ants, Galileo, and Gandhi.

Operate like ants

Ants are known for their hard work and seemingly chaotic colonies. Ant colonies, however, operate within a sophisticated system of what are effectively shared goals and overarching operating principles that inform their actions. Individual actions occur within the context of complicated dynamics throughout the colony. The impacts of one ant's work are most accurately understood within the context of the group's efforts and the systems (both "social" and ecological) in which the ants live.

Similarly, for businesses, it takes a common understanding of sustainability and overarching operating principles to begin moving in the direction of sustainability. The shift toward sustainability will be clear not merely from the actions of a few companies adopting new practices but within the broader context of sectors and economies adopting new models for addressing human needs and desires. For businesses, this shift will mean forging unusual partnerships and collaborations that reflect new understandings of linkages and "ripple effects" between businesses and across broader social, economic, and ecological systems.

Innovate like Galileo

Broad-based action is necessary for innovating and shifting society towards sustainability. It is, however, insufficient. Galileo-like brilliance will also be essential, grounded in examination of systems and generation of new ways of understanding system dynamics. Simply put, a new perspective on the economy and businesses must be based on intelligent questioning, theorizing, and testing. Only through such discovery will we create new business paradigms, principles, and practices that work with ecological dynamics and foster socially vibrant, resilient, and just systems.

These new principles will not only be rigorous and rooted in scientific methods of examination but will also help guide companies in the direction of sustainability. The principles will be no more constraining to businesspeople than is the law of gravity to engineers. Just as engineers must work *with* the system in which their designs are built, so too must businesspeople. It is therefore best to know about these systems and their operating principles when designing enterprises, so that trade and commerce can work *within* (rather than against) the full range of ecological, social, and economic dynamics at play in the world.

Lead like Gandhi

Yet collaboration and innovation alone are the ingredients of many contemporary businesses. Few are sustainable. The distinguishing element needed for businesses to shift towards sustainability is best expressed through the determination, focus and compassion of Mohandas K. Gandhi and other leaders who succeeded in bringing about fundamental shifts in society. Facing a formidable challenge, Gandhi maintained a bold vision and acted with deep compassion and concern for all life. He succeeded because of his uncompromising compassion and determination. The transformation of business and society towards sustainability will need these same attributes in the face of the seemingly impossible.

Sustainability-oriented business similarly offers an opportunity to lead positive change rather than to follow it. For companies, the opportunity lies in having a sustainability-inspired vision of the enterprise and rooting it in compassion and respect for all species of the present and future. This approach increasingly has the winds in its sails as the public demands responsible, honest, transparent companies.

Integrating the lessons of Nature, genius, and compassion

These initial elements of the sustainability story are like all good stories. They have an essence and defy efforts to take them apart. The individual components lose their magic when viewed alone. As the stories of new businesses continue to develop, they will increasingly show that it takes the integration of the characteristics of ants, Galileo, and Gandhi to move toward sustainability.

In the following pages you will read about a wide range of work on sustainability and business. The book has been divided into five parts to present a set of theories emerging about sustainability and its application: to business strategy and operations, to financial-sector practices, to accountability and reporting drivers, and to pathways towards organizational change. Together, these parts show the current range of sustainability theories and applications.

What this book contains

Introduction and Part 1:
the transition to sustainability-oriented enterprises

Both the Introduction (Chapter 1) and Part 1 (Chapters 2–4) provide context and highlight some of the new ways of thinking about business and sustainability issues. In the Introduction, Ray Anderson describes his experience with leading Interface, Inc., a commercial carpet company, towards a sustainability-focused business model.

In Chapter 2, Gretchen Daily and Katherine Ellison draw attention to the role that ecological systems play in undergirding social and economic systems. They argue that we should value ecosystem services (such as clean air and water) as an integral part of our economy and society.

In Chapter 3, I provide an overview of the sustainability field and various approaches for integrating these concepts into businesses. I also offer a growing set of indications that changes are already under way in the private sector.

In Chapter 4, Karl-Henrik Robèrt discusses The Natural Step's sustainability framework used for integrating ecological and social issues into decision-making processes.

Part 2: case studies of evolving business initiatives

In Part 2 (Chapters 5–8), the "ant colony" begins to emerge through case studies that show how sustainability concepts are being applied to a range of businesses. In Chapter 5, David Hudson and Lynelle Preston examine Hewlett Packard's dematerialization efforts. Through a detailed analysis Hudson and Preston reveal that important ecological gains can be made, especially through a service model, but they caution that decreases in material use in one product may be undercut if total production continues to rise.

In Chapter 6, Derek Smith describes efforts to integrate sustainability practices throughout a medium-sized business, Norm Thompson Outfitters. He argues that the process has fundamentally been about change management, *not* environmental management.

In Chapter 7, Cecilia Danks, Martin Goebel, and Karen Steer explain innovative solutions to increasing the scale of small, place-based companies and accessing mainstream markets without compromising the ecological and social aspects of sustainability. By drawing on the examples from the wood products, beef, and agriculture sectors, Danks *et al.* show that small businesses in rural communities throughout the US Pacific Northwest are organizing in production and marketing alliances—mirroring their own "ant colonies"—that follow sustainability-oriented principles and practices in order to sell their products under specialized or joint labels.

In Chapter 8, the chief executive officer of sustainability-focused Verdant Power, Matt Klein, lays out a new set of financing mechanisms that leverage the integrated (social, ecological, and financial) focus at the core of the business.

Part 3: case studies from the financial services sector

In Part 3 (Chapters 9 and 10), another component of the emerging "ant colony" can be seen through changes in the financial sector. Alois Flatz, the director of research and development (R&D) for Sustainable Asset Management, writes about the Dow Jones Sustainability Index and the process of reflecting sustainability concerns within a financial index, in Chapter 9.

In Chapter 10, Jennifer Sokolove examines Shorebank Enterprise Pacific and explores the provision of finances and credit in relation to new sustainability-oriented companies in the Pacific Northwest region of the USA.

Part 4: reporting and accountability

Part 4 (Chapter 11) draws out the early, still-developing characteristics of Gandhi and the role they play in informing sustainability—in this case, through accountability and reporting. Allen White, of the Global Reporting Initiative, explains the factors that have led to the shift to greater accountability and sustainability reporting.

Part 5: pathways forward to organizational and societal change

The final part, Part 5 (Chapters 12–14), completes the story of how to begin changing a complex organization towards sustainability. In Chapter 12, Juli Torok and I summarize work on organizational change.

In Chapter 13, Hilary Bradbury describes the important role of personal engagement in the work of sustainability-oriented organizational and corporate change.

In the final chapter (Chapter 14), I draw the strands of the book together, arguing that we should see this set of stories as an integrated whole that begin to reveal the systems-based approach that this field of work requires.

The shift has begun

The sustainability initiatives described in this book are at various stages of development and integration. As a set, however, the chapters illustrate that a shift towards sustainability-informed practices is under way across sectors and business sizes. It can no longer be said that the only companies responsive to the issues are under pressure from regulators and activists. Rather, these chapters reveal that sustainability concepts and practices are now fully emerging and are beginning to permeate enterprises across the economic landscape. Sustainability-oriented change is slowly becoming a reality. These changes will redefine successful 21st-century companies not only in terms of financial performance but also in terms of social and ecological factors.

The story of our future lies ahead and is only now beginning to be written. The cases in this book show glimmers of the changes to come. It will be innovators with strokes of genius, a focus on interrelated ecological, social, and economic systems, and deep-seated compassion and determination who will continue writing the story.

Sissel Waage
The Natural Step
San Francisco, CA
February 2003

1
Introduction
Envisioning the prototypical company of the 21st century

Ray Anderson
Interface, Inc., USA

It is a special privilege for me to write this Introduction. I have a deep appreciation of Dr. Karl-Henrik Robèrt's work as the founder of The Natural Step, the organization through whose efforts this book exists. I hope to provide a framework for what follows in this extraordinary collection of real examples of the rethinking and reshaping of economic enterprises that have been inspired by sustainability principles. I shall draw heavily on my experiences in my own enterprise, Interface, Inc., and will define the essential role The Natural Step plays in the ongoing transformation of my company toward sustainability as we seek to build an economically, ecologically, and socially sound enterprise.

One way or another, each of the enterprises described in this book has, of its own volition, begun to work through the complex process of integrating sustainability principles into its business philosophy and practices. I offer at the outset, by way of the Interface example, the general model that each of the organizations discussed throughout this book has undertaken in its own unique way. I hope, in the process, to provide a clear picture of how the entire industrial system must change to survive.

Others make the case that such change must happen; this book makes the case that such change is happening. The individual examples underscore the wisdom that physicist Amory Lovins, co-founder of the Rocky Mountain Institute, often expresses: "If it exists, it must be possible." Alan AtKisson, a sustainability advocate, advisor and author (see AtKisson 1999), offers a metaphor of ameba-like progress among early movers—people and companies—who are the "pseudopods" reaching out to establish a new foothold for moving the "body" of the industrial system to a new state—harmony with the natural world on which the entire economic system is utterly dependent.

As I write, I am wearing two hats. The first is that of an entrepreneurial industrialist, the founder of Interface, Inc., a start-up-from-scratch venture that has grown to be a billion-dollar, global manufacturer of carpets, textiles, and architectural products. The second hat is one that I share with every living creature, that of an astronaut on Spaceship Earth.

However, the mind beneath those two hats is one. It is reconciled to the inseparability and interdependence of the world of business and the natural world. This view may not be held by many, or even most, of my peers in the business world. I did not always hold it myself.

For the first 21 years of my company's existence I never gave one thought to what we were taking from the Earth to feed our petroleum-intensive manufacturing processes, or what we were doing to the Earth with our waste, emissions, and effluent. It was not until August 1994 that my own change occurred, when I read a book that changed my view of the world, my life, and, eventually, my company's very nature. The book was Paul Hawken's *The Ecology of Commerce* (1993).

I had been asked to make a speech to a newly formed company task force that was convening to assess our company's worldwide environmental position. The task force was assembled in response to growing customer questions about what Interface was doing for the environment. At the time, we had no good answers. In thinking about that speech, which I really did not want to make, I could not get beyond, "We obey the law; we comply."

At that propitious moment, as if by pure serendipity, Hawken's book landed on my desk. Reading it, I quickly came to a chapter entitled "The Death of Birth." That phrase, coined by the biologist E.O. Wilson to describe species extinction, felt like the point of a spear, a spear that I feel in my chest to this day. It was an epiphanal experience. For the first time in my life I became sensitized to the responsibility that we *homo sapiens*—astronauts on Spaceship Earth—have for the damage we are doing to our spacecraft and, as a consequence, to ourselves and to the countless creatures that share with us the thin shell of life that is the biosphere.

Absorbed in Paul Hawken's treatise, I was convicted as a plunderer of the Earth and as part of the system that is systematically fouling the passenger capsule of Spaceship Earth. Over time, that conviction has grown and grown. One needs only to take the long view—the truly long view of evolutionary time—to know that the present take–make–waste linear system, driven by fossil fuels, wasteful and abusive of a finite biosphere, simply cannot go on and on and on.

Well, I made that speech, drawing freely on Hawken's material. I shocked the entire task force with the challenge to lead our company to environmental sustainability and, through our example, to lead the entire industrial world to a new model for an industrial enterprise.

But, how to even think about sustainability? How to define it for ourselves? How to begin to move in that direction? And, just as important, how to communicate such a vision or present a plan of action to our company's 6,500 people, few of whom had ever heard the word "sustainability," much less thought about how to meld it into their work lives? These were the daunting questions with which I wrestled for a year, while the task force members went back to their businesses with my challenge to lead. Only one thing was really clear: this was a mountain to climb, a mountain much taller than Everest and infinitely more difficult. We named it "Mount Sustainability."

For that year, while I struggled with my questions and while the task force members confronted the status quo in their individual businesses, I spoke to our people at every opportunity to bring them along on the climb. It was easy to articulate the "why?" of the imperative to climb this mountain, but not so easy to offer "hows." I am sure our people, for the most part, discounted my ranting as the program of the month that would surely go away in time, because it was just too hard to really do. It was too hard to even think about doing. It was the early days of the sustainability movement and there was no "how-to" manual.

But I stayed on the case. I read. I learned. I retained the best advisors that I could find. I engaged members of the task force to help work out ways to do something, anything, to make a start. And, gradually, a plan took shape. The plan clicked into place in my mind one night as I was watching the movie *Mind Walk* (Bernd Capra 1991), based on Fritjof Capra's book, *The Turning Point* (1988). Capra had written about and in the film Liv Ullman, the actor–scientist, was talking about the interconnectedness of all things. Although they were describing things at the subatomic particle level, I began to think about the connections between Interface and its various constituencies. That thought process resulted in the schematic shown in Figure 1.1, depicting our company in terms of its connections to its customers and its suppliers (the supply chain), to its communities, and to the Earth (to the lithosphere [the Earth's crust] and to the biosphere).

The circle at the center of the diagram represents Interface. Inside that circle are its people, capital, and processes. Economists often put "technology" where I have put "processes," but, to my mind, "processes" is the broader word and better choice. At the core are the company's values. Of course, this diagram describes every organization. The combination is unique for each company, but the general picture is the same for all. Yet no company stands alone. Any company is connected to a number of important constituencies. In our case, Interface is part of a supply chain, with suppliers and customers. Products flow through that supply chain in one direction; money flows in the other direction.

The supply chain does not stand alone either. It is connected to some other important constituencies. Our suppliers are dependent on Earth's lithosphere for organic and inorganic materials. A very small amount of our raw material is natural, coming from the biosphere. Our processes are, unfortunately, connected to Earth's biosphere by the waste-streams and emissions that we produce. And the products we make, at the end of their useful lives, go to landfill or incinerators, creating a further pollution load for Earth's biosphere.

We are connected to our community as well. Our people come from the communities in which we are located. Their wages return to the community's economy. Our capital comes from a sector of the community—the financial sector. If we are fortunate enough to earn sufficient profits, dividends are returned to those investors, along with interest to our lenders and, we hope, capital appreciation to our shareholders. Government is part of community, too. We are connected to it through laws, regulations, and, of course, the taxes we pay.

With these linkages in place we have the typical company of the 20th century and early 21st century. There are good linkages, bad linkages, and some missing

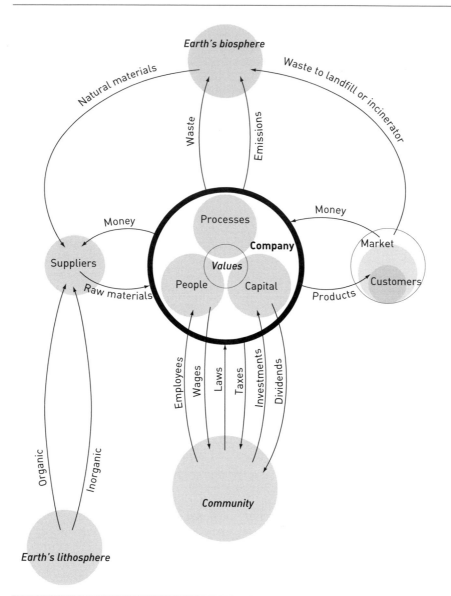

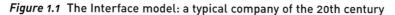

Figure 1.1 The Interface model: a typical company of the 20th century

linkages that should be added. If you are a businessperson, this diagram will describe your organization as well and every one of your suppliers and customers. This is a diagram of the ubiquitous, unsustainable enterprise and its unsustainable supply chain.

In a general sense, it is a diagram of the entire industrial system. Each supplier is an organization with people, capital, processes, and values. So, too, is each customer. The diagram is a description of the whole industrial system that has arisen out of the first industrial revolution—taking by extraction from the Earth; making by linear, fossil-fuel-driven, abusive processes; and wasting through emissions and waste-streams—all to deliver products that end up in landfills and incinerators. And notice the relationship with the community—it is very "arm's-length," especially with its employees:

- With employees: "we will offer you wages for work"
- With investors: "send us your money"
- With governments: "give us your laws, take our taxes, and go away"
- With the community: "send us your people"

As for Interface, if this diagram is all there is to describe the company, then Interface is just typical. However, we are trying to transform our company into something different. I have called that new organizational state the "prototypical company of the 21st century." Let us see what that means, step by step. How do we get there? What is the plan?

Scaling the seven faces of Mount Sustainability

We are pursuing this goal—of becoming the prototypical company of the 21st century—on seven fronts simultaneously, although we are at different stages of progress with each. You might say we are climbing the "seven faces" of that mountain. We hope the seven climbs will meet at the point at the top, symbolically representing zero environmental "footprint." The system conditions of The Natural Step define that point, and define sustainability for us. Through hundreds of projects, our research subsidiary is driving this effort. Every part of the business is engaged right down to the factory floor to create that prototypical company of the 21st century.

Face 1: zero waste

The first face of the mountain is shown in Figure 1.2. It is the face of "zero waste." In pursuit of zero waste, to attack an unwanted linkage to the biosphere—that is, to put an "X" on the unwanted "waste" linkage in the diagram—we have launched an effort we call QUEST, an acronym for "quality, utilizing employee suggestions and teamwork." This initiative is our total quality management program and

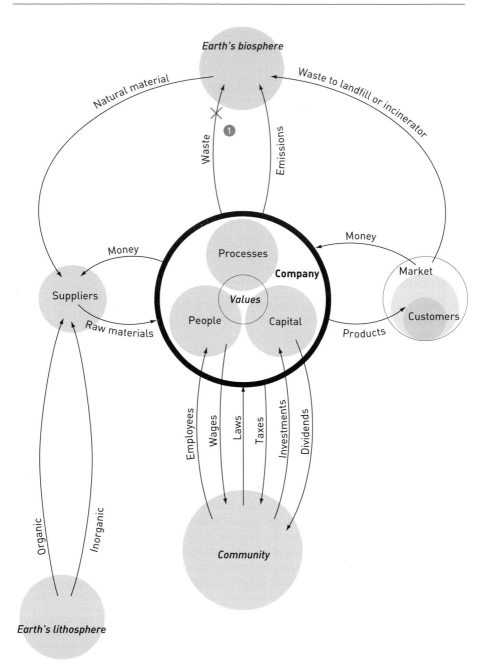

Note: the linkage targeted at this face is labeled **❶**; the cross indicates an attack on that linkage, to move towards zero waste

Figure 1.2 **The Interface model, face 1: zero waste through QUEST (quality, utilizing employee suggestions and teamwork)**

much more. Quality, to us, means zero waste of any kind. Any waste is bad—a mispriced invoice or a misdirected shipment, as well as scrap or defect. Anything that we do not do right the first time, any cost that goes into our product that does not produce value for our customers, is waste. Against ideal operational standards—which would have zero waste—we identified US$70 million in waste in 1994, representing 10% of sales, a figure that has grown in absolute terms as the business has grown.

We were on a mission to cut waste by half by the end of 1997. However, it took us six years to reach an index of 0.49 (51% reduction), yielding US$165 million in savings up to that point. Although we lost ground against the index in 2001 and 2002, with poor operating schedules resulting from economic slowdown, we have added US$44 million to savings against the baseline of 1994, bringing the cumulative total to US$209 million (see Fig. 1.3). This amount is in real money: hard dollars. It is paying for the rest of the revolution that we are engineering in our company, which we call EcoSense. One result has been an overall reduction of scrap to landfill of more than 60% from 1994 levels, and by 80% or more for most operations. QUEST has provided 28% of operating income over the nearly eight-year period.

We reframed QUEST for the second and third three-year periods. We found, after the early savings, that with a larger company there was still US$80 million (per year!) in waste. We will pursue this initiative until all waste is driven out of our company, which will require reinvention of our company over and over. Therefore, we must be a "learning company," which calls for great focus on our people and their development. It also means an unrelenting striving for perfection, or zero waste.

Face 2: benign emissions

The second face of our mountain is the face of "benign emissions," at which we begin to attack another unwanted linkage to the biosphere. We inventoried every smokestack and every outlet pipe in our company to see what and how much was being emitted. Since then, we have continually reduced emissions. Including acquisitions since 1994, we started with 292 smokestacks. Over the period 1995–2002 we shut down 109 smokestacks (a 39% reduction). I hope to live to see the last one closed. Furthermore, a total of 22 effluent pipes has been reduced to a total of 10 such pipes (a 55% reduction). Factories with no outlet stacks or effluent pipes—that is the vision!

However, we know that to prevent toxic emissions altogether we must go upstream and prevent those toxic substances from entering our factories in the first place. What comes in will go out—as product, waste or emissions. We are staggered by how difficult this undertaking has proven to be. The inputs to our factories (and everyone else's) are replete with substances that should never have been taken from the lithosphere in the first place. Nature put some of it there 3.85 billion years ago and it should be left there; we could not have evolved in its presence. Filters are not the answer; end-of-pipe solutions are not sustainable. What do you do with the dirty filters? The first and second laws of thermodynamics tell us there is no place called "away" to throw them. So we have learned

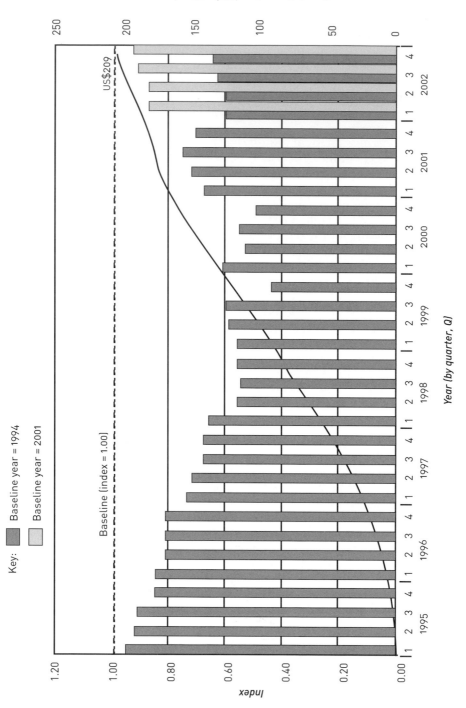

Figure 1.3 Interface, Inc.: cumulative results of QUEST (quality, utilizing employee suggestions and teamwork), from the first quarter (Q1) of 1995 to the fourth quarter (Q3) of 2002

to put the filters in our brains, not at the end of the pipes, and to work upstream on the inputs.

Face 3: renewable energy

The third face is that of "renewable energy," where, to climb to the top, we must, in time, use solar, wind, and hydrogen to run our processes, with the possibility of gas turbines and biomass in the short-term. This shift will chip away at numerous unwanted linkages, both to the lithosphere and to the biosphere. There is good news on this front. Power from photovoltaic cells is coming down in cost. Wind power is already competitive with fossil fuels. Fuel cells are improving rapidly.

At Interface, our first large photovoltaic project was a 127 kWp (at peak sunlight) to produce the world's first Solar-made™ carpet. Our specifier customers love the idea. Who cares if the electricity costs a bit more? It is the right thing to do. We have contracted in Canada, the United Kingdom and Holland for green power, mostly wind and biomass. It costs a premium, but with reduced usage through efficiencies it is the right thing to do—and the smart thing. Solar-made™ carpet sells in Canada and Europe, too.

Thus, encouraged by the marketplace, we have declared all fossil fuel energy to be waste under QUEST—first, to be reduced to the irreducible minimum through efficiency improvement, then to be replaced by renewable energy. The initial emphasis is on efficiency. Energy saving is far less costly than energy generating, by any means.

Face 4: closed-loop recycling

The next face to scale is "closed-loop recycling," during which we further reduce unwanted linkages and bring new linkages into being. Through this work, two cycles are introduced. First, we introduce a natural, organic cycle that uses natural raw materials to make compostable products ("dust to dust"); second, we introduce a technical cycle, giving human-made materials and precious organic molecules life after life through recycling.

However, the recycling operation must be driven by renewable energy, too; otherwise, we will use more fossil fuel to supply the process with energy than we will save in petrochemical-based materials in the first place. Recycling without renewable energy is a misplaced focus, but, if we can get it right, we will never have to take another drop of oil from the Earth. Cutting the fossil fuel umbilical cord is also a part of the vision, along with factories without stacks. Standing in the way, however, is the next face: transportation.

Face 5: resource-efficient transportation and logistics

"Resource-efficient transportation (logistics)" is the face that is least within our control. We can video-conference to avoid making unnecessary trips for meetings and we can drive the most efficient vehicles available. We can site our factories close to their markets and plan logistics for maximum efficiency. But, unless we choose to shut down contact with our customers and go out of business we are dependent on the transportation industry for more sustainable logistical options. Isn't everybody? I see this face as one of the hardest to conquer.

Yet Peter Russell's "global brain" (1995) is waking up. Honda and Toyota have introduced hybrid gas–electric cars. German companies are working on jet engines that use hydrogen. Daimler-Benz has invested millions in a fuel-cell venture in Canada. Amory Lovins is developing his "hypercar" (Hawken *et al.* 1999).

When we have done all else to reduce the greenhouse gases associated with transportation, we will close the remaining "carbon gap" with carbon offsets. "Trees for travel" and other offset programs will have to bridge the gap if we are to realize carbon-neutral, and thus climate-neutral, transportation. So, for every 4,000 miles one of us flies in a commercial jet, we plant a tree. When that tree is fully grown, in 200 years or so, Earth will have got even for that trip. This, you see, is a long-term strategy.

Face 6: the sensitivity hook-up

The "sensitivity hook-up," our sixth face, spawns numerous new and desirable connections: service to and investment in the community, especially in education, together with closer relations with suppliers, customers, and among ourselves. It is getting everybody on the same plan, understanding where we are going and why. These efforts lead to increased awareness of the thousands of little things we can all do to inch toward sustainability, breaking unwanted connections. Ties to the community, to our suppliers and customers and within our organization are all changed and strengthened. The principles of natural capitalism (Hawken *et al.* 1999) and the system conditions of The Natural Step become at once our shared framework and our compass, pointing the way and acting as a magnet, drawing us toward the summit of the mountain. The ISO 14001 environmental management system is a given, a map for tracking progress. We have coupled it with The Natural Step for a goal, a destination.

One result of Interface's commitment to involving its employees in sustainability efforts was that *Fortune* magazine selected us as one of the 100 best companies in the USA to work for in 1997 and 1998. Our people said so, citing the galvanizing effect of climbing "Mount Sustainability" on our organization, and validating Maslow's (1987) contention that people will rally around a higher purpose in their personal lives and their work.

Face 7: the redesign of commerce

The seventh, and final, face calls for the "redesign of commerce" itself, which probably hinges on the acceptance of entirely new notions of economics, especially prices that reflect full costs—internalizing the externalities associated with hydrocarbons—to create ecologically and socially honest prices. To us, it will mean shifting emphasis from products to services. Therefore, we have invested in downstream distribution, installation, maintenance, and recycling—all aimed at forming "cradle-to-cradle" relationships with customers and suppliers. We want to build relationships based on delivering, by way of service agreements, the services our products provide—color, texture, warmth, acoustics, comfort, cleanliness, ambience, esthetics, and functionality—rather than selling the products themselves. The result is a further breaking of the undesirable linkages to the lithosphere and to the biosphere (see Fig. 1.4). In addition, another highly desired result is increased market share at the expense of inefficient, slow-to-adapt competitors.

We see many changes since we began the climb up the mountain. Numerous "✕"s on a linkage indicate where we are attacking the unwanted linkages. There are also many new connections, depicting renewable energy, closed-loop material flows, more vital connections throughout the supply chain and with the community, and the service component that overshadows products.

View from the summit

Success on all seven fronts—or a successful climb on all seven faces—will bring us to the summit of Mount Sustainability and our goal of becoming the prototypical company of the 21st century. The schematic in Figure 1.5 shows what this new enterprise will look like. Such a company will have a number of characteristics. It will be strongly service-oriented by means of products that deliver service. It will use resources efficiently, waste nothing and be cyclical (no more linear take–make–waste processes of the first Industrial Revolution). It will be driven by renewable energy (minimized, and thus afforded, through efficiency). It will be strongly connected to its employees and constituencies—with engaged communities, engaged customers, and engaged suppliers who have bought into the vision. What we believe will emerge is our own "ecosystem" of connected constituencies, with cooperation replacing confrontation. This company will be way ahead of all regulations, rendering the regulatory process irrelevant. Its values will have shifted, too. It will be committed to taking nothing from Earth's lithosphere that is not rapidly and naturally renewable and to doing no harm to Earth's biosphere. The undesirable linkages will all be gone. New, vital linkages will be in place.

The prototypical company will be sustainable and just. It will serve as an example for all and will be doing well by doing good. It will be winning in the marketplace, but not at Earth's expense nor at the expense of our descendants. Rather, its success will be at the expense of inefficient competitors. And it will be growing, too, even in a no-growth world, by taking market share from inefficient, unsustainable competitors. All the while, this emerging new enterprise will ensure that there is declining throughput of virgin materials, eventually reaching zero throughput. Only zero throughput of extracted natural capital is sustainable over evolutionary time (the true long run)—a radical thought, but a necessary objective, not just for Interface but for the entire industrial system.

Progress to date and an invitation to join the expedition

Our goal is for Interface to reach the summit by the year 2020. We are getting ready for the day when the price of oil reflects its true cost and all prices are ecologically and socially honest and when virgin petrochemical-based materials become very

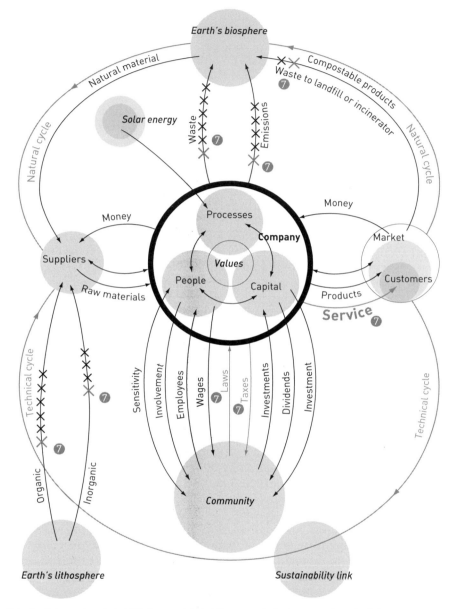

Note: the linkages targeted at this face are labeled ❼; crosses indicate an attack on the linkage, to move towards the redesign of commerce

Figure 1.4 **The Interface model: the redesign of commerce**

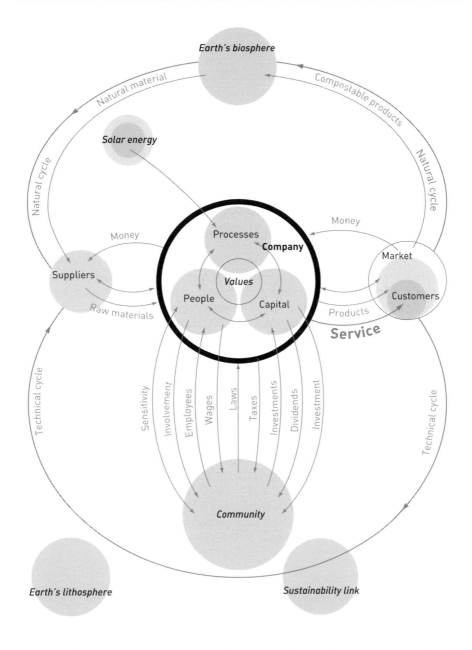

Figure 1.5 The Interface model: a prototypical company of the 21st century

dear. That is the day we will be ultra-successful in the marketplace, because we believe our customers will join in and climb this mountain of sustainability with us. Doing well by doing good is cause and effect, effect and cause—a positive feedback loop that is good for Earth.

The restorative company will add to this diagram the one missing linkage—that is, reinvestment in natural capital to restore the biosphere. This reinvestment will begin to repair the damage inflicted on Nature over the nearly 300 years of the industrial age.

How are we doing at Interface? This is a work in progress. Although we will not be satisfied until we reach the point where we leave "zero footprint," at the top of Mount Sustainability, the progress in the first eight years of implementation of the plan has been remarkable. The carbon intensity of Interface is down 33% (in terms of pounds of extracted petrochemical stuff per dollar of revenue), which includes all the petrochemical-derived material and energy extracted from Earth and processed through the entire supply chain to produce revenue for Interface. Greenhouse gases are down 30% in absolute terms.

This is the Interface plan and the Interface model for a sustainable industrial enterprise. It describes how we intend to get from here (unsustainable) to there (sustainable). In the eight years that we have spent first planning then figuring out how to integrate sustainability into our business, we have learned, without a shadow of a doubt, that this approach is a better business model, in the strictest business sense. People, process, product, profit, and purpose are all well served by proper attention to place, our Spaceship Earth. Doing well by doing good is a new and better way to bigger profits and to greater, more genuine, shareholder value. In the most difficult economic conditions of our corporate existence over these past few years, the model has proven not only its viability but also its superiority. To businesspeople everywhere, I urge you to take the step. Just try it; I think you will like it.

An industrial system that simply cannot go on and on must change. I believe every enterprise that is to survive must climb this same mountain, and its same seven faces. Together we must map out and climb the eighth face—to restore the health and productivity of the biosphere as well as the social sphere.

Read on now and see these inspiring examples of how other organizations are approaching this awe-inspiring climb. I hope you will start making your plans for joining us at the top. There will be room for everyone who makes it there.

Part 1
The transition to sustainability-oriented enterprises

All truths are easy to understand once they are discovered.

Galileo Galilei[1]

In the transition to sustainability-oriented enterprises, analytical breakthroughs have already begun. This part describes a few of the new frameworks that have been developed to understand and communicate the connections between ecological, social, and economic systems. The relevance and accessibility of these new ways of thinking is increasing through ongoing refinement.

1 www.quotationspage.com/quotes/Galileo_Galilei

Understanding Nature's services to societies*

Gretchen Daily
Stanford University, California, USA

Katherine Ellison
Investigative Journalist, California, USA

Nature's first green is gold.

Robert Frost[1]

When three-year-old Becky Furmann got the "poopies" and became dehydrated, her doctor urged her to drink water. He had no way of knowing that water had caused the rare illness that would kill her. As the chubby blond child grew thin and pale, her sufferings were finally confirmed as the ravages of *Cryptosporidium parvum*, a parasite almost unheard of until April 1993, when it slipped through one of the two modern filtration plants in Milwaukee, Wisconsin, and entered the city's water supply. Becky had been born with human immunodeficiency virus (HIV), which weakened her immune system, yet she had seemed otherwise healthy until then. Cryptosporidiosis sealed her fate. "She tries to ask us to kiss it and make it better, and we can't," said her father, near the end.

In all, Milwaukee's cryptosporidiosis epidemic led to more than 100 deaths and 400,000 illnesses. The victims had been betrayed by their water—and by their faith in the technology keeping it safe. What's more, they had plenty of company throughout the world.

With the start of the 21st century, every year more than 3 million people were dying of diseases spread by water, and another 1 billion were at risk, lacking access to water suitable to drink. As Milwaukee's disaster showed, the problem wasn't limited to developing countries. Some 36 million Americans were drinking water

---

*   From *The New Economy of Nature: The Quest to Make Conservation Profitable* by Gretchen
     C. Daily and Katherine Ellison. Copyright © 2002 Island Press. Reprinted by permission
     of Island Press/Shearwater Books, Washington, DC, and Covelo, CA.
1   Frost 1979.

from systems violating United States Environmental Protection Agency (EPA) standards. One million Americans were getting sick every year from the contamination, and as many as 900 were dying from it. Fecal bacteria, heavy metals, arsenic, and pesticides had become familiar ingredients in many US water supplies, and, as happened in Milwaukee, sometimes the highest-technology methods couldn't keep the contaminants out. Breakdowns were becoming a serious problem as mechanical systems aged and many strapped local governments deferred maintenance, to the point that the American Water Works Association estimated it would cost $325 billion to rehabilitate the country's dilapidated mechanical systems to ensure safe drinking water for everyone.

This crisis, and particularly this specter of expense, led the city of New York in 1997 to embark on a bold experiment that would reveal the value of what had been a mostly hidden but huge gift of Nature. With billions of dollars and the drinking water of nearly 10 million people at stake, planners weighed the costs and benefits of two alternative solutions to their water problem—constructing a filtration plant or repairing the largely natural filtration system that had been purifying the city's water all along. Nature won. And, in a turn of events that would have global implications, it won on economic grounds.

The battlefield on which this victory was achieved is the Catskill/Delaware Watershed, the heart of New York's purification and delivery system, named for the two major rivers flowing from it. The rural landscape is famed as a scene of great beauty, with sun-struck slopes, glistening streams and trees that explode in color each fall. Less well known is that it's also a highly efficient and valuable machine.

The cogs are 2,000 square miles of crop-filled valleys and mountains blanketed in forest, all connected by meandering streams feeding into an extensive system of 19 reservoirs. For nearly a century, the complex natural system has been delivering water of exceptional purity to the people of New York City and several upstate counties. In recent years, it has produced as much as 1.8 billion gallons per day, serving New Yorkers with a healthy drink whose taste and clarity have been the envy of mayors throughout the United States. And, unlike the case in most other large US cities, New York's tap water has never passed through a filtration plant.

Instead, the water, born as rain and melted snow on mountaintops as far as 125 miles away from those who will ultimately drink it, is naturally cleansed as it makes its way downhill toward the reservoirs. Beneath the forest floor, soil and fine roots filter the water and hidden microorganisms break down contaminants. In the streams, plants absorb as much as half of the surplus nutrients running into the waterway, such as nitrogen from automobile emissions and fertilizer and manure used on nearby farms. In open stretches, wetlands continue the filtering as cattails and other plants voraciously take up nutrients while trapping sediment and heavy metals. After reaching the reservoirs, the water is further cleansed as it sits and waits. Dead algae, floating branches and leaves, and remaining particles of grit slowly sink to the bottom. Some pathogens left in the water may bind to the grit and settle, too.

This mostly natural process—supplemented by small doses of chlorine and fluoride at the end of the water's journey—worked beautifully for most of the 20th century. But then signs appeared of some mechanical failures. The trouble was relentless new development: roads, subdivisions, and second homes were popping up all over the watershed, most of which is privately owned. Failing septic systems were leaking raw sewage into streams. Farming and forestry were also taking a toll, with lawn chemicals, fertilizers, pesticides, and manure all being washed into the reservoirs at an unprecedented rate.

By 1989, these problems could no longer be ignored. The United States Congress that year amended the Safe Drinking Water Act, putting into motion a major review of the country's drinking water systems. New York City was faced with the potentially enormous cost of an artificial water filtration plant, estimated at as much as $6–8 billion, plus yearly maintenance expenses amounting to $300–500 million. That price tag meant potential catastrophe for New York's budget, and city officials were determined to avoid it. With vigorous lobbying, they won agreement from federal regulators to try the alternative of a watershed protection program capable of guaranteeing water quality indefinitely. Rather than pay for the costly new filtration plant, the city would spend the much smaller amount of about $1.5 billion to protect the upstate watershed, including buying tracts of land as buffers and upgrading polluting sewage treatment plants. The EPA, in turn, would grant a five-year reprieve of its order, with the possibility of renewal.

The scheme was seriously challenged from the start. Powerful developers filed suit, claiming that property values would plummet as the city imposed restrictions on new construction. Environmentalists criticized the city's efforts as too weak. Nonetheless, the unprecedented agreement was a milestone in a world in which Nature's labor has too long been taken for granted. A major government body had acted as if an ecosystem—the watershed—were worth protecting in its natural state for the economic benefits it gives society. And it had invested in its restoration as if it were in fact a precious piece of infrastructure.

New York City planners had joined a new and diverse movement of prospectors for "green gold." Like the miners of yore, they were out to extract value from Nature and were in a rush to do so against competing forces. But, rather than aiming pickaxes and dynamite at a non-living, finite trove of gold, they wielded scientific studies and restoration projects, for the assets they sought were alive and renewable and would, if managed properly, continue to yield wealth for many years to come.

For most people who were paying attention, this came as a revelation. Conservation could save money—a lot of money. Trees, for example, could be worth something more than timber, acquiring financial value for the gifts they give while standing and part of a healthy, functioning forest. Land could have financial value apart from its potential to have something mined from it or built or farmed on it. The labor of ecosystems previously regarded as "free" might even be quantified in some way, recorded on balance sheets, and formally considered in decision-making.

Around the world, in city offices and university conference halls, among small groups of community activists and at the World Bank, scientists, legal scholars, bureaucrats, and professional environmentalists debated the implications of New York's experiment. Could it possibly work? Did scientists know enough about the mechanics of watersheds to give reliable advice on their management? And assuming the approach turned out to be justified, how widely could it be replicated?

In fact, without clear answers to these questions, and in many cases without knowing much about New York, governments around the world—in Curitiba, Brazil; in Quito, Ecuador; and in more than 140 US municipalities, from Seattle, Washington, to Dade County, Florida—were starting to calculate the costs of conserving watersheds and compare them with the costs of building mechanical plants. In a bold departure from business as usual, they were taking stock of their natural capital. In the process, they were learning how ecosystems—environments of interacting plants, animals, and microbes, from coastal tide pools to Loire Valley vineyards to expanses of Amazonian rainforest—can be seen as capital assets, supplying human beings with a stream of services that sustain and enhance our lives. These "ecosystem services" provide not only food and wine but also cleansing of Earth's air and water, protection from the elements, and refreshment and serenity for human spirits.

As the saying goes, a woman's work is never done—nor fairly compensated—and this is nowhere truer than in the case of Mother Nature. Much of Nature's labor has enormous and obvious value, which has failed to win respect in the marketplace until recently.

Forests, for example, not only help purify water but also reduce potential harm from flooding, drought, and mudslides. They shelter people from winter storms and summer heat and provide homes for many of Earth's other living inhabitants. Most dramatically, they help stabilize climate by absorbing heat-trapping carbon dioxide (CO_2) from the atmosphere.

Wetlands provide a similar range of valuable services. Along river floodplains, they slow and diminish the flow of water, protecting homes and roads from flood damage. In the process, they also purify the water. Along coastlines, wetlands and similar habitats nurture young fish, oysters, and other seafood. Coral reefs offer stunning beauty and recreational opportunities while supplying people with 10% of the fish consumed globally.

In farming regions, hedgerows and remaining native habitats support bees and other insects that pollinate crops. All told, the harvest of about one in three food crops worldwide—from alfalfa to watermelons—is possible thanks to the work of pollinators. And, finally, all ecosystems foster genetic diversity, maintaining a "library" of genes with values yet to be discovered for future medical and industrial products.

Historically, all these labors of Nature have been thought of as free. And, with the exception of the production of a few specific goods, such as farm crops and timber, the use of Nature's services is actually quite startlingly unregulated. Despite our assiduous watch over other forms of capital—physical (homes, cars, factories), financial (cash, savings accounts, corporate stocks) and human (skills and knowledge)—we haven't even taken measure of the ecosystem capital stocks that produce these most vital of labors. We lack a formal system of appraising or monitoring the value of natural assets, and we have few means of insuring them against damage or loss.

Although governments have negotiated a wide array of global and regional agreements to protect certain ecosystems from degradation and extinction—such as the Ramsar Convention on Wetlands, the Convention on Biological Diversity, and the Convention on the Law of the Sea—these agreements are mostly weak, lacking the participation, resources, and systems of incentives and enforcement they need to be effective.

Even more striking is how rarely investments in ecosystem capital are rewarded economically. Typically, property owners are not compensated for the services the natural assets on their land provide to society. With rare exception, owners of coastal wetlands are not paid for the abundance of seafood the wetlands nurture, nor are owners of tropical forests compensated for that ecosystem's contribution to the pharmaceutical industry and climate stability. As a result, many crucial types of ecosystem capital are undergoing rapid degradation and depletion. Compounding the problem is that the importance of ecosystem services is often widely appreciated only on their loss.

The source of this predicament is easy to comprehend. For most of humankind's experience on Earth, ecosystem capital was available in sufficient abundance, and human activities were sufficiently limited, that it was reasonable to think of ecosystem services as free. Yet, today, Nature everywhere is under siege. Each year the world loses some 30 million acres of tropical forest, an area slightly larger than Pennsylvania. At this rate, the last rainforest tree will bow out—dead on arrival at a sawmill or in a puff of smoke—around the middle of the 21st century. Biodiversity—short for biological diversity, the amazing variety of life on Earth—is being reduced to the lowest levels in human history. Homo sapiens has already wiped out one-quarter of all bird species, and an estimated 11% more are on the path to extinction, along with 24% of mammal and 11% of plant species. One-quarter of the world's coral reefs has been destroyed, with many others undergoing serious decline. To top it off, we're taking fish out of the sea for consumption faster than they can reproduce. Dramatic as they are, these global statistics mask the accelerating loss of local populations of species—the individual trees that help keep water pure, the individual bees that pollinate our crops.

An overriding force behind this liquidation of ecosystem capital is the tremendous human demand for food and fiber—wheat, rice, cotton, timber, and so on. To produce these commodities, people have already dramatically transformed half of the planet's ice-free land surface, from natural landscapes to farmland, ranchland, and tree plantations. In many parts of the world, these activities are undermining the very resources that support them, depleting soil fertility and water supplies. Yet pressures are enormous to expand and intensify this production, despite its obvious toll.

The 21st century began with a growing sense among scientists that crucial thresholds had been reached and time to fix things was running out. We were operating beyond the limits of what Nature could sustain, conscious that we couldn't keep it up, but with no plan under way to change our course. As Stanford University biologist Peter Vitousek has said, "we're the first generation with tools to understand changes in the Earth's system caused by human activity, and the last with the opportunity to influence the course of many of the changes now rapidly under way" (Vitousek *et al.* 1997).

This increasingly apparent deadline has begun to inspire a shift in thinking for many scholars, most notably economists. To be sure, economists have long been concerned with issues of resource scarcity and limits to human activities. That's why their field was dubbed "the dismal science." Yet, throughout the 1960s, 1970s and 1980s, most economists clashed with ecologists. Economists accused ecologists of being alarmist about adverse human effects on Earth and of proposing costly and unnecessary measures of protection. Meanwhile, ecologists charged economists with promoting "growth" at any price and misusing partial indicators of well-being, such as the gross national product, that are blind to wear and tear on the planet.

This conflict began to ease in the late 1980s, however, with efforts to forge a new discipline integrating ecology and economics. An early participant in this movement was Stanford professor and Nobel laureate Kenneth Arrow (Arrow *et al.* 1995), who for decades has been disturbed by the way economics dismisses "externalities," activities of which there are two types. Positive externalities are activities that benefit people who don't pay for them; negative externalities harm people who don't receive compensation.

An example of a positive externality is modern Costa Rica's careful stewardship of its forests—a striking turnabout from the rampant deforestation that lasted into the 1980s. The new conservation policies contribute to sustainable development in the region while also helping to stabilize the global climate and maintain biodiversity. Yet, for the most part, only Costa Ricans pay to preserve these widely enjoyed benefits. In contrast, a negative externality occurs when Americans drive gas guzzlers. This activity contributes to air pollution, potential climate change, and the risk of the US government being drawn into foreign conflicts over oil. Yet, even though these negative consequences affect large numbers of people, the drivers—since US gas is cheap and relatively untaxed—don't pay the costs.

"Internalization" of such externalities—enactment of a system of fair pricing and fair payment—is badly needed, but it will not be simple. Arrow has tried to meet the challenge in part by joining other economists and ecologists in a growing effort to "rethink economics," a process fortified by their yearly meetings on the island of Askö in the Stockholm Archipelago (Daily *et al.* 2000).

Another major player in these meetings has been Cambridge University professor Partha Dasgupta, the recent president of both the British and the European economics associations. Born in India, Dasgupta has devoted much of his career to studying the interplay of overpopulation, poverty, and environmental degradation. He remembers being stunned, at a United Nations meeting in 1981, when economists from developing countries stood up one by one and told him they couldn't afford to protect their environments. The encounter, he later said, gave him "some measure of how far we had yet to go. We must stop viewing the environment as an amenity, a luxury the poor can't afford" (Dasgupta 1993). Quite to the contrary, Dasgupta is convinced that the local environment is often the greatest asset for poor families because they have few alternatives for income if it fails (Dasgupta 1993). The rich, by contrast, have a global reach for all sorts of ecosystem goods and services, as revealed by their dinner tables laden with fresh fruit, fish, spring water, and flowers from all over the planet. Ultimately, though, the rich are also vulnerable to faltering ecosystem services and the social instability that can arise as a result.

Important as they clearly are to rich and poor alike, ecosystem services typically carry little or no formally recognized economic value. As Columbia University economist Geoffrey Heal points out, economics is concerned more with prices than with values or importance. "The price of a good"—say, a loaf of bread or a car or piece of jewelry—"does not reflect its importance in any overall social or philosophical sense," says Heal. "Very unimportant goods can be valued more highly by the market—have higher prices—than very important goods" (Heal 2000a, 2000b).

This contradiction isn't new. Economists throughout the 18th and 19th centuries were perplexed by the paradox of diamonds and water. Why do diamonds command a much higher price than water, when water is obviously so much more key to human survival? The answer, proposed by Englishman Alfred Marshall, is now common knowledge (Heal 2000a, 2000b): price is set by supply and demand. In the case of water, the supply (at least in Marshall's England) "was so large as to exceed the amount that could possibly be demanded at any price," Heal explains (Heal 2000a, 2000b). "Consequently the price was zero; water was free. Now, of course, the demand for water has increased greatly as a result of population growth and rising prosperity, while the supply has remained roughly constant, so that water is no longer free" (Heal 2000a, 2000b). Diamonds, by contrast, started out scarce: the desire for ownership always exceeded their supply. Their market price was thus high—set by rich people competing for the few diamonds available.

Ecosystem assets have the importance of water and are gradually acquiring the scarcity of diamonds as the human population and its aspirations grow. As they become more like diamonds, they take on increasing potential value in economic terms. But major innovations to our economic and social institutions are needed to capture this value and incorporate it into day-to-day decision-making.

The main challenge in the pursuit of this goal is that most ecosystem services are currently treated as "public goods," which if provided for one are provided for all, no matter who pays. An example is air quality: if a government spends on reducing pollution, it helps taxpayers and non-taxpayers alike. That leads to a problem of "free-riders," in which some people benefit without charge from services paid for by others. And this is particularly true with the services provided by Nature. Although we've engineered a financial system so sophisticated as to include market values for feng shui masters and interest rate derivatives, we've not yet managed to establish them for such vital and everyday services as water purification and flood protection.

The big challenge now is how to measure, capture, and protect these newly discovered values before they are lost. There's been an urgent flurry of calls to do just that since the late 1990s, yet the quest to realize the value of Nature's services is anything but new. Even Plato drew attention to the links between the clearing of forests in Attica and the drying of local springs (Hillel 1991). And, in the 1860s, US statesman George Perkins Marsh lamented how "rivers famous in history and song have shrunk to humble brooklets" in the deforested lands of the once powerful Roman Empire (Marsh 1864).

Still, not until New York made its historic decision to invest in its watershed did it seem possible that big governments would catch on, supporting the concrete results of Nature's work with cash on the table. Replicating that endeavor to any great extent, by conserving not only watersheds for water purity but also wetlands for flood control, and forests for climate stabilization and biodiversity conservation, would require a tremendous amount of new scientific understanding of ecosystems—of their functioning, of their susceptibility to adverse human effects and their amenability to repair, and of the pros and cons of replacing them with technological substitutes. More important, it would require a willingness to look at the world's economy in an entirely different way, starting with the assumption that ecosystems are assets whose output has concrete financial worth.

It's not that we don't value these services at all. It's clear that we're willing to pay. We buy costly water bottled from faraway, pristine springs, send checks to support endangered species, pay premiums for homes next to preserved "open space," and part with outlandish sums to travel to places where we can still catch glimpses of untrammeled Nature. All the same, we still think of conservation basically as something to do for moral or esthetic reasons—not for survival and certainly not for profit.

Nevertheless, the record clearly shows that conservation can't succeed by charity alone. It has a fighting chance, however, with well-designed appeals to self-interest. The challenge now is to change the rules of the game so as to produce new incentives for environmental protection, geared to both society's long-term well-being and individuals' self-interest.

A great unanswered question is whether the drive for profits, which has done so much harm to the planet, can possibly be harnessed to save it.

Market values for such essential gifts of Nature as clean water and fresh air are well under way. Understanding them is key to making the best of them and, as the eminent biologist Edward O. Wilson has urged (Wilson 20002), to giving economist Adam Smith's "invisible hand" a green thumb.

3

Reconsidering business from a systems perspective
The shift to sustainability-oriented enterprises and financial services

Sissel Waage
The Natural Step, USA

Two of the most powerful drivers of change within modern economies are the explosion of digital technologies and the shift toward sustainable development. Both require us to rethink the nature of goods and services; both have the capacity to transform the relationship between governments, companies, citizens and consumers.

James Wilsdon and Paul Miller[1]

When Tim Brown became the president of IDEO—a prominent product design firm—he asked employees what they wanted the company to become in the years ahead. The answer took him by surprise. Studio heads and designers at all levels were concerned with the environmental impacts of their products and the growing human needs globally. In short, the employees were concerned with sustainability issues. Many perceived that their biggest impact on the world was production of more landfill.

As the volumes of modern industrial products have grown and their usage time has shrunk, the throughput of materials has increased enormously. Today in the USA many products have only a six-month "lifespan" (Hawken *et al.* 1999: 81). Designers at IDEO recognized these dynamics and expressed interest not only in incrementally decreasing material use but also in taking a much greater leap to revolutionize modern product design. These employees wanted their products to be restorative of ecological systems and to have relevance to (and accessibility for) the vast percentage of the world's population struggling to meet basic human

---

1   Wilsdon and Miller 2001: 2.

needs. However, they had a simple problem. It was unclear how to integrate environmental and social issues methodically and systemically in their decision-making processes and current work.

This interest in rethinking modern businesses and decisions in terms of environmental impacts and human needs is emblematic of a growing awareness of the integrated concept of sustainability—in terms of ecological, social, and economic factors. It represents the goal of addressing key societal issues. Drawing on the words of Dee Hock, founding chief executive officer (CEO) of VISA International, it offers the early movement toward "the organization of the future [which] will be an embodiment of community based on shared purpose calling to higher aspirations of people" (quoted in Kiuchi and Shireman 2002: 160).

A growing body of work has emerged to inform such a transition in the business world. Sustainability-focused business tools and approaches offer decision-makers a way to structure their thinking about how companies are imbedded within—and deeply reliant on—environmental and social systems. The boundaries between specific companies, systems of commerce, broader social dynamics, and ecosystems are far more permeable than many existing mental models reflect. Ecological systems, human societies, and businesses are fundamentally intertwined. We all need oxygen produced by plants. Commerce fundamentally relies on healthy workers as well as on available natural resources. Together, these elements affect the bottom line in very real ways, whether or not they are accounted for in financial reports. Clarity on how to mesh this understanding with business decision-making has grown significantly over the past decade.

What follows is an overview of the expanding body of sustainability concepts. It is not exhaustive but, rather, touches on some of the key developments. Indications that a shift is already under way are also drawn out through examples of the growing interest in applications of sustainability within businesses.

Paradigm shifts in science and business: the increasing relevance of sustainability concepts

> When paradigms change, the world itself changes with them. Led by a new paradigm, scientists adopt new instruments and look in new places. Even more important, . . . scientists see new and different things when looking with familiar instruments in places they have looked before. It is rather as if the professional community had been suddenly transported to another planet where familiar objects are seen in a different light and are joined by unfamiliar ones as well . . . We may say that after a revolution [or paradigm shift] scientists are responding to a different world.
>
> *Thomas Kuhn*[2]

2 Kuhn 1962: III

Thomas Kuhn's work describing paradigm shifts marked a fundamental change in the way scientific conceptual development was understood. He argued that paradigm shifts most commonly occur when anomalies are discovered and an increasing number of critical questions are asked about the way in which a set of dynamics is explained. As a previous theoretical framework becomes less useful, new theories are proposed.[3] Some of these new approaches represent distinct breaks, or nonsynchronous leaps, in current thinking. Eventually, a new theory is proposed, and accepted, as a more compelling way to understand the dynamics. These paradigm shifts reform scientific fields. Kuhn asserted that, following such a "revolution" in thought, previous measurements and tools may become irrelevant and need to be replaced by entirely new parameters and approaches (Kuhn 1962: 129). In this sense, paradigm shifts have the potential to change our understanding of which factors are important and of what actions should be taken in a specific context.

For example, Copernican astronomy, and Galileo's work on proving these theories, represented a paradigm shift. Theories fundamentally changed (albeit slowly) as new concepts were accepted. Often, in the wake of these shifts, preexisting boundaries, dynamics, and factors were also reconsidered.

A similar shift is occurring in relation to understanding the imbeddedness of economies, and businesses, within broader social and ecological systems. This shift began in the 1980s, as the term and concept of sustainable development became well publicized in the *World Conservation Strategy*—a report by a group of high-profile non-profit organizations (including the International Union for the Conservation of Nature [IUCN] and the World Wide Fund for Nature [WWF]) and the United Nations Environment Program (UNEP)—and in the report of the 1987 World Commission on Environment and Development (WCED 1987).[4] In international policy circles, sustainable development became the organizing concept for considering economic growth and use of natural resources. The most commonly cited definition is from the WCED report, which states that sustainable development "meets the needs of the present without compromising the ability of future generations to meet their own needs" (1987). These needs—of present and future generations—are commonly expressed in terms of ecological, social, and economic issues.

The importance of the sustainable development concept has grown dramatically in recent years. Scientists are increasingly in agreement that ecological systems are being changed as a result of human resource-use practices. Numerous trends of concern have emerged. For example, in areas around the world, water withdrawal exceeds the rate at which groundwater reserves can be replenished.[5] Globally, 35% of the most important commercial fish stocks show a pattern of declining yields, and an additional 25% are being fished at their biological limit

---

3   As Kuhn (1962: 67) explained, "Newton's new theory of light and color originated in the discovery that none of the existing pre-paradigm theories would account for the length of the spectrum, and the wave theory that replaced Newton's was announced in the midst of the growing concern about anomalies in the relation of diffraction and polarization effects to Newton's theory."

4   This report is also referred to as the Brundtland Report, after the Norwegian former Prime Minister, Gro Harlem Brundtland, who chaired the commission.

5   See www.wri.org/wri/trends/fragment.html.

and are vulnerable to declining numbers.[6] Over 50% of the world's wetlands have been destroyed during the past century. Half of the remaining coastal wetlands are likely to be lost by 2080 as a result of agriculture, urban sprawl, and rising sea levels (Renner 2001).

The effects of these and of many other alterations to ecosystems are already being felt and will become increasingly significant as vital ecological services become endangered. For example, as a Worldwatch Institute scientist explains, wetlands currently play a key role in "regulating water flow and providing flood control, recharging groundwater supplies, retaining essential soil nutrients, buffering other ecosystems against contaminants and offering habitat for diverse biological communities" (Renner 2001).

An international team of researchers has estimated that these and many other ecosystem services are worth, on average, US$ 33 trillion per year: a number derived from assessments of what it would cost to provide all these services through human projects and technology use.[7] The costs estimated are nearly twice the value of the global gross national product (GNP). Yet, at present, any damage caused to these services is often simply considered an externality. One of many problems with this perspective is, as researchers unequivocally assert, "the decay of ecosystems sets the stage for more frequent and more devastating 'un-natural' disasters [which are] natural disturbances made worse by human actions" (Renner 2001).

The ramifications of an increasing number of natural disasters exacerbated by altered ecosystems could be significant for society. The potential of sea level rise as a result of climate change is a cause for concern, particularly in light of the fact that 33% of the world's population lives within 100 km of a coastline. The economic effects are likely to be considerable and will continue to disproportionately impact the economically poorest regions. To demonstrate, according to a report by Abramovitz for Worldwatch Institute, between 1985 and 1999 the world's wealthiest countries sustained considerable economic losses as a result of natural disasters, representing 2.5% of gross domestic product (GDP). However, the world's poorest countries endured an economic toll of natural disasters representing 13.4% of their GDP (Abramovitz 2001). Abramovitz (2001) concludes that "more and more of the devastation wrought by such natural disasters is 'unnatural' in origin, caused by ecologically destructive practices."

In addition to these concerns, ecological changes can have cascading effects on public health which, in turn, have further economic implications. As Renner, a Worldwatch Institute analyst, explains:

> The deterioration of critical ecosystems like wetlands and coral reefs can boomerang: communities have less protection against extreme weather events, and disease vectors are able to spread more easily, compromising human health and well-being . . . Environmental crises and health epidemics translate into rising economic costs in the form of property losses from natural disasters and skyrocketing healthcare bills (Renner 2001).

6   Food and Agriculture Organization, cited at www.wri.org/trends/fishloss.html.
7   See www.wri.org/wri/trends/ecoserv.html.

Region	Cost (US$ billions)
Asia	409.8
North America	304.4
Europe	112.4
Caribbean	30.0
Central America	22.3
Oceania	16.5
South America	16.4
Africa	6.8

Table 3.1 Global economic losses resulting from natural disasters, 1985–99

Source: Abramovitz 2001

These issues can become particularly stark in the context of impoverished areas where people cannot meet their basic human needs—even in the current context, without the burden of additional natural disasters. Furthermore, the total number of people in these challenging circumstances continues to grow.

The 2002 *Human Development Report* of the United Nations Development Program states that 52 countries ended the 1990s poorer than when that decade began (UNDP 2002). In that ten-year period, the number of refugees and internally displaced persons grew by 50%. The number of people living in "extreme poverty" increased in many regions, including Africa, Latin America, Eastern and Central Europe, the Former Soviet Union, and the Arab States. Public health concerns also grew. HIV (human immunodeficiency virus) and AIDS (acquired immune deficiency syndrome) are extremely serious issues. Access to clean water and food remains an enormous concern, as every day 5,500 children die from diseases caused by water and food polluted with bacteria (UNICEF/UNEP/WHO 2002). Access to basic healthcare is poor in many areas. As Donnelly in a 2003 *Boston Globe* article explains:

> Yesterday, 24,000 people worldwide could have been saved by basic [health]care. The same number could have been saved the day before, and the day before that. In all, over the last year, 8.8 million lives were lost needlessly to preventable diseases, infections, and childbirth complications (Donnelly 2003).

At the same time, nations that offer foreign aid—including European countries and the USA—provide farmers in their own countries with subsidies often greater than their total aid to poor countries. These subsidies have continued to shape the economic dynamics between nations in the southern and northern hemispheres. In many cases, they also favor large-scale agriculture, affecting small family farmers in northern-hemisphere countries.

Within Western Europe and North America, poverty also exists in greater degrees than previously thought.[8] For example, the US Bureau of the Census reports that in 2000 over 11% of the population was living in poverty (Dalaker 2001). Also, a US "hunger belt" was highlighted in a January 2003 National Public Radio report that focused on poverty in Western rural counties from New Mexico to Washington State.

Overall, Sakiko Fukuda-Parr, the lead author of the 2002 UNDP report, asserts that there are "growing divisions between those who prosper in this new world and those who do not" (UNDP 2002). The implications are that:

> Globalization is forging greater interdependence, yet the world seems more fragmented—between the rich and the poor, between the powerful and powerless, between those who welcome the new global economy and those who demand a different course.
>
> The anti-globalization movement, the most significant social movement of our times, is demanding greater social justice, not just handouts for the poor. All this adds up to a world in urgent need of a political order that can achieve greater inclusion, an order in which all people and countries can have a say in decisions that affect their future, and one with rules and institutions which command trust among all people and countries (UNDP 2002).

These examples show the complex interplay between social, economic, and ecological systems. All commerce and economic activity is imbedded within, and is fundamentally reliant on, ecological and social systems. The three—society, the economy, and ecology—can be understood as nested systems. Robustness and resilience in all three create the potential for feedback loops that are positive throughout. The concerns about sustainability relate to the increasingly worrying specter of feedback loops that support negative, undesired outcomes, and increase the likelihood that a range of problems (in terms of ecological, social, and economic factors) will worsen over time. In response to these concerns, there is an expanding awareness that sustainability issues must be considered and that businesses must become a part of the solution.

Business becomes part of the solution: developing new sustainability-oriented decision-making tools and approaches

Eco-efficiency was one of the early, widely recognized frameworks developed to apply a portion of sustainability concepts to the private sector. The term was coined prior to the 1992 United Nations Conference on Environment and

---

8   A report issued in 2000 by the Organization for Economic Cooperation and Development asserts that poverty in Western Europe and North America is "far wider than previously calculated" (Oxley *et al.* 2000).

Development (UNCED) in relation to businesses contributions to sustainability issues. "Eco-efficient companies" were defined, in a ground-breaking 1991 book *Changing Course*, as "those which create ever more useful products and services—in other words, which add more value—while continuously reducing their consumption of resources and their pollution" (Schmidheiny and BCSD 1991).

A number of studies have documented the bottom-line benefits of minimizing emissions, diminishing material and energy use, designing for re-use and recycling and identifying substitutes for hazardous materials. Such actions typically reduce the cost of goods sold, thereby directly improving both operating and EBITDA (earnings before interest, taxes, depreciation, and amortization) performance. For example, Textron's Bell helicopter unit reported savings of US$100 million in 2000 by recollecting waste sludge and salvaging magnesium hydroxide for re-use in its electroplating processes (Deutsch 2001). Similarly, 3M's famous Pollution Prevention Pays (3P) program resulted in over US$800 million in savings (WBCSD 2000a). The positive effects on firm expenditure increased awareness of "green" issues as strategic and operational decisions (Richards 1999).

Both the concept of eco-efficiency and the many examples of successful applications have been important in proving the relevance of environmental issues to business operations. However, the challenge is that if eco-efficiency is too tightly focused on resource inputs then it will address only a small portion of the broader (unsustainable) systems. That is, within a narrow application of eco-efficiency, resource and energy use, as well as waste and environmental impacts, may be lessened only within one product line, one division, or one firm. Significant issues are likely to remain if there is a net increase in the number of products made and if substitutions away from certain substances do not occur (for more information, see Chapter 4). In addition, within a tight focus on eco-efficiency, the social aspects of sustainability may not be addressed at all. The result may be little or no net decline in waste, emissions, and other impacts, as well as little or no attempt to address the social aspects of the issues. Thus, the problem with a tightly focused eco-efficiency concept is that in optimizing only a subset of the system the broader dynamics of the whole system may not be considered. Recent conceptual work on eco-efficiency has recognized these issues and broadened the term to mean "more value with less impact" (Lenhi 2000: 257).[9] The challenge is in ensuring that applications of the concepts are similarly expanded to include a fuller set of issues and a systems view.

Another response to these issues has been from analysts who assert that there is a growing need to significantly decrease net resource use by a factor of 10 overall, and by a factor of 4 as a short-term goal (Schmidt-Bleek 1994; von Weizsäcker *et al.*

9   In 1993 the term was defined by participants in a multi-stakeholder workshop with which the World Business Council on Sustainable Development (WBCSD) was involved. It was defined as follows: "Eco-efficiency is achieved by the delivery of competitively priced goods and services that satisfy human needs and bring quality of life, while progressively reducing ecological impacts and resource intensity throughout the life-cycle to a level at least in line with the Earth's estimated carrying capacity. In short, it is concerned with creating more value with less impact" (WBCSD 2000b: 4). "Eco-efficiency leads to more value from fewer resources, through redesign of products and services and through new solutions" (WBCSD 2000b: 6).

1997). These researchers state that eco-efficiency needs to become much more expansive in its approach, widespread in its application, and aggressive in addressing the growing resource demands relative to available resources.

During the early 1990s the field of industrial ecology emerged, offering another approach. The theory, and examples, promoted closed-loop business and industrial systems, the idea being premised on the concept of no waste (e.g. see Allenby and Cooper 1994; Allenby and Richards 1994; Ayres 1989; Graedel and Allenby 1995; McDonough and Braungart 1998, 2001; O'Brien 1999; Socolow *et al.* 1994).

At the same time, in the late 1980s and early 1990s, The Natural Step framework and system conditions for sustainability were developed (Holmberg and Robèrt 2000b). This effort was launched from the realization that much of the environmental debate focused on disagreements among scientists rather than the considerable areas of agreement. The debate suffered from a lack of overarching, commonly agreed-on, scientifically based principles of sustainability. The process began in 1989. A Swedish oncologist, Dr. Karl-Henrik Robèrt, collaborated with other scientists to develop a clearly articulated set of core, scientifically based, sustainability principles. Together, this group authored a consensus document that described the basic knowledge of the biosphere's functions and human interactions in relation to sustaining life on Earth. In the early 1990s, Dr. Robèrt worked with physicist Dr. John Holmberg to further build on this work and define a set of system conditions for a sustainable society, based on the laws of thermodynamics and natural cycles (see Box 3.1). The system conditions were developed by taking a systems perspective and by considering the desired end-point—sustainability. In addition, these system conditions have several important attributes. They are general enough to be relevant for all activities and fields, yet concrete enough to guide thinking and decision-making. They also do not overlap. Overall, when applied in the context of The Natural Step framework—which includes the principles as well as the approach of "backcasting" (see Chapter 4)—decision-makers are offered greater clarity on how to move forward with efforts to dematerialize, substitute inputs, support changes in land and natural resource management practices, and integrate social aspects of sustainability.[10]

In a sustainable society:

1. Nature is not subject to systematically increasing concentrations of substances extracted from the Earth's crust.

2. Nature is not subject to systematically increasing concentrations of substances produced by society.

3. Nature is not subject to systematically increasing degradation by physical means.

4. The ability of humans to meet their needs worldwide is not systematically undermined.

Box 3.1 The Natural Step's four system conditions

10 In February 1997, 20 prominent scientists from the USA and Canada gathered for three days to examine the science behind The Natural Step framework and assess its

Throughout the 1990s, a range of other approaches emerged to address various levels of planning within the context of moving towards sustainability. Most notably, recent work on "natural capitalism" builds on eco-efficiency and industrial ecology by laying out specific strategies with which to "reduce environmental harm, create economic growth and increase meaningful employment" (Hawken *et al*. 1999: 11). Specifically, natural capitalism calls for four iterative changes in society's businesses and organizations (see Box 3.2). The first strategy, to promote a "radical increase in resource productivity," is fully aligned with goals of eco-efficiency. Thus, within the context of natural capitalism theory, tightly focused work on increasing eco-efficiency can be understood as an initial step in the direction of much more far-reaching shifts. The second strategy, to explore the possibilities of biomimicry, resonates with industrial ecology research and writing, with the goal of "redesigning industrial systems on biological lines" in order to enable "the constant re-use of materials in continuous closed cycles, and often the elimination of toxicity" (Hawken *et al*. 1999: 10-11). The third strategy is to establish a service and flow economy by creating systems that ensure that goods are circulated rather than used and thrown out. Finally, the fourth strategy relates to reinvesting in ecological systems in order to ensure that society is "sustaining, restoring and expanding stocks of natural capital" (Hawken *et al*. 1999: 10-11). Together, these strategies offer a "roadmap" for moving toward sustainability.

Another conceptual contribution to the field was development of the term "triple bottom line" (Elkington 1997). The term fundamentally questions the single (financial) bottom line. It argues for the importance of considering environmental and social costs and returns, along with standard financial accounting, to determine the bottom line. In reality, all these factors have always affected businesses. That is, all companies produce, and are affected by, financial, environmental, and social impacts in their operations. For example, the relevance of sustainability concepts to business is evident in the reports of large companies held liable for millions of dollars in clean-up costs of sites used by contract manufacturers filing for bankruptcy (GEMI 2001). In addition, these impacts are manifest in the damage to reputation that companies experience after human rights violations or when environmental issues are highlighted. And thus, the single bottom line will increasingly reflect ecological and social returns.

Over the past decade, the sustainability field has matured. The questions emerging from this area of work are intended to spark business innovation through examining "functional needs" and addressing these needs through services that de-couple growth from resources (WBCSD 2000a: 12). For example, sustainability analysts ask: Are people buying large appliances or merely seeking ways in which

validity. The group summarized its findings and issued the following statement (Natural Step 1997): "We believe that without solutions to the problems addressed by The Natural Step Framework, both human civilization and biological diversity are seriously threatened. The development of appropriate solutions to these problems requires the support and contributions of the global community of scientists and engineers. We further believe that the application of The Natural Step's four system conditions is a valid approach for addressing these problems, and is especially useful for organizing information regarding sustainability. To be effective the conditions must also be augmented by the evaluation of the environmental impacts of specific substances and practices."

The four strategies of natural capitalism are to:

- Promote a radical increase in resource productivity.

- Explore the possibilities of biomimicry. Biomimicry can be described as the redesign of industrial systems along biological lines, changing "the nature of industrial processes and materials, enabling the constant re-use of materials in continuous closed cycles, and often the elimination of toxicity" (Hawken *et al.* 1999: 10).

- Develop a service and flow economy. A service and flow economy "calls for a fundamental change in the relationship between producer and consumer, a shift from an economy of goods and purchases to one of service and flow" (Hawken *et al.* 1999: 10). Hawken *et al.* go on to say that, "in essence, an economy that is based on a flow of economic services can better protect the ecosystem service on which it depends."

- Invest in natural capital. This can be done by reinvesting in "sustaining, restoring and expanding stocks of natural capital" (1999: 11).

Regarding these four strategies, Hawken *et al.* (1999: 11) assert that "all four changes are interrelated and interdependent; all four generate numerous benefits and opportunities in markets, finance, materials, distribution, and employment. Together they can reduce environmental harm, create economic growth, and increase meaningful employment."

Box 3.2 The four strategies of natural capitalism

Source: Hawken *et al.* 1999

to wash clothes efficiently and refrigerate food? (Hawken *et al.* 1999). The field emphasizes exploration of the ways in which to provide services rather than products (Hawken *et al.* 1999; Senge and Carstedt 2001). This model shifts away from thinking about business as continually having to procure and produce items, to companies that maintain items in use over time (Hawken *et al.* 1999; Senge and Carstedt 2001). Thus, sustainability leaders seek creative approaches to building businesses around decreased material throughput, continued flow of goods into products (in cycles with little or no waste, operating on sustainable sources of energy) and the focused provision of the services that consumers seek (Allenby and Richards 1994; Hawken *et al.* 1999). In addition, however, the sustainability field highlights another element—the consideration of social systems—and thus an essential element of these issues is ensuring that the economic system is restorative not only of natural systems but also of social systems.

However, even within the sustainability field, this set of social issues has received the most critique and the least consistent and substantive integration into businesses. These challenges permeate society, ranging from labor and production practices, through infrastructure siting strategies, to relationships with communities, vendors, and many others within the complex supply, use, re-use, and disposal chains of economies. Social aspects of sustainability span from labor conditions and wages, to accessing natural resources (e.g. food, water) as well as educational, informational, and other socioeconomic resources. For example, relevant questions relate not only to what the mine workers or apparel manufacturing employees are paid but also to how the product and production processes affect the conditions in which these individuals (and all communities exposed to the full life-cycle impacts of the products) live. In the case of a manufacturing plant, questions above and beyond the obvious wage issues are many and include: Is the room or factory well ventilated for workers? Is it producing untreated waste that is entering the community's water system? Are children employed? Is there a local school that they could be attending? If not, why not? When these products are disposed of—possibly in communities far from where they were made—do they break down and emit further chemicals that are intruding on groundwater aquifers and/or airsheds? What is the effect on public health? How does the extraction/ transport/manufacturing/recycling/disposal of the product affect socioeconomic relations? Does it limit people's ability to address human needs (through either direct or indirect effects)?

As in ecological systems, these social dynamics occur within a series of nested spaces and places, each of which has ripple effects. Privileged access and use can positively influence accrual of benefits and enable a buffer from impacts. For example, poverty has been shown to track the existence and reinforcement of access problems (e.g. see Romm and Sy 1996). These include access to all resources— natural resources (food, water, etc.), informational and educational resources, financial resources, and many others types of resources. This dynamic is clear in less affluent communities, where there is seldom money to influence policy or invoke legal rights in a court of law. De facto rules, in the form of physical force or cultural norms, have the potential to shape social relations more strongly than can codified laws. Within these contexts, social networks can become very important in accessing resources of all kinds. For example, if people cannot get a bank loan, they borrow from a lender who knows them (though she or he may charge extremely high interest rates). Access to resources thus becomes a set of replicating dynamics that are imbedded within and shaped by a complex set of factors.

Given this range of social aspects of sustainability, the challenges for considering the issues systematically, without becoming overwhelmed, appears immense. There is, however, a substantial literature on (and guidelines about) the social aspects of sustainability, including human needs, human rights, labor and worker rights, access issues, social capital development, and other aspects of the socioeconomic elements of sustainability.[11]

The most recognized approaches begin with the international human rights standards, presented in the United Nations Universal Declaration of Human Rights (UDHR), which was widely adopted following World War II.[12] Additional international documents also address the social aspects of sustainability. For example, the conventions of the International Labor Organization (ILO) focus on

---

11 For introductory lists of existing principles and guidelines, see www.business-humanrights.org.

12 With regard to the most basic human needs, the Declaration unequivocally states, in Article 25(1): "Everyone has the right to a standard of living adequate for the health and well-being of himself [and herself] and of his [and her] family, including food, clothing, housing and medical care and necessary social services, and the right to security in the event of unemployment, sickness, disability, widowhood, old age or other lack of livelihood in circumstances beyond his [or her] control" (www.un.org/Overview/rights.html).

labor issues, including child labor, freedom of association, working hours, and health and safety. More recently, an increasing number of non-governmental organizations have begun to develop guidelines for business operations. Amnesty International has established a set of principles concerning the link between business and human rights.[13] The Social Accountability 8000 standard has also addressed social and human issues as applied to the workplace.[14] The Global Reporting Initiative (GRI)—developed over the past decade to create an international standard for corporate social responsibility (CSR) and sustainability reporting—recommends the use of specific social indicators based on the ILO's Tripartite Declaration (ILO 1991), the Guidelines for Multinational Enterprises, from the Organization for Economic Cooperation and Development, which provide international standards for business in terms of social issues (OECD 1994), and the UDHR. Although the GRI 2000 guidelines focused on workplace and human rights, more recent work on the GRI has refined these indicators and has led to the development of a third level, community–society–development.[15]

All this work marks the beginning of a shift to sustainability-oriented business theory that is informing new practices. This shift is premised on an understanding of business as nested within—and fundamentally reliant on—broader social and ecological systems. If one realm is compromised, the soundness of the other interrelated elements is at risk. All this work has offered a language and a growing body of analytical tools to facilitate the integration into business decision-making processes.

The sustainability field matures: integrating various principles, strategies, approaches, and tools

Today, companies considering how to integrate sustainability factors into their decision-making face a complex field of concepts, standards, and guidelines, including: the ISO 14001 standard on environmental management systems, life-cycle assessment (LCA), ecological footprinting (Rees and Wackernagel 1994), Factor 4 (von Weizsäcker *et al.* 1997), Factor 10 (Schmidt-Bleek 1994, 1997), sustainable technology development (Weaver *et al.* 2000), natural capitalism (Hawken *et al.* 1999), and The Natural Step Framework (Holmberg and Robèrt 2000b). There has been a proliferation of macro-level principles (e.g. the United Nations UDHR, The Natural Step Framework strategies (e.g. cleaner production, natural capitalism), as well as issue-specific and industry-specific criteria and

13   For more information, go to www.amnestyusa.org/business/checklist.html.
14   For additional information, go to www.cepaa.org.
15   Although the GRI states that a company has a decreasing level of responsibility between the first item (labor) and the third item (community–society–development), it is proposed that all three should be considered in the assessment of a firm. In addition, supplier performance is highlighted as a key element of social impacts, thereby leading to the business and its suppliers being included in reporting on each of the three realms (for more information, see GRI 2002b).

guidelines (e.g. Forest Stewardship Council certification [www.fscoax.org], green-energy certification [e.g. USA Green-e; www.green-e.org], and a variety of eco-labels [e.g. German "Blue Angel," *Blauer Umweltengel*, www.blauer-engel.de]). For many business decision-makers it is unclear what connections (if any) exist between these approaches and how to begin assessing the sustainability-related aspects of their products. It is also not immediately evident what questions should be asked of vendors in requesting products that are more sustainable when considered from a full systems-based perspective.

Yet, for environmental, human rights, and integrated sustainability specialists, there are sound reasons as to why sub-fields and focused efforts exist rather than tightly integrated approaches. Single-industry and issue-focused approaches are essential for specificity. Broader frameworks and principles are necessary for highlighting systems, connections, and overarching limits. Work on these distinct levels is often both complementary and conceptually interrelated. The problem—particularly for many end-users, including businesspeople—is that these linkages have not been clearly drawn out and are not readily apparent.

The need to highlight interrelationships between existing sustainability assessment approaches has begun to be addressed by an international group of leaders of environmental and sustainability thought, including pioneers of the environmental footprint concept, the Dutch Sustainable Technology Program, the Factor 10 and MIPS (material input per unit of service) concepts, natural capitalism, The Natural Step, and the Zero Emission Forum. The group gathered in May 2000 to synthesize existing work through discussion of the commonalities and differences between the various philosophies and efforts. One result of these discussions was a joint paper outlining "relationships, synergies and diversity among their approaches" (Schmidt-Bleek and Robèrt 2001; Robèrt *et al.* 2002). The document—co-authored by representatives eight organizations—underscored the importance of a systems approach and clearly articulated principles, objectives, and tools.[16] The Natural Step framework offered the overriding principles, whereas natural capital, ecological footprint, LCAs and other and approaches offer key additional tools (Robèrt *et al.* 2002). Overall, the group agreed that the utility of these principles, strategies, and tools can increase when they are aligned with a full systems perspective as provided by The Natural Step Framework (for a further explanation of the resulting "map" of the field, see Chapter 4).

With an increasingly clear theory of how economic systems are imbedded within, and reliant on, ecological and social systems as well as what approaches

16 The group also wrote that: "Each of the sustainability **objectives** described by the [Natural Step] System Conditions can be further divided into two basic mechanisms: **dematerialization** (i.e. reduction of material flows), and **substitution** (i.e. exchange of type/quality of flows and/or activities). These two aspects of sustainability can be used in parallel and on different scales, e.g. from changing amounts *and* types of fuel in the same process (e.g. from petroleum fueled, to more efficient bio-fueled, vehicles), through a more radical change of the whole process (e.g. from combustion engines to more efficient and cleaner fuel cells), to completely new and less resource demanding and more ecologically/socially sound ways of satisfying the same human need (e.g. from a road-transport dependent business model that does not integrate social costs in developing countries, to licensing and fair trade utilizing information technologies)" (Robèrt *et al.* 2002: 200).

and tools can be used to act on this information, a paradigm shift has begun in the way business is understood.

Business interest in sustainability: indications of a shift to sustainability-oriented enterprises

There are a growing number of indications that business is currently undergoing a paradigm shift toward sustainability-oriented models and practices. The first is the increasing number of companies issuing CSR reports and drawing on the GRI.[17] For example, in 2001, Ford, McDonald's, Nike, and Starbucks each issued their own CSR reports. Although the definitions of "responsibility" and the information reported vary widely across a range of companies, the fact that time and money is being invested in this effort reveals a growing sense that there is a need to weigh in the company's position on sustainability-related issues. In addition, a growing number of businesses are seeking sustainability advisory services, including: CH2MHill, Collins Pine Company, IKEA, Nike, Scandic Hotels, and Starbucks (for more information on each of these cases, see Nattrass and Altomare 1999, 2002). An ever-increasing number of case studies of related efforts are emerging (e.g. see Gordon 2001; Holliday *et al.* 2002; Nattrass and Altomare 1999, 2002). Also, a *Wall Street Journal* and Harris Interactive Business School Survey in 2000 found that "77% of corporate recruiters said it is important to hire students with an awareness of social and environmental responsibility" (Alsop 2001: B12).

Further indicating a shift to sustainability, a 2000 PricewaterhouseCoopers (PwC) report stated:

> There is undoubtedly a rapid progression to greater focus and accountability on corporate sustainability or the environmental and social issues. With this comes the need to engage with stakeholders and demonstrate performance and transparency . . . *Failure to address the issue will result in greater cost, not least in relation to reputation, and could even lead to organizations not being allowed to operate* (PwC 2000 [emphasis added]).

The report concludes that "to add business value, organizations need to integrate environmental and social strategies into their core business strategy in a proactive and innovative manner" (PwC 2000).

Financial-sector indications of an emerging paradigm shift include the creation of the Dow Jones Sustainability Group Index, which, as of 31 October 2002, managed close to €2 billion. This index is premised on the recognition that companies addressing sustainability "have superior performances and favorable risk/return profiles because sustainability is a catalyst for enlightened and disciplined management, a crucial success factor."[18] In addition, over the past 15 years, investments

---

17 For more information on CSR reports, go to www.csrwire.com. On GRI guidelines, go to www.globalreporting.org.
18 See www.sustainability-index.com.

screened for social responsibility have grown considerably. In the USA, these funds increased from US$59 billion in 1984 to US$2.16 trillion in 1999 (Worldwatch Institute 2001). This amount represents US$1 out of every US$8 under professional management in the USA that is now subject to some level of corporate responsibility screening (Worldwatch Institute 2001). Sustainability-conscious investors are also increasingly using their money in new ventures that align with their goals. For example, over a ten-year period, the Investors' Circle[19] has facilitated the investment of over US$80 million in 130 socially responsible companies and small venture funds. Although screening methods vary, and few, if any, companies truly are sustainable, the fact that a market for these new financial instruments exists is telling that the time is ripe for change (see Box 3.3).

Rationale for a shift toward sustainability

The reasons for the emergence of sustainability-oriented business are many (see Box 3.4). In some instances, the shift is initially grounded in savings from eco-efficiency improvements that inform early stages of sustainability efforts. In the words of Peter Senge, a senior lecturer at the Sloan School of Management at the Massachusetts Institute of Technology, and Goran Carstedt, a former senior executive at Volvo and IKEA, for most businesses:

> The primary output of today's production processes is waste. Across all industries, less than 10% of everything that is extracted from the Earth (by weight) becomes usable products. The remaining 90% to 95% becomes waste from production . . . So while businesses obsess over labor and financial capital efficiency, we have created possibly the most inefficient system of production in human history (Senge and Carstedt 2001: 28).

These linkages—between waste, production, and costs—have built the business case for eco-efficiency, supporting the relationship between financial and environmental performance. It is now a well-documented relationship. For example, a survey of over two dozen academic studies shows strong empirical evidence of ties between environmental and economic performance (Wagner 2001). This study clearly showed that markets react positively to good corporate environmental deeds (such as signing the CERES [Coalition of Environmentally Responsible Economies] principles[20]) and negatively to bad ones (such as oil spills, findings of contamination, and so on). Similarly, multiple regression analyses find a generally positive and causal relationship between environmental and economic perfor-

---

19 The Investors' Circle is a non-profit organization that serves as a "national network of angel and institutional investors, foundation officers and entrepreneurs who seek to balance financial, social and environmental returns." The organization is "dedicated to catalyzing the flow of capital to private companies that deliver commercial solutions to social and environmental problems" (www.investorscircle.net).

20 www.ceres.org

Those organizations adopting sustainable business strategies today have favorable winds at their back. Customers, governments, investors, non-governmental organizations (NGOs), and multilateral organizations are all driving forces for sustainability. Individual and institutional investors are shifting their money toward socially responsible funds. NGOs are monitoring corporate operations and demanding accountability. Multilateral organizations—such as the Commission on Biodiversity, and the Global Reporting Initiative (GRI)—are pushing sustainable agendas.

Companies pursuing sustainability are poised to take advantage of these market forces. They also may realize other gains:

- According to Morningstar, socially responsible investment funds are at least 30% more likely to get a top 5-star rating than are non-socially responsible investments (Morningstar ratings measure risk and revenue potential; go to www.morningstar. com).

- Pressure from environmental NGOs ensured that trade and the environment were linked for the first time in the North American Free Trade Agreement (NAFTA; see Baker Fox 1995) and affected the negotiating positions of governments at the meeting of the World Trade Organization (WTO) in Seattle (see Bayne 2000).

- Some 60% of consumers have looked for products with ethical qualities, and 5% do it consistently, according to a study by the UK-based The Co-operative Bank (Cowe and Williams 2000).

- Research confirms that a majority of retail consumers will buy "greener" products, given equal price and quality (SustainAbility 2001: 23).

- Customers are willing to punish businesses that behave unethically, and expect transparency, honesty, and humility from businesses (Creyer and Ross 2001: 28).

In addition, these companies may also position themselves to participate in vast new markets. Sustainability-focused business models will be essential in addressing the needs of the 4 billion people currently making less than US$1,500 a year (Pralahad and hart 2002).

Box 3.3 Sustainability, market forces, and opportunities

Author: Frank Marquardt

---

mance showing that pollution prevention activities have a positive influence on financial performance—as measured by return on assets, return on sales, and return on investment. Perhaps most importantly, this review of the data revealed that conclusions about corporate benefits from environmental management practices are not tied to one or two examples but literally to dozens. The result is clear: "eco-efficiency works and builds value for customers and stakeholders" (DeSimone *et al.* 1997: xx).

However, going beyond a tight focus on eco-efficiency and becoming proactive on broad sustainability issues is essential. As DeSimone *et al.* argue:

> The secret is moving away from [a] compliance-focused, crisis avoidance mentality and seeing good environmental *and* social performance as the essential foundation for the market and public reputation and the motivated and confident staff that creates success in today's business environment (DeSimone *et al.* 1997: xx [emphasis added]).

Sustainability-focused enterprises elevate the importance of their social and environmental performance to a level usually reserved exclusively for economic performance. These investments are paying off in the form of:

- Cost savings
- Competitive advantage
- Consumer loyalty and trust
- Shareholder value

First, sustainability-focused re-engineering of energy and material flows can significantly reduce operational costs while increasing access to capital by lowering risks. Numerous organizations have cut operational costs through sustainable practices. To give two examples:

- 3M has saved more than US$810 million since 1975 through its Pollution Prevention Pays program (www.3m.com)
- Interface saved more than US$165 million between 1994 and 2000 by re-engineering production and by redesigning processes to reduce waste (www.interfaceinc.com).

Also, a *Business Week* ranking showed that 100 of the best-performing technology companies are either focused on achieving internal efficiency or selling services that enable others to be more efficient (Burrows and Green 2001).

Second, sustainability-oriented organizations position themselves to adapt to competitive pressures through innovation, focusing on technologies and systems that use financial, natural, and social resources in an efficient, effective, and economic manner, thereby creating new business options and the ability to respond to change. For instance, a UK study by Innovation through Partnerships showed that the core of innovation is a dynamic and resilient relationship between a company and its stakeholders; see http://strategis.ic.gc.ca/epic/internet/incsr-rse.nsf/vwgeneratedintere/rs00083e.html. Such companies also find it easier to attract and retain high-caliber employees. For example:

- A study by Rutgers University found that firms applying "high-performance work practices" have a 7.05% decrease in employee turnover with a US$3,814 increase in profits per employee (see Huselid 1995).

- A study by Students for Responsible Business found that 82.7% of MBA respondents would choose an offer for a more socially responsible company if the salaries offered were equal, and more than 50% were willing to accept a lower salary in order to work for a company with a good sustainable development reputation (Albion 1996).

Third, sustainable business practice enhances brand equity and reputation:

- A study by Cone-Roper found that 86% of consumers have a more positive image of a company if they see it doing something to make the world a better place (Creyer and Ross 1997).

- A study by DePaul University found that the average reputation score for a company with a strong commitment to business ethics was between 4.7% and 6.7% higher than for companies without this commitment (Verschoor 1998).

Last, research shows that companies pursuing a sustainable business strategy have significantly greater shareholder value than their peers:

Box 3.4 **The case for sustainability** (continued opposite)

Author: Frank Marquardt

● A study by IFC Kaiser—one of 330 companies within the S&P (Standard and Poor) 500—found that a 50% improvement in environmental management systems and environmental performance resulted in a 13.2% decrease in the beta statistic, a measure of sensitivity of stock used by analysts (Ameer *et al.* 1996).

That sustainability makes economic sense should not be surprising. Economic systems grow out of environmental and social systems. In the past, drawing down the "capital" of ecological and social systems led to financial gain. Today, these habits are increasingly leading to financial hardship—boycotts, fines, ruined reputations, and loss of the "license to operate." The pressures on companies to take responsibility for their impacts on the communities and environments they touch, and not simply on their economic results, are growing.

There is a simple reason why this is so. The scientific evidence showing that Nature's life-support systems are deteriorating is overwhelming. As consumption has increased, many ecosystem services have steadily become threatened. Stakeholders are realizing that, unless these types of behavior change, social and ecological systems will become increasingly vulnerable.

Box 3.4 (continued)

Another motivation for integrating sustainability concepts into business is the long view on business resource use. For example, the CEO of DuPont, Chad Holliday, has unequivocally stated in an article in the *Harvard Business Review* that:

> We have become increasingly aware of an inescapable and disturbing fact: We will not be able to sustain our businesses over the long haul because they are based on two assumptions that no longer hold. One is that cheap, unlimited supplies of hydrocarbons and other non-renewable resources will always be available. The other is that the Earth's ecosystems will indefinitely absorb the waste and emissions of our production and consumption (Holliday 2001: 130).

This statement starkly notes that the size and impact of businesses today is so significant that limits can be perceived. And these limits reveal fundamental boundaries for all companies. Reflecting these challenges, Holliday (2001: 130) further asserts that "companies will not succeed in the 21st century if the world's ecosystems continue to decline and if societies fail." This statement clearly reflects acknowledgment of companies' imbeddedness in broader ecological and social systems.

The role of sustainability in sparking innovation is another reason to rethink a company in terms of integrated financial, social, and ecological issues. For example, the 2000 PwC report, *Creating Business Value through Corporate Sustainability*, tightly links the importance of innovation to investor interest in non-financial measures for assessing organizational value.[21] It also asserts:

21 The PricewaterhouseCoopers report states that other non-financial measures used in assessing future earnings include: "quality of the corporate strategy and strategic goals; organizational ability to execute the corporate strategy; organization innovation; management credibility; [and] employee productivity" (PwC 2000: 1).

> Organizations that can move beyond compliance, address process
> efficiency issues [and] execute comprehensive and innovative corpo-
> rate strategies responding to new challenges and opportunities are
> more likely to realize competitive advantages and increased share-
> holder values (PWC 2000: 4).

Overall, sustainability initiatives focus on considering new ideas and approaches,
with the potential of leveraging new markets and first-mover advantages.

This emphasis on innovation through sustainability resonates with increasing
work on the role of non-financial factors in shaping investors' decisions. A continuing flow of new ideas will define leading businesses. Similarly, assessing the new
trends and maintaining key intangible advantages will define the cutting edge,
particularly in light of Ernst & Young's assertion that financial measures are often
lagging indicators (Ernst & Young 1997: 2).

The importance of continuous innovation, and other intangible factors, is
perhaps best articulated by an analogy and the assertion of a New York University
Professor of Accounting and Finance that: "To claim that intangible assets should
be measured and valued, while intangibles should not—or could not—is like
stating that 'things' are valuable, while 'ideas' are not" (Baruch Lev, quoted in Ernst
& Young 1997: 1). Sustainability concepts and practices offer a new set of intangibles that have the potential to differentiate businesses.

Another way of assessing the gains accrued by integrating sustainability concepts into business decisions is clear in the factors that go into the bottom-line
calculus, as laid out in Table 3.2.

For companies based in the USA and Europe, these factors have combined with
pressure from activist organizations, consultations with non-profit organizations
on integration of sustainability into business strategy and operations[22] and regulatory change (particularly in the European Union). All of these elements are
providing motivators to shifting towards sustainability-oriented business.

For this broad spectrum of reasons, an increasing number of companies are
experimenting with multi-pronged sustainability initiatives. These efforts seek not
only to exceed current regulations but also to explore the integration of social as
well as ecological factors into business. In this process, sustainable development
has firmly entered the corporate lexicon for the 21st century.

Conclusions

**Foresight is the key to survival. Managers able to perceive trends
and weak signals where others see only noise or chaos can capi-**

---

22   These voluntary advisory services offer technical information and analytical tools to
     guide environmental and sustainability-based decision-making and are provided by a
     range of non-profit organizations, including Business for Social Responsibility, the
     Environmental Defense Alliance for Environmental Innovation, The Natural Step, the
     Rocky Mountain Institute, Natural Capital Group and the Management Institute for
     Environment and Business at the World Resources Institute.

Traditional factors	Commonly recognized additional factors	Seldom recognized additional factors[a]
● Revenue ● Cost of sales ● Profit margins ● Cash flow ● Earning of net income ● Debt–equity ratio ● Price–earnings ratio	● Lawsuits ● Liabilities ● Fines ● Savings from efficiencies[b] ● Increased productivity, quality and consistency ● Ability to attract and retain the best employees ● Public and community relations improvements as a result of being a leader in environmental and social concerns ● Product differentiation and new market identification and development	● Reliable sources and flow of natural resource inputs ● "Social license to operate" in a city, state, region, or nation ● Innovation and productivity among workers ● Local-community public health ● Stability of socioeconomic context in which the business operates

[a] Related to systems thinking and sustainability
[b] For example, from reduced use of energy and resources

Table 3.2 Considering the full range of factors that affect the bottom line

Source: adapted from Tom Van Dyck, US bancorp Piper Jaffray, from a speech given at the Bioneers Conference, October 2001

talize on the changing nature of the market to reposition their firms before new entrants become a serious threat . . . Today's corporations can seize the opportunity for sustainable development.

Stuart Hart and Mark Milstein[23]

The focus needs to be on "whole system innovation:" identifying how e-commerce can contribute to more complex webs of sustainable innovation around energy, transport, production and consumption.

James Wilsdon and Paul Miller[24]

23   Hart and Milstein 1999: 24.
24   Wilsdon and Miller 2001: 14.

Given the changing business context and the increased importance of ecological and social impacts of decision-making, there is significant opportunity for firms that begin taking steps towards changing their strategies and operations. First, companies can question current boundaries of how they analyze their "responsibility" and impact, by assessing the full set of cascading effects of their decisions. This process will enable decision-makers to better understand what costs are hidden by current approaches to tracking and accounting. Second, business leaders can envision a viable enterprise that designs problems out of the system from the start, by integrating economic, ecological, and social sustainability factors into the core value proposition, strategy, and operations. Third, decision-makers can create a plan for moving the business of today in the direction of a sustainable business of tomorrow. Last, companies can invest in research and development focused on specific issues, such as developing and testing sustainability-based materials, products, and business models that will push the boundaries of currently accepted practice by greatly decreasing (and ultimately eliminating) environmental and social impacts.

A growing number of companies are acknowledging the relevance of sustainability concepts to their business. For example, BP chairman John Browne has stated, "there are good commercial reasons for being ahead of the pack when it comes to issues to do with the environment" (quoted in Senge and Carstedt 2001: 25). In addition, many companies have for many years been grappling with questions of how to address labor and other social issues. All these companies are in the rough waters of transition and shifts. None has yet figured out how to fully integrate these issues into its core business and reinvent its strategy and operations. However, an increasing number of firms have taken steps to recognize that new models of business are needed: ones that can define success in terms of financial as well as social and ecological parameters.

The powerful combination of business and sustainability will grow through the 21st century. Investment in sustainability-based strategies and approaches offers a unique leadership opportunity to businesses. The current business focus on efficiency allows for the introduction of new ways of thinking about improvements, from dematerialization through decreased energy use and cleaner transport. Sustainability, however, calls for innovation on a much greater scale, through integration of economic, ecological, and social impacts of business decisions. Leaders in integrating these issues into enterprises will fundamentally redefine what businesses are and how business is done.

Integrating sustainability into business strategy and operations

Applying The Natural Step approach and Framework and backcasting from principles of sustainability

Karl-Henrik Robèrt

Blekinge Technical University and The Natural Step, Sweden

Most businesspeople are familiar with CFCs (chlorofluorocarbons) and how they eventually became doomed as an input to modern industrial products. The scientific data linking the compound to damaging the ozone became overwhelming and, at great cost to a number of companies, replacements were sought.

Although the story is well known, few are fully aware of the great irony of its history. CFCs were originally introduced as being environmentally "perfect," because they were non-toxic and non-bioaccumulative. In light of those two parameters, the compound seemed relatively safe. However, the problem was that scientists did not yet understand other factors and dynamics within the Earth's complex systems. The effects on the ozone layer were not originally known.

CFCs represent one of many examples of decisions—in this case about "safe" materials—that have been made on a large scale, only to be followed by a late awakening and significant costs to society and individual organizations. PCBs (polychlorinated biphenyls), DDT (dichlorodiphenyltrichloroethane) and methyl mercury are other examples of compounds that have been linked to biological impacts, including diminished fertility in mammals and birds. Researchers have also detected bromine organic antiflammables in human blood, documented that plastic additives act as endocrine disrupters, identified that antibiotics in biota lead to a growing number of antibiotic-resistant strains of microbes, and linked kidney dysfunction to cadmium that humans have ingested in foods. All these examples show that society is repeating the same kinds of mistakes over and over again, without considering the lessons of industrial history.

Industrial history has shown that impacts generally occur through very complex interactions in the biosphere, which generally cannot be determined beforehand. At best, a certain impact can—after it has occurred—be clearly linked to a certain activity or process. However, these findings are usually associated with delays between the time of initial use of the compound and the discovery of its impacts.

Given this situation, it seems advisable to develop another approach to planning and decision-making that could more adequately take into account these realities. Such an alternative approach would not be based on an exhaustive understanding of all variables, because that is unlikely to occur, as the CFC case vividly shows. Rather, an alternative method could be based on the discovery, and disciplined use of, principles by which sustainability-oriented decisions—such as the selection and management of materials—are determined upfront and "upstream," or at the original point of decision of whether or not to use a particular input instead of after damage has already occurred.

As mentioned in Chapter 3, in the late 1980s a group of Swedish scientists set out to develop just such an approach. Since then, The Natural Step framework for strategic sustainable development has been developed and published in numerous scientifically peer-reviewed papers (e.g. see Holmberg and Robèrt 2000a; Robèrt 1994, 2000; Robèrt *et al.* 2002). The Natural Step Framework has been applied within businesses to enable decision-makers to understand sustainability issues and begin planning based on these new insights (Bradbury and Clair 1999b; Nattrass and Altomare 1999, 2002). In this chapter I describe the Framework and offer examples of its application.

Backcasting from principles of success: introduction to The Natural Step Framework and approach

The Natural Step Framework is built on "backcasting" from "basic principles of success," as explained in Box 4.1. The methodology has been elaborated from back-casting from scenarios (Robinson 1990), a planning approach that begins with envisioning a picture of success. This scenario approach is similar to working on a

Backcasting is a planning procedure by which a successful outcome is imagined in the future, and decision-makers ask: "What was it that we did today that allowed us to get to this outcome?"

The basic principles of success are principles that are:

- Necessary, and sufficient, to enable a successful outcome (i.e. social and ecological sustainability), independent of scale or field of activity
- Sufficiently concrete to guide problem analysis and creative solutions
- Mutually exclusive, to enable clear understanding and to allow for the development of metrics for the comprehensive monitoring of the process in relation to the goals

Box 4.1 Backcasting from principles of success

jigsaw puzzle while being guided by a specific image of the finished puzzle. The picture helps the person doing the jigsaw to deal with its complexity and clarify the actions needed to move toward the desired result. Similarly, the scenario aids the decision-maker in understanding the goal(s) that she or he is moving towards.

However, backcasting from scenarios raises several difficulties when it is applied to sustainable development. The first relates to the challenge of developing detailed descriptions of scenarios on which many people will agree with regard to a successful sustainable outcome. The second, and related, shortcoming within the sustainability context is that there is often resistance to making very detailed plans in light of ongoing technical developments that may subsequently change the planning conditions. Third, and finally, this technique often becomes mired in the question of how we know whether a detailed description of a sustainable enterprise or society really is sustainable. Decision-makers appear to face great uncertainty, particularly in relation to sustainability issues.

These shortcomings, however, can be addressed by an adapted approach of backcasting from basic principles of success. This approach resembles a game of chess rather than a jigsaw puzzle. It is the principles of success—such as the principle of checkmate—that guides the game. This approach offers a dynamic way in which to engage in planning, whereby each move takes the current situation of the game into account while at the same time optimizing the possibility of winning, which can come about in many different ways. One of several advantages of this method is that it is easier to agree on basic principles for success—as well as some actions that can serve as stepping stones in the general desired direction—than it is to agree on detailed descriptions of a final outcome.

These basic principles of sustainability can be derived and elaborated as "first-order" mechanisms—that occur "upstream" at the first level of approximation—to create ecological and social *un*sustainability. The principles are based on an understanding of ecological and social dynamics and the complexities of these interconnected systems.

Understanding complex systems and thinking "upstream:" the rationale for the principles of The Natural Step Framework

Within a planning framework for complex systems it is essential to keep five hierarchical levels apart and not to confuse them with each other (Robèrt 2000):

- Level 1: systems
- Level 2: success
- Level 3: strategy
- Level 4: actions
- Level 5: the toolbox

These five levels are illustrated in Figure 4.1. For example, the use of renewable energy belongs to the action category (level 4), not the success category (level 2). A change to renewable energy is not a principle, but something that we do. Although it is an important step forward, a shift to renewable energy may lead to significant ecological impacts, such as the flooding of areas (in the case of hydropower), or deforestation (in the case of extensive use of biomass fuel sources). Therefore, this action is not in itself a principle for sustainability. Rather, renewable energy should be introduced in a way that will comply with the principles of sustainability.

This example highlights that the success level is at the heart of planning. It should inform strategies, actions, and tool design. This level is developed through backcasting from the principles of success, or, by imagining that the conditions for success are complied with and then asking, "What shall we do now to optimize our chances of reaching this successful outcome?"

In the case sustainability, as further detailed in Figure 4.2, to arrive at a principle definition of success (level 2), we must know enough about the system (level 1), which consists of the biosphere and human societies as well as the interactions and flows of materials between the two. Since the concept of sustainability (level 2)

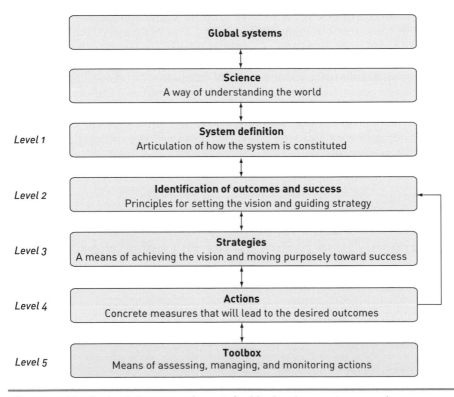

Figure 4.1 The logic of the strategic sustainable development approach to decision-making

Source: Robèrt *et al.* 2002

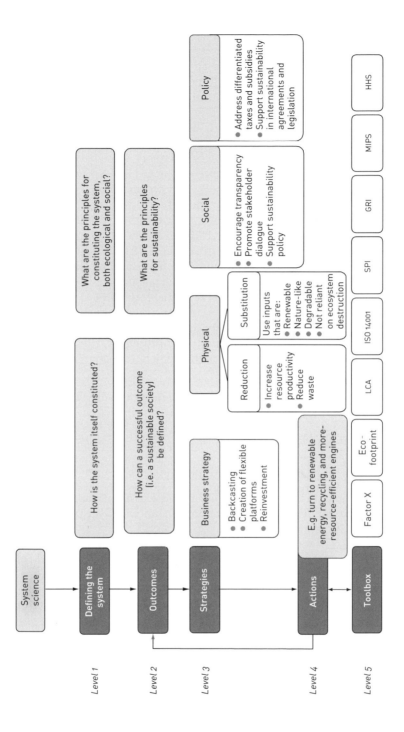

Figure 4.2 Overview of the strategic sustainable development approach to decision-making

Source: Robèrt et al. 2002

becomes relevant only as we understand the *non*-sustainability inherent in the current activities of society, it is logical to design principles for sustainability as restrictions that determine what human activities must *not* do in order to avoid destroying the interrelated ecological and social systems.

CFCs provide a good illustration of this issue. Given that in the relatively recent past many people thought that CFCs were "harmless," it is incumbent on us to ask what compounds are perceived as harmless today but that may be understood differently tomorrow. In what ways—expressed as principles—could we destroy the systems' (the biosphere's and society's) ability to sustain us? The answers to this question should be looked for at their sources, or "upstream," in the complex relationships and cause–effect chains, where basic errors of societal design trigger numerous negative impacts that occur later "downstream." To correct errors at this systems level—or "upstream," in cause–effect chains—is the only way to address current problems and avoid new problems. By understanding this level (i.e the basic rules of the game, from a biophysical and societal perspective), we will be able to ask the right questions and to structure the available details in a way that makes sense for decision-making.

Scientists understand, and increasingly agree on, key mechanisms that are resulting in non-sustainability. In terms of basic principles, these issues can be grouped into three separate mechanisms by which humans can destroy the biosphere and its ability to sustain society:

- A systematic increase in the net concentration of matter that is introduced into the biosphere from outside sources

- A systematic increase in concentration of matter that is produced within the biosphere

- A systematic degradation by physical means

Together, these first three basic principles provide a framework for ecological sustainability that implies a set of restrictions within which sustainable societal activities must be incorporated.

The sustainability of society depends also on addressing human needs through the maintenance and robust functioning of social systems, including formal institutions as well as the informal structuring of civil society as a whole. These issues relate not only to sustaining society but also to complying with the above three ecological constraints. Therefore, these interrelated social and ecological dynamics necessitate a fourth basic condition that takes into account the social aspects of sustainability.

Finally, by adding "not" before each of these mechanisms, it is possible to identify a set of basic principles for defining sustainability in the system (i.e. the biosphere and society). These four principles are articulated as system conditions in:

- *System condition 1: the first principle relates to societal influence on the biosphere as a result of the accumulation of lithospheric material (material from the Earth's crust).*

   The balance of flows between the biosphere and the lithosphere must be such that concentrations of substances from the lithosphere do not systematically increase in the whole biosphere, or in parts of it. This balance can be influenced in two ways: first, through upstream decisions about what and how much to mine from the Earth's crust; second, by society's ability to safeguard, re-use, and continually cycle existing mined materials through recycling and other measures.

Over the long term, the sustainability of concentrations of materials from the lithosphere that are in the biosphere will depend on properties such as eco-toxicity—understood in a broad sense to include effects on geophysical systems—and bioaccumulation. Owing to the complexity and delay mechanisms in the biosphere, it is often very difficult to foresee what concentration will lead to negative impacts. A general rule is not to allow deviations from the natural state that are large in comparison with natural fluctuations. However, even more importantly, such deviations *should not be allowed to increase systematically*. Therefore, what must be achieved at the very least is a halt to systematic increases in the net concentration of matter that is introduced to the biosphere from the Earth's crust.

● *System condition 2: the second principle focuses on societal influence on the biosphere as a result of the accumulation of substances produced in society.*

This mechanism differs functionally from the first, as production refers to the combining of elements into compounds, whereas system condition 1 reflects the net input of elements. More specifically, the flows of molecules and nuclides that leak from societal activities must not be so large that they can neither be integrated into the natural cycles within the biosphere nor be deposited safely into the lithosphere. The balance of flows must be such that concentrations of substances produced in society do not systematically increase in the whole biosphere or in parts of it. As well as the upstream influence on this balance through production volumes and the characteristics of what is produced, such as the degradability of the produced substances, the balance can also be influenced by the quality of final deposits and our ability to safeguard the flows through measures such as recycling and thermal treatment.

In a sustainable society:

1. Nature is not subject to systematically increasing concentrations of substances extracted from the Earth's crust.

2. Nature is not subject to systematically increasing concentrations of substances produced by society.

3. Nature is not subject to systematically increasing degradation by physical means.

4. The ability of humans to meet their needs worldwide is not systematically undermined.

Box 4.2 The Natural Step's four system conditions

Just as there are differences in the properties of different metals, the qualitative differences between various compounds are also complex. There is therefore a need for us to take into account even subtle differences and consider carefully the respective flows of these materials and the practices used to deal with them.

- *System condition 3: the third principle relates to societal influence on the biosphere by physical means. It covers all kinds of destructive manipulation, displacement and harvesting of natural capital and natural flows within the biosphere.*

  This condition implies that the resource basis for productivity in the biosphere—such as thickness and quality of soils, availability of fresh water, protection of biodiversity, and so on—is not systematically degraded by over-harvesting, mismanagement and other ecological impacts by physical means (e.g. through disruption of groundwater flows, or through displacement, such as placing asphalt over productive ecosystems).

- *System condition 4: the final principle relates to social dynamics and the production of services for humans. The challenge is to meet the human needs of our society locally and worldwide.*

  The term "human needs" is defined here not only in terms of basic physical needs (such as for food and fresh water) but also in terms of broader "constitutional" needs that that must be satisfied for humans to stay mentally and socially healthy (such as the protection of human life, understanding, identity, and so on; for references on this subject, see Cook *et al.* 2002).

Taken together, the first three system conditions define an ecological framework for any sustainable society, and the fourth principle is the basic social condition. This fourth system condition interacts with the other three in a dynamic way. In addition, if the purpose of society is to meet human needs—worldwide, today, and in the future, while conforming to the ecological constraints given by the first three principles—then sustainability implies that we also need improved means of dealing with social issues such as "equity" and "fairness" from the perspective of human needs. It is an ineffective use of resources, from the perspective of humanity, if one billion people starve and lack access to safe drinking water while at the same time another billion use more resources for low-value activities such as sitting in traffic jams. These issues could begin to be addressed by keeping the basic needs of humanity in mind—all people, now and in the future—in planning and decision-making processes.

Consideration of these basic principles of sustainability also makes it easier for us to draw conclusions upstream in complex cause–effect chains or at the sources of problems. For example, consider the principle of conservation of matter—that which is introduced into society has a tendency eventually to leak out into ecosystems. From a backcasting perspective, this reality leads to questions such as: "Do we use persistent compounds that are foreign to Nature?" "Do we incur social costs through the purchase of specific materials and products made (particularly those from the developing world)?" These questions, and many others sparked by this approach to thinking, open up the mind to a wide-screen perspective and should have at least as high priority as the question "Do we emit this or that eco-toxic substance?" The problem is that the latter question covers only those substances and activities that have already surfaced as problematic, whereas the first set of questions completes the picture at the basic principle level, helping us to avoid new problems that will otherwise surface in the future.

Applying The Natural Step Framework: a strategic sustainable development decision-making process

The Natural Step has placed these principles into a framework for sustainable development that is used in conjunction with backcasting techniques. Actions are launched, step by step, in a strategic way to serve as viable "stepping stones" towards compliance with the sustainability principles. The framework is systematized as an approach to facilitate brainstorming sessions and team planning, as presented below, in the "A–B–C–D" methodology.

Phase A: explaining the framework

The process begins with phase A, in which the framework (containing the system conditions) is explained to offer a shared mental model for "community building" among the participants of the planning process. This step enables the group to play the "game" of sustainable development by the same rules.

During the process, a few metaphors are used to explain the relevance of sustainability to all participants in the group. For example, non-sustainable development can be perceived as a situation where society enters deeper and deeper into a metaphorical "funnel" in which there is declining potential for quality of life, within society at large as well as within individual companies and organizations. Specifically, pollutants and gases that induce climate change are increasing in concentration, and the productivity of ecosystems is decreasing, which means that there are greater throughputs of resources to obtain the same harvest or catch. At the same time, human global population is growing, as are income gaps and economic disparities. The overall result is that, per capita, the resource potential for living prosperous lives is systematically declining as all the world's inhabitants move deeper and deeper into the "funnel" of declining resources. This set of dynamics is even more evident when we consider that legitimate demands from the "have-nots" of the world are on the rise. Use of The Natural Step approach and framework enables decision-makers to decrease the risk of "hitting" the walls of the funnel, such as by increasing the costs to source natural resources, manage waste, fight legislation, control negative press about corporate impacts, or lose market share to other firms that develop solutions that have positive effects—financially, socially, and ecologically.

This metaphor vividly explains the need for the integration of sustainability factors into decision-making processes. It also highlights that the application of sustainability concepts, and The Natural Step Framework, does not depend on altruistic motivations or a reliance on the saving of money and resources through greater efficiency. Rather, there are significant business benefits in integrating the full scope, or range, of sustainability issues into business decisions.

Nonetheless, some companies argue that it is not worth acting proactively and integrating sustainability into decision-making processes because the timing for such negative events is difficult to determine. However, this argument actually works the other way around. That is, the business risk for being part of the problem—by continuing with inherently non-sustainable practices—will systematically increase in the future as the "walls of the funnel" continue to tighten. To change a company to fully integrate sustainability principles will require time. Few firms can rapidly alter their dependence on non-sustainable energy systems, infrastructure, technologies, and management routines, and even fewer will be able to (re)build a brand and positive reputation, or control negative press, overnight. Rather, what a firm does today influences its chances for success tomorrow. All these issues are discussed in this first phase of the process.

Phase B: assessing the organization's position

The second phase, phase B, includes conducting an assessment of where an organization is "today" in terms of sustainability. This task is done by analysing all current flows and practices that are critical from a sustainability perspective and by developing a set of diagrams and lists to represent these flows and practices. At the same time, the group considers all the assets that are in place to deal with problems.

This assessment process can be ongoing. For example, through the life-cycle of materials—from resource extraction, through transport, processing, and use, to disposal—the four system conditions can be used as a guide to discover flows and management routines that are critical from a sustainability perspective. Questions may emerge over whether or not a substance is persistent and foreign to Nature. Solutions are sought in combinations of dematerialization and substitution of each critical flow, as described below. In addition, when new products are planned, this way of thinking can inform all stages of a traditional product design cycle— from investigation of needs, through the production and marketing of a prototype of the principle product, to the production and marketing of the final product.[1]

Phase C: creating solutions and visions

The third phase, phase C, involves the creation of solutions and visions for "tomorrow," through application of the constraints arising from the system conditions

---

1   In conjunction with ten small to medium-size companies, The Natural Step is currently developing this way of planning into a concrete tool for sustainable product development. An essential aspect of this study is to identify hierarchies of relevant questions for each system condition.

and suggested solutions listed and scrutinized. This process is undertaken at a brainstorming session where top management is actively engaged. At this point, no significant constraints are applied other than looking only at what is theoretically feasible.

Phase D: setting priorities and taking action

Finally, the fourth phase, phase D, involves making priorities from the list developed in phase C and launching concrete programs for change. This step provides the framework with its strategic component. Suggestions from the list generated in phase C are prioritized. Selection of activities to be launched relatively early on—to serve as stepping stones for further improvements—should be based on responses to the following three questions:

- *Does this measure move in the right direction with regard to all system conditions?* Sometimes a measure represents a trade-off, moving in the right direction with respect to one of the system conditions but at the expense of some of the others. Asking this question enables decision-makers to see the full picture and to find complementary measures that may be needed in order to take all system conditions into account. Consequently, this question often increases the length of lists of opportunities and potential solutions.

- *Does this measure provide a stepping stone for future improvements?* It is important that investments be further elaborated or completed in line with the system conditions, so that they do not lead to dead ends. For example, it would be unwise to invest heavily in a technology that will cause fewer impacts on Nature in the short term but that will be difficult to adapt later on or that may be difficult to move away from in order to achieve ultimate and complete compliance with the system conditions.

- *Is this measure likely to produce a good return on investment soon enough to fertilize further processes for future improvements?*

It is the combination of answering "yes" to each of these three questions that provides the strategic element of the Framework. Each suggested investment is scrutinized with regard to its potential to reduce impacts, allow the organization to progress further towards sustainability, and secure the funding of ongoing work, particularly within a business context.

Utilizing the strategy

For use throughout the process, the system conditions can be "translated" into objectives that are relevant to the individual organization (see Box 4.3). For an organization that does not want to be a problem in the system, a logical and ethically relevant translation would be to add the words *our contribution* into the phrasing of the system conditions.

The ultimate sustainability objective of our organization is to:

- Eliminate our contribution to systematic increases in concentrations of substances from the Earth's crust

- Eliminate our contribution to systematic increases in concentrations of substances produced by society

- Eliminate our contribution to systematic physical degradation of Nature

- Eliminate our contribution to the undermining of humans' ability to meet their needs worldwide

Box 4.3 Sustainability objectives for companies based on The Natural Step's four system conditions

Overall, each individual organization must draw its own conclusions from these basic principles with regard to problems, solutions, goals, and objectives. However, the framework provides a systematic way of guiding this intellectual process, through an "A–B–C–D" process.

Integrating sustainability thinking into action: the dynamics of dematerialization and substitution

Each of the system conditions represents a basic principle for sustainability. To comply with the system conditions in the future management of materials requires combined dematerialization and substitution (Robèrt *et al.* 2002). These actions mean that, when society is managing materials in a sustainable way, minerals and metals (system condition 1) and chemicals and unintentionally produced compounds (system condition 2) are no longer increasing in concentration in the biosphere. That is, all compounds will have ceased to increase systematically, not only those that are currently causing identified impacts. Furthermore, renewable materials will not be over-harvested and/or purchased from poorly managed ecosystems or from companies that are failing to restore ecosystems (system condition 3). In addition, infrastructure for transport will not be growing systematically and eroding the landmass of productive ecosystems (system condition 3). Finally, materials will not be wasted and/or made inaccessible by other means to less affluent people. Nor does the extracting, manufacturing, transporting, warehousing, distributing, and marketing of any items contribute to social behavior or abuses that undermine people's capacity to address their human needs and live a fulfilling life (system condition 4).

In turn, from an industrial perspective this future will require dematerialization by means of higher resource productivity and less waste. Such dematerialization (e.g. by recycling or making improvements to designs) will allow for greater material performance per utility unit, avoiding accumulation of waste (system conditions 1 and 2) and reducing the physical pressure on productive ecosystems (system condition 3). These actions will increase resource productivity and reduce waste, which will feed into the possibility of achieving sufficient resources for people on a global scale (system condition 4).

Substitution will also be needed, as many of the currently used materials and management routines are so problematic from a sustainability perspective that they will be too expensive to safeguard within the constraints provided by the system conditions. Examples of materials that will need to be substituted with respect to the first three system conditions include:

- System condition 1: heavy metals that are usually very scarce in eco-systems (e.g. cadmium; see Azar *et al.* 1995)

- System condition 2: chemicals that are relatively persistent and foreign to Nature (e.g. bromine-containing organic anti-flammables)

- System condition 3: materials that are extracted in ways that do not restore natural systems (e.g. strip mining, and the harvesting of timber from poorly managed ecosystems)

Such flows should not only be dematerialized—necessary during the transition period—but also, in the end, be phased out and substituted with other materials and practices.

New materials should be selected in a way that maximizes the benefits for global society and presents opportunities for future generations that will be easier to adapt within the constraints of the system conditions. This means that the flows of certain other materials may not be dematerialized but will be increased in relation to current use in order to arrive at a sustainable society. Other materials may be scarce and foreign to Nature, and yet their respective flows may be essential for sustainability and consequently need to be increased in a sustainable way (i.e. safeguarded by extraordinary societal means and "closed-loop" processes). Examples might be scarce metals in thoroughly recycled photovoltaic cells.

The practice of dematerialization and substitution are not only important independently but also are interrelated in a dynamic way that should be utilized in planning. For example, the less degradable a material is, the more it must be safeguarded and/or dematerialized within the "technosphere," or industrial systems, particularly if it is relatively scarce in natural systems. For scarce metals the assimilation is slow and occurs as sedimentation and biomineralization. For chemicals that are relatively persistent and foreign to Nature, assimilation occurs also as degradation with relatively long half-lifetimes.

Finally, it is essential to note that there are economic relationships between dematerialization and substitution. For example, when very profound dematerialization is not sufficient to achieve sustainability goals—perhaps because materials are relatively non-degradable and/or impact levels in natural systems have already been exceeded (e.g. in the case of CFCs or PCBs)—then substitutions may be relatively expensive early on. This cost ratio is a function of the early production volumes of the substitutes, which are likely to be relatively small in the initial stages of a transition. Furthermore, these changes will often require investment in new infrastructure. One example is the development of new coolants in refrigerators; in the shift away from CFCs, new refrigerators must be designed to use those new coolants. To make the substitutions affordable the implementation of new technologies is often made possible through various types of dematerialization, such as the achievement of greater resource productivity and the production of less waste within the new and more expensive production lines and products (Holmberg and Robèrt 2000a; Robèrt *et al.* 2002). In short, dematerialization supports substitution, and substitution will prompt dematerialization.

Examples from industry

Electrolux

One example of these dynamics and planning with sustainability in mind is the way in which Electrolux phased out the use of CFCs. The introduction of hydrochlorofluorocarbons (HCFCs) would have meant an improvement in relation to the use of CFCs in terms of effects on the ozone layer. However, use of The Natural Step Framework, and backcasting from the system conditions, led to the following questions being asked:

- Can we assume that HCFCs will be used on a large scale in the future?

- If not, would the developed technology for HCFCs be applicable to other substances that would be less problematic from the system condition point of view?

These questions led to a completely different strategy towards sustainable use of hydrocarbons, with use of the compound R134a as a flexible platform—or stepping stone—towards compliance with the system conditions, mainly the second system condition (Robèrt 1997). Though this compound has a relatively low degradability and does not fit the long-term goal in itself, it could be used as an incremental step toward a new type of white good. This new type of white good was designed specifically to be adaptable for the next generation of degradable hydrocarbons that Electrolux was developing.

This process led Electrolux to become the first in launching a whole family of freon-free refrigerators and freezers. The result was an increased market share in several important markets. The company also developed a new overall business strategy, based on the system conditions, which eventually encompassed a subtle balance of strategically chosen dematerializations and substitutions, for a number of product lines, under each system condition (Electrolux 1994).

IKEA

Another example of systematic planning of this type is the methodology by which IKEA introduced its particular brand of low-energy lamps on the market. The trade-offs between wasting energy on the one hand and increasing pollution with mercury on the other have different dimensions and cannot be compared with

Replacing an incandescent lamp with a CFL [compact fluorescent lamp] will give considerable savings in energy consumption and electricity costs (roughly a factor 5) and a considerable increase in product life (factor 8–10). But the high price has been an obstacle for the private households to dare to prove these facts to themselves in practice. The typical price level in Sweden at the time was SEK120 ($15) for an 11 W CFL (corresponding to a 60 W incandescent lamp). The reason for the high price has evidently been that the lamp manufacturing giants have large production facilities for incandescent lamps and don't want to compete with themselves by marketing CFLs at low prices. [However,] the problem is even more complex, since CFLs have higher mercury contents than incandescent lamps.

The trade-off problem is between higher use of mercury (system condition 1), lower expenditure of energy (mainly system conditions 1 and 2) and higher costs for the lamps, lowering their availability to the public (system condition 4).

A more creative methodology than trying to estimate if the impacts outweigh the benefits is to start the planning procedure from a point where the trade-offs do not exist—backcasting from the system conditions to find a strategy to comply with [all of] them. In short, these were the moves that followed from a specific planning process.

[First,] we identified a producer who could provide a good enough combination of the listed criteria to serve as a platform. We wanted a good reliable CFL with a maximum of 3 milligrams [mercury] per lamp, which can be compared with the requirements in the European Union environmental labeling system for such lamps, which is a maximum of 10 milligrams on the global market (factor 3). A Chinese manufacturer, outstanding both from product design and production technology points of view, could meet those requirements in the same time [and offer a] competitive price. [Second,] we let this producer, and [its] competitors, know that as long as [they] were ahead of the competitors [with regard to] price, energy expenditure and mercury contents, [then they] would continue to do business with IKEA. We then visited the supplier's RD&E department and discussed possibilities for further reducing of the mercury content and other potential environmental improvements. We documented our visit on video and the edited videocassettes were later distributed to all our Swedish stores.

Finally, we informed customers about the very serious environmental dangers with mercury and offered them to take back (free of charge) all their used light sources containing mercury to the IKEA stores. We made a contract with a major recycling company (RagnSell) to take care of all such returned light sources with mercury, including all those we generate ourselves in stores, warehouses, and offices. [Some] 98%–99% of the mercury is recovered by a specialist company in Germany. Together with SSNC we made a thorough review also of this company and documented this on the videocassette mentioned above.

As a result of this campaign the private household sales of CFLs in Sweden have increased considerably. The competition had to decrease their prices. Our CFL sales have increased.

We think that our campaign has been good for everybody—for the customers and for the country (we need to save energy in order to close down nuclear reactors)—except the manufacturers and importers of incandescent lamps. We calculated that, if every Swedish household replaced 20 pieces of 60 W incandescent lamps with 11 W CFLs, the resulting yearly energy savings would equal the production of one of the Swedish nuclear reactors.

Case study 4.1 IKEA: the introduction of low-energy lamps

Source: Russel Johnsson, 2002, personal communication

each other by scientific means. The problem was dealt with through backcasting and jointly expressing a vision that, in the future, lamps would be very energy-efficient yet would not contribute to increasing concentrations of mercury or any other pollutant, while also making perfect business sense and appealing to customers, even those with a "thin wallet." How could IKEA produce a flexible platform to arrive at this point? The story is presented by the head of environmental affairs at that time, Russel Johnsson (see Case study 4.1).

Discussion and conclusions

The Natural Step Framework and approach are elaborated from the constraints determined by basic principles of sustainability. Backcasting from the basic principles of sustainability is a framework that covers the relevant aspects of how to plan ahead in a complex system, such as for societies within the biosphere. The approach brings a sustainability perspective to analyses of current practices and materials, to suggested solutions and visions and to the strategic evaluation of various solutions and paths to move towards sustainability. Also, this approach brings a new perspective to opportunities for improved economic outcomes.

A framework for sustainable development is neither an alternative to scientific studies and facts nor a substitute for specific concepts and tools that inform actions. All these elements are essential. A framework stitches it all together, creates comprehension and provides direction to the planning process. Without a full systems-based approach and framework, it is difficult to:

- Ensure that all aspects of the sustainable use of materials are considered from a full systems perspective

- Enable decision-makers to assess current data and information on sustainability in a structure that is relevant to strategic decisions

- Discover areas where more information is necessary—or unnecessary—for making relevant decisions

- Focus problem-solving upstream at the source of problems, in order to design problems out of the system

- Evaluate alternative material solutions and visions from a strategic point of view, so that "blind alleys" can be avoided

- Deal with trade-offs in a strategic way

- Build creative assessment and problem-solving communities through shared mental models

- Involve all aspects of business in a cohesive manner, including: leadership, management, programs of activities, product development, choice of materials, and indicators

Sometimes, there are many possible choices that fit the presented framework and can serve as strategic "stepping stones" towards consonance with the system conditions. How can a decision-maker determine priorities among the various options? Is it possible to come up with checklists or manuals to support decision-making beyond the overall framework, with its guidelines for dematerialization and substitution throughout the life-cycle of materials? Given that complete compliance with the system conditions is the ultimate goal, on what grounds can trade-offs during the transition be managed? How are uncertainties with regard to compliance with the principles addressed?

From other complex systems, such as a game of chess, a couple of essential conclusions can be drawn that answer these questions. First, once basic rules are clear, the individual's potential to deal with trade-offs and optimize chances of success in multidimensional and complex situations is very great. Second, one of the most essential elements for utilizing this potential, and becoming "professional," is to learn and become more and more experienced. Last, beyond a certain level of specificity, checklists confuse people more than they help.

Therefore, it is unlikely that very detailed checklists or manuals can replace any of the time-consuming training it takes to be a professional planner in a complex system. The reason is that when decision-makers choose between various strategic options for sustainable development there are many categories of criteria in play simultaneously that present themselves as "gray areas," so that each situation has a tendency to be "unique" (for examples of categories of criteria, see Box 4.4). In other

---

Seven of the most obvious and important categories of decision criteria are described below.

Category 1: certainty of current data and information

This category varies between:

- No knowledge about risks, or even about the very existence of a material or compound (meaning that there is zero influence on decisions)
- Certainty, so that the categories described below are allowed to determine the outcome of planning

Between these extremes, a gray zone influences decisions in a relative manner. The "precautionary principle" has been launched to deal with this gray area and is further informed by categories 2 and 3 described below.

Category 2: seriousness

This category communicates directly with the first. The extremes in this category lie between:

- Full knowledge of very serious social and/or ecological impacts
- Full knowledge of completely benign impacts

Between these extremes we again have a gray area, this time expressed as the "degree of potential danger." The greater the seriousness of the potential impacts, the smaller the certainty needs to be to provide a rationale for undertaking proactive measures.

Box 4.4 Categories of decision criteria relevant to sustainable development
(continued over)

Category 3: urgency

The combined result of the first two categories is now integrated into the time perspective. The extremes are:

- Certain information on very serious impacts that will occur very soon
- Vague information on very benign effects that might occur in the distant future

Again we have a gray area between these extremes—multidimensional in nature.

Category 4: the relative contribution to the problem by individual players

This category reflects the moral dilemma. The greater an organization's contribution to a problem, the greater the ethical demands on that organization to do something about it. For obvious reasons, this contribution often lies somewhere within a gray area. Uncertainty here should not be used as a means of dodging responsibility. We are dependent on the system and should be prepared to be held accountable for impacts we inflict on the biosphere.

Category 5: the efficacy of possible solutions

This category can be subdivided into two interrelated categories:

- Technical potential
- Economic potential

The technical potential relates to whether or not an actor has access to effective means to deal with a problem. The potential of providing a substantial contribution to a solution is a driver for activity, and vice versa. Needless to say, reality often presents itself somewhere in a gray zone.

Regarding the economic potential, even if very effective measures exist to solve the problem it is not certain that contributions to solving the problem will be particularly attractive or even possible from an economic point of view. The extremes lie between the following two situations:

- There is a net income from the measures. (In this case, there may not be any other drivers.)
- The pure costs are so great that the measure is not within the realm of a realistic budget.

Category 6: market visibility

This category varies between high and low visibility, respectively. It also has a complex ethical dimension.

With regard to negative impacts, a decision may be made *not* to take measures to solve a problem because there is a high probability of avoiding being caught. This is an unethical and ultimately flawed decision. The same applies to paying "lip service" to solving the problem and "showing off" without any greater engagement with the real cause of the problem. If, however, the high visibility of very good actions is allowed to influence decisions for marketing reasons, it may be a good thing not only for marketing but also for the creation of role models and leaders within society.

Category 7: clustered risks

The list of categories above is complex enough. However, it deals with the risks of only one identifiable material or problem. In reality, sustainability risks that are linked to individual materials and products present themselves as clustered risks when seen from the perspective of the whole life-cycle of the product—from resource extraction to end-use and disposal of products.

Box 4.4 (continued)

words, attempts to come up with very detailed, layered, "hands-on" manuals—on top of a framework of basic principles—have a tendency to result in so many feedback loops and footnotes and exceptions that they risk causing confusion rather than helping the reader.

The conclusion is clear. It is not possible to create upfront comprehensible, easy-to-handle, and detailed checklists or manuals for the management of complex systems. Problems are generally multidimensional, and each dimension presents itself as a gray area.

Instead, the overall recommendation would be to make principles for success very clear upfront as well as to create smart overall strategies and guidelines to approach those principles (i.e. to apply a framework to decisions as a shared mental model among team members) and then to get on with learning and playing the "game." This process allows for deep experience to be gained and used in seeing the larger picture for reaching the goal and selecting stepping stones in that direction.

Finally, as the process unfolds—and as the marginal costs in relation to utility and profit decreases, as more and more "low-hanging fruit" is picked—it is likely that a need for more sophisticated tools will evolve, including ISO 14001, life-cycle assessments, tools for product development, and purchase manuals. To ensure, however, that all efforts continue to move in the same direction, all these tools should be informed by the same framework that informs the business program— backcasting from basic principles of success.

Part 2
Case studies of
evolving business initiatives

For while the giants have just been talking about an information
superhighway, the ants have actually been building one.

The Economist 1995[1]

The process of applying sustainability concepts and frameworks to business is
already under way. The chapters in this part describe a range of implementation
efforts. The case studies serve to reveal new ways of doing business, and cover:

- A large company (Hewlett Packard; Chapter 5)
- A medium-sized company (Norm Thompson; Chapter 6)
- Small companies (the Healthy Forests, Healthy Communities partnership; Oregon Country Beef; Stahlbush Farms; Chapter 7)
- A start-up company (Verdant Power; Chapter 8)

As a set, these examples demonstrate how sustainability concepts are informing new
ways of operating and, in some cases, new overarching business strategies.

---

1   "The Accidental Superhighway," *The Economist: A Survey of the Internet*, 1–7 July 1995
    (quoted at http://alpha.zimage.com/~ant/antfarm/read/quotes. html).

Sustainability and dematerialization at Hewlett Packard

David Hudson and Lynelle Preston
Hewlett Packard, California, USA

> Environmental protection is a complex undertaking, but the laws
> of Nature are simple. We will provide leadership on the journey to
> an environmentally sustainable future.
>
> *Carleton S. Fiorina*[1]

It seems that, overnight, companies are addressing and pursuing sustainability and sustainable development. Is this really new for businesses? In many cases, the principles of sustainability are in fact radically shifting how companies think about future business success. At Hewlett Packard, however, although the focus on sustainability at a corporate strategy level is relatively new, in many ways the concept of sustainability is not. Rather, it is the logical extension of a long history of corporate citizenship deeply ingrained within the company's culture and values.

We begin this chapter with a brief description of how citizenship has been integrated into Hewlett Packard's core strategy since the company's early days, and how it is now evolving into sustainability. The focus then shifts to the environmental aspect of sustainability and, more specifically, to Hewlett Packard's dematerialization initiative. We then describe the role of dematerialization in information technology (IT) and highlight four specific case studies. We conclude the chapter with a discussion of the future implications of dematerialization in the context of sustainability.

1   www.hp.com, 2002.

From citizenship to sustainability

> Among the . . . objectives Bill Hewlett and I set down was one recognizing the company's responsibility to be a good corporate citizen . . .
>
> I recall a conference I attended in the late 1940s that included people from various industries and organizations. We began talking about whether businesses had responsibilities beyond making a profit for their shareholders. I expressed my view that we did, that we had important responsibilities to our employees, to our customers, to our suppliers, and to the welfare of society at large. I was surprised and disappointed that most of the others disagreed with me. They felt their only responsibility was to generate profits for their shareholders.
>
> *David Packard*[2]

The concept that a company has responsibilities toward all its stakeholders, not just shareholders, is not new for Hewlett Packard. Throughout the leadership transitions, this idea of citizenship has remained a core element.

Following the recent merger with Compaq in 2002, Carly Fiorina once again reinforced Hewlett Packard's commitment by defining citizenship as one of four key corporate strategies and designating a senior vice-president to deliver on this objective. At the same time, Fiorina formed a corporate social and environmental responsibility group that includes both a corporate social responsibility program and a program called Environmental Strategies and Sustainability. Although these programs previously existed elsewhere in the company, combining them under senior-level leadership illustrates the heightened level of priority and significance.

What is the relationship between citizenship and sustainability? Being a good corporate citizen means acting as a responsible member of a local or global community. Sustainable development is more specific, referring to a comprehensive, integrated approach to development that does not compromise the health of the environment or the lives of future generations. Although it has not always been recognized, citizenship and sustainability are interrelated. As the debate intensifies about whether our current patterns of human production, consumption, and development are environmentally and socially sustainable, it is becoming increasingly clear that to be a leading corporate citizen requires proactively addressing sustainable development.

Hewlett Packard recognizes that contributing effectively to the challenges of sustainable development is extremely complex and the solutions will not be easy or immediate. In fact, many analysts predict that the shift to sustainability will require changes similar in scale and scope to those of the Industrial Revolution. (Hawken *et al.* 1999: 1-21). For this reason, Hewlett Packard believes that delivering sustainable solutions offers tremendous business opportunity and potential for business leadership in the 21st century.

---

2   Packard 1996: 165-66.

With regard to the social challenges of sustainability, Hewlett Packard recognizes that the IT industry has brought prosperity to millions, but millions more live in poverty without access to technology and the economic opportunities it can provide. Hewlett Packard's e-inclusion program works in developing nations and underserved communities worldwide to close the gap between technology-empowered and technology-excluded communities. Although the urgency of basic needs—such as, food, water, shelter, and health—cannot be underestimated, IT can be instrumental in improving access to related services such as agriculture, education, and healthcare. Hewlett Packard's vision for the e-inclusion program is a future in which all people have access to the social and economic opportunities of the "digital age" and can contribute to building a sustainable future.

In terms of ecological systems, being a sustainable company means delivering value to customers without degrading the environment. Hewlett Packard is developing programs that reduce its ecological footprint (Wackernagel and Rees 1996) as well as those of its customers and partners. Hewlett Packard's dematerialization initiative—aimed at reducing materials use and using less-harmful materials—is an example. As a manufacturer, some of Hewlett Packard's most significant environmental impacts occur through the materials used in its products. Dematerialization is a key strategy to reducing those impacts.

In early 2002, Hewlett Packard launched its dematerialization initiative. The first phase was to increase understanding of dematerialization efforts already occurring at Hewlett Packard through analysis of several case studies. The second phase, already under way, is to translate this knowledge into programs and policies to further promote dematerialization and reduce materials-related environmental impacts.

The dematerialization initiative at Hewlett Packard

> The urgent challenge for our developed consumer economies is to reduce our ecological footprint.
>
> Technology can dramatically improve efficiency and dematerialize many activities. Inventing business models for selling services rather than material goods is also an essential element of success.
>
> *Anne Livermore*[3]

During the past century, materials use has exploded throughout the industrialized and developing worlds. Current usage patterns have reached levels many experts believe are not sustainable (Geiser 2001: 367-91). As a result, dematerialization has become a pressing environmental and social imperative.

Business forces, however, are also driving the materials use and reduction trends at a unit level. In the world of IT, customers constantly demand smaller, more

---

3   Anne Livermore, Executive Vice-President, Hewlett Packard Services Organization, in an address to United Nations Economic and Social Council, New York, September 2000.

powerful products. As electronics take-back legislation is globally enacted, dematerialization also reduces long-term recycling costs. An important example is the proposal for a Directive on Waste Electrical and Electronic Equipment (WEEE) recently adopted by the European Commission, which will mandate producer end-of-life responsibility for all electronics products.[4] Reducing materials use lowers both direct and indirect costs, thereby enhancing the bottom line.

Dematerialization at Hewlett Packard is guided by the following precepts:

- Take the entire life-cycle into account: the total materials consumed throughout an IT product's life-cycle—including extraction of raw materials, manufacturing, distribution, use, and recycling or disposal—far exceed the product mass alone. For example, it is estimated that a computer itself represents less than 2% of the materials consumed by that computer through its life-cycle (Hilty *et al.* 2000: iii). Although we strive to assess the impacts of materials over the product life-cycle, practical obstacles do exist, including the cost and relatively high levels of uncertainty associated with life-cycle data (Schaltegger and Burritt 2000: 240-57).

- Consider absolute materials use: increasing materials efficiency per unit of product may not reduce material use overall, because the increased quantity of units produced might outweigh the efficiency gains per unit. This dynamic is closely related to the "rebound effect," in which efficiency causes prices to drop, lower prices stimulate demand, which in turn leads to increased production. Recent paper-use trends illustrate this interrelationship. According to research by the Rocky Mountain Institute (RMI),[5] although word processing held great promise for reducing paper use by digitizing documents, computer-related use of paper has grown steadily during the past few decades, largely as a result of the decreasing cost and increasing convenience of printing. Hewlett Packard's dematerialization initiative takes the rebound effect into account by focusing both on per-unit and absolute material use.

- Recognize that materials vary in impact: the total quantity of materials used is only one factor in assessing adverse environmental impacts. Different materials may have distinct impacts. The dematerialization initiative considers not only the mass of materials used but also the types of materials applied in Hewlett Packard products and the impacts associated with specific materials.

4   See http://europa.eu.int/comm/environment/docum/00347_en.htm.
5   See www.rmi.org/sitepages/art7037.php.

Dematerialization in the information technology sector

In some respects, dematerialization is intrinsic to IT, as smaller and faster machines continually redefine the cutting edge. An off-the-shelf laptop purchased today has thousands of times the processing power, weighs just a few pounds and consumes less than one-thousandth the electricity than one produced in the 1940s. Not only do IT products dramatically reduce in size and mass over time, but IT breakthroughs also replace material-intensive products and processes used by people throughout the world. E-mail vividly illustrates the potential of IT to enable broader dematerialization within society, as in many cases it has replaced physical mail.

However, countervailing pressures exist, primarily as a result of total volume and industry growth. Vividly illustrating this dynamic is that, in 2002, a mere 25 years after the advent of the personal computer (PC), cumulative sales hit 1 billion units. According to research from Gartner and Intel (reported in IDG News Service Monday 2002), in the next six years, another billion units will be sold. The pace of innovation, and the resulting technology obsolescence, further increases the demand for new machines and the number of units that are taken out of service annually. Indeed, IT products can become technologically outdated several years before the end of their useful lives. At present, it is estimated that only 10–20% of computers in the USA are recycled,[6] compared with approximately 84% of appliances.[7] This combination of high turnover and low recapture rates translates into low material productivity. It also highlights the need for IT companies to seriously tackle product end-of-life solutions as one key strategy for increasing material productivity.

Hewlett Packard dematerialization case studies

During the spring of 2002, Hewlett Packard's Environmental Strategies and Sustainability Group analyzed examples of dematerialization currently occurring throughout the company. Cases were chosen to represent the range of Hewlett Packard's business activities, including products, supplies, product-based services, and future innovations. Some examples, such as those occurring in "inkjet supplies," were largely the result of deliberate attempts to improve environmental performance. Others, such as "all-in-ones," "e-pcs," and "managed print services," were driven primarily by business variables such as customer preference and product differentiation.

6   In 1999, Stanford Resources Inc. estimated that, of the 31.4 million PCs shipped in the USA in 1997, only 3.2 million PCs (10.2%) would be recycled in 2000 (note: 2000 is compared with 1997 because the average lifetime of a computer is assumed to be 3–5 years). By 2005, the expected rate is expected to increase to 19% compared with 2002 shipments.

7   According to the Steel Recycling Institute, the US recycling rate for appliances in 2002 was 84.1%.

Case studies were developed based on interviews with more than 40 Hewlett Packard staff throughout the company as well as on extensive internal and external research. In each case, material and energy savings were analyzed, as well as economic value added to the customer and to Hewlett Packard. Summaries of each of these case studies are given below.

All-in-ones

Hewlett Packard produces a popular line of multifunctional devices called "all-in-ones" (AiOs), that integrate printers, scanners, copiers, and sometimes faxes into a single device. Although AiOs were created primarily to save customers space and to increase functionality and convenience, they also offer potential to reduce environmental impact. AiOs capitalize on the fact that stand-alone devices have many components in common, including imaging mechanisms, paper feeds, power supplies, and casings. Combining these devices provides comparable functionality while eliminating redundant components, thereby reducing overall materials use. In addition, packaging and energy use decrease significantly.

The dematerialization analysis compared AiOs with the comparable stand-alone devices, using Hewlett Packard product environmental profiles (for more information, see www.hp.com). For example, the AiO G55 was compared with the sum of the Deskjet 970 printer, the Color Copier 180 and the Scanjet 2200 Cl. Specific information was gathered on product weight, energy use in standby mode, cardboard packaging weight, and plastic packaging weight for every AiO and its corresponding stand-alones.[8]

It was found that AiOs significantly reduce the amount of materials and energy required to deliver a given functionality. For example, as shown in Figure 5.1, the AiO G55 weighs 19.4 lb (42%) less than the sum of the weight of its comparables. The G55 also uses 3.9 fewer pounds of packaging and consumes 7.5 fewer watts of electricity in standby mode. AiOs that include faxes (the majority) realize even greater savings.

Despite these important decreases in material use, other key considerations remain from a sustainability perspective. For example, not every customer purchasing an AiO would have otherwise purchased all comparable stand-alones. Owing to the cost and space savings, some customers buying AiOs purchase an item with greater functionality than they would otherwise have done.

Even taking this rebound effect into account,[9] however, total materials and energy savings in 2001 were still dramatic, consisting of approximately 18,000 tons

---

8   In this case, we are looking only at product and packaging mass and energy use in operation and not at all materials and energy consumed throughout the product's life-cycle.

9   To consider this rebound effect, the analysis segmented the AiO market into two main groups: home consumers and office users, with the office user group including home offices and small businesses. An AiO manager provided the approximate percentage breakdown of these two groups and the typical purchasing behavior of segments within each group. For example, one subset of home consumers typically purchases a printer only, whereas another subset purchases a printer and one other device.

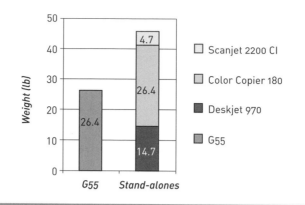

Figure 5.1 Comparison of the weight of the Hewlett Packard all-in-one G55 (giving the functionality of a scanner, copier, and printer) with the combined weight of comparable, individual products (the Deskjet 970 printer, the Color Copier 180, and the Scanjet 2200 Cl)

of product, 5,000 tons of packaging and more than 100,000 MWh of electricity.[10] Although the issue of obsolescence remains, the AiOs nonetheless demonstrate the potential of intelligent design to reduce environmental impact in relative and absolute terms.

E-pcs

E-pcs are a line of small form-factor PCs designed for the business environment that were created to conserve desktop space, simplify serviceability, and increase ease of use. The streamlined design of the e-pc consists of only three components—hard disk drive, system chassis, and power supply. Although the driving force behind e-pcs was not environmental performance, the environmental benefits are significant.

To analyze e-pc materials and energy savings, we compared the "average" e-pc with the "average" Vectra, a Hewlett Packard line of full-sized business PCs.[11] The average e-pc weighs less than half as much as the average Vectra—10.2 lb compared with 23.1 lb—and uses 30–40% less packaging.[12] The smaller form factor also results in lower shipping and warehousing costs. In addition, e-pcs consume about 6% less electricity in use than do Vectras.

10 For the AiO analysis, we assume AiOs are identical to comparable devices in terms of life expectancy and recyclability.

11 The "average" e-pc was calculated by averaging the mass, packaging, and energy consumption values of the e-pc40 and the e-pc42, based on Hewlett Packard product environmental profiles (see www.hp.com). These values were compared with those of the "average" Vectra—the average of the Vectra XE 310, the Vectra VL 420, and the Vectra VL 800.

12 This analysis considers only product mass and not total life-cycle material consumption. It also assumes e-pcs and Vectras offer similar user functionality and disregards any potential differences in their ability to be recycled.

One sustainability-related challenge, however, is that e-pcs achieve these reductions through a much simpler design that limits expandability and the ability to add hard drives, CD-ROM drives or other devices. Lack of expandability in turn affects materials efficiency, because expansion can extend a product's useful life.

Even taking this into account, however, the e-pc remains 75% more efficient in material use—a saving of 7.6 lb per unit. In 2001, e-pc savings totaled several thousand tons of hardware, hundreds of tons of packaging and more than 4,000 MWh of electricity.[13]

These environmental benefits are matched by strong customer value. The Gartner Group recently performed a study comparing the total cost of ownership of small form-factor PCs with that of traditional PCs. The conclusion is that small form-factor PCs, such as the e-pc, can save companies US$1,000 per computer over a three-year life-cycle.[14] Benefits include factors such as decreased maintenance costs and reduced energy use.

The e-pc demonstrates the complexity of analyzing materials efficiency and introduces the counter-intuitive claim that in some cases by limiting expandability one may actually increase materials efficiency. When a trade-off exists between size reduction and expandability, the critical factor is that the materials saved through the smaller design must exceed those forgone through expansion-related life extension. This ratio will vary product by product, and analysis requires detailed assumptions regarding expected product use.

Inkjet supplies[15]

The term "inkjet supplies" refers to the ink cartridges used in Hewlett Packard inkjet printers. Owing to high unit volumes, even minor design changes in ink cartridges can result in sizable environmental and human health benefits.

One example of these benefits is clear from Hewlett Packard's redesign of its cartridges to eliminate the need for an adhesive. When heated to high temperatures, this adhesive forms an extremely strong bond between component parts. The strong bond made it difficult to recycle the cartridges. In response, Hewlett Packard's design and manufacturing engineers created product components that snapped together mechanically. Elimination of the need for adhesive increased the recyclability of the cartridges by approximately 25%. It also saved Hewlett Packard US$2.4 million over four years as a result of reduced costs for manufacturing, capital equipment, and operations and maintenance.

---

13   To match e-pc materials efficiency, the Vectra would need to increase its life-span by 126% (more than doubled) through expansion. In reality, Vectra users extend product life-span through expansion only by an estimated 30%, so e-pcs remain 75% more efficient in material use. This translates to a saving of 7.6 lb per unit.

14   According to the Hewlett Packard web page at www.hp.com/desktops/news/webnews/news010409.html#FOOT1.

15   The text for this section on inkjet supplies is taken primarily from the article, "Integrating Environmental Product Design into Inkjet Printing Supplies," written by Hewlett Packard Product Stewards Lynn Laszewski and Tim Carey (Laszewski and Carey 2002).

Inkjet cartridge packaging changes also led to significant savings. When customers purchase printers, inkjet cartridges are provided in the printer box. Previously, the cartridges included were contained in the same packaging designed for retail sales to protect the cartridges from damage during shipping and display. Such packaging was unnecessary, as cartridges sold inside the printer box are already protected. A simpler package was created. Information insert design was also simplified. Overall, approximately US$0.17 of packaging material has been eliminated from each cartridge sold with a printer. The new design has resulted in weight savings of 2.6 million lb of paper and paperboard and has diverted 3 million lb of packaging from landfill in 15 months.

These examples demonstrate the benefits of introducing environmental objectives into the design process itself as well as the overlap between environmental and business objectives. Indeed, the search for environmental benefits may uncover clear business benefits, such as reduced costs through material savings.

Managed print services

A final example of dematerialization at Hewlett Packard concerns managed print services (MPS), an outsourced printing service for large companies. Through MPS, Hewlett Packard assumes control of the design, implementation, and maintenance of a company's printing services and charges that company on a usage basis. The service reduces the customer's capital expenditure and resources dedicated to maintaining its distributed printing and imaging environment.

This business area has experienced rapid growth over the past two years (2001–2002). As a product-based service, the value of a product is delivered without actually selling the product itself. This business model has significant potential to reduce materials use because the service provider assumes extended responsibility for the product. The product itself becomes a cost center, increasing the service provider's incentive to design efficient products that are easily maintained and to recapture as much value as possible at the end of the useful life of the products.

Product-based services may save materials and energy in several respects. It may do so through:

- Improved product design. MPS staff members have responsibility for Hewlett Packard printers throughout the life-cycle of those printers and, in the process, gain extensive breakdown and service data. As MPS bears the cost if it deploys printers that require frequent service, a strong incentive exists to share performance-related information with product designers to minimize service issues. This communication does indeed occur within the MPS product chain, as representatives from functional groups, including designers, meet regularly to discuss these issues.

- Optimized product operation. as MPS employees maintain the customer's printers, these machines are more likely to operate smoothly. In addition, this service also decreases malfunctions, reduces materials use, and extends the life of the product.

- A reduced number or volume of products manufactured. Right-sizing and optimizing a printer fleet reduces the number of printers needed at a company site. For example, one contract with a division of a large corporation decreased the total number of printers and imaging devices from approximately 3,600 to 1,400, a 61% reduction. In general, 50% reductions are common.

- Increased recycling of machines. Printers within the MPS system have a very high recycling rate, extending the useful life of printers and printer components. Second-generation uses include refurbishment of the product, the breakdown of the product for parts and recycling, movement of the product within Hewlett Packard, or sale into secondary markets. Hewlett Packard believes its efforts in this area lead the market.

Overall, it has been estimated that in 2002 MPS will reduce printer mass on clients' sites by nearly 3,000 tons, will increase toner cartridge recycling by tens of thousands of units, and will save more than 700 tons of paper (this assumes an estimated 5% increase in duplexing). Customers may save up to 30% in total printing costs, largely by outsourcing printer environment design, administration, and technical support needs to Hewlett Packard. Factors that increase customer lifetime value include guaranteed sales of supplies, a service annuity and the opportunity to use updated technology.

Conclusions and implications for the future

The Hewlett Packard dematerialization initiative has confirmed that improvements to product design have the potential to greatly reduce the environmental impact not only of the company but also of its customers. The rationale for action was, in the case of reducing materials through invention of AiOs and e-pcs, driven primarily by business objectives. The inkjet supplies example, however, demonstrates the benefits of integrating environmental objectives into the design process itself and extending responsibility for environmental performance beyond environmental staff to designers and business managers. Each of these cases highlights the need to make environmental design considerations an integral part of the standard product development cycles at Hewlett Packard.

The dematerialization case studies vividly show the need for analysis across a product's entire life-cycle to fully understand environmental impacts. Although ad hoc analysis of specific products or components does yield useful information, it often reflects only a fraction of the total impact. With products and supply chains as complex as those in IT, measurement of full life-cycle impacts requires substantial commitment and resources, yet is critical if impacts are to be reduced effectively.

Another conclusion from the research is that energy and materials fall into overlapping categories. Substantial energy is required to produce many materials, and substantial amounts of materials are required to generate energy. As a result, efforts to increase energy efficiency constitute an effective dematerialization strategy, and dematerialization is an effective energy-reduction strategy. Overall, Hewlett Packard's work on dematerialization has underscored the importance of addressing these two areas in an integrated fashion.

The dematerialization initiative also revealed that not only products but also the business models used to deliver those products to customers have a significant impact on environmental performance. The MPS case demonstrates that customers, Hewlett Packard, and the environment can all benefit from moving beyond product-based to service-based business models. Hewlett Packard plans to investigate opportunities to further this trend in other areas of its business.

A final conclusion is that to optimize decisions according to sustainability principles and parameters, a manufacturer must record, analyze and understand its materials impacts thoroughly. In the same way that a company cannot maximize its profits without rigorously tracking its finances, it cannot hope to maximize its environmental and social performance without comparable rigor and precision applied to other areas. Therefore, one outcome of the research is recognition of the need for a robust environmental performance tracking system. This system will collect the detailed data required to measure and assess environmental impact and performance accurately.

This research is just one step towards inventing a sustainable future. The dematerialization initiative was part of Hewlett Packard's strategy for environmental sustainability, but the social implications of this work also are apparent. An examination of the environmental impacts of materials and production processes is closely related to concern for human health issues as well as for broader question of equity. Thus, the social and environmental challenges are not distinct but rather interwoven.

The journey ahead is both daunting and exciting, requiring the highest level of commitment combined with a tireless effort and the best of our collective intelligence. Hewlett Packard—a company of inventors with a legacy of doing good—welcomes this challenge.

6
Engaging in change management
Transformation through sustainability strategy at Norm Thompson Outfitters

Derek Smith
Norm Thompson Outfitters, Oregon, USA

> **Vision without action is a daydream.**
> **Action without vision is a nightmare.**
>
> *Asian proverb*

Companies that seek major change in any aspect of their business often start with a noble vision, generally based on a founder's or key decision-maker's philosophy. This vision is often followed by some action or achievement of a few significant outcomes, which may or may not be linked to a longer-term set of measurable objectives. Unless effective change-management principles are put into place to push companies beyond these initial steps, activities that require major change frequently fizzle out. This should be of noteworthy concern to those companies pursuing sustainability.

All organizations—from multinational chemical companies to regional non-profit organizations—face the dilemma of productively linking vision and action. Both research and applied work within companies has shown that to create true, lasting, institutional change, both vision and action must be tightly intertwined and performed in tandem. Since the pursuit of sustainability generates major change in an organization, this vision–action bond is critical.

In this chapter I focus on explaining the case of a journey toward sustainability through organizational change at Norm Thompson Outfitters, a US$200 million catalog retailer that sells apparel, gifts, gourmet foods, household items, and outdoor gear in its Norm Thompson, Solutions, and Early Winters brands.

I begin by describing the fundamental role of cultural change in shifting businesses toward sustainability. The case of Norm Thompson is then presented with specific attention to the approach and the shift from a single issue—of the building of a new headquarters—to a broader-based approach that addressed the core elements of the business and employee jobs. It describes the challenge of fundamentally changing core strategies and operations and adopting sustainability-informed product development to purchasing procedures. I argue that successful redirection of these critical functions is dependent on changes in collective human behavior within the organization, which is a complex and dynamic undertaking. Overall, this case study offers insights that may help existing businesses determine an appropriate approach for integrating sustainability into their operations.

Integrating sustainability into decision-making: the role of cultural change

Few, if any, companies have become leaders in customer service, quality or other valued competencies without mapping out a strategy that respects and builds on internal values and norms. Given this tight link between culture and change, transformation of an entire company is a process in shifting its belief systems and objectives. Such a change necessitates an enormous commitment of time and careful planning, as well as resources and creativity.

Early on in the effort at Norm Thompson, the vice-president of human resources emphasized that past research in organizational change has shown that complex initiatives often take five to seven years—depending on size, complexity, geographic dispersion, and other factors—for a company culture to fully embrace a major new strategic endeavor. This immediate awareness of the pace of change, and the need for ongoing dedication to the process, informed Norm Thompson executives' expectations and underscored the need for careful planning and for longer-term horizons. Other key elements of organizational change theory informed the work in its earliest stages, including the need for clear direction and support from the top leadership, a sense of urgency, and a systematic and multidimensional plan. Finally, the intention was to seek, and demonstrate, change occurring throughout the organization.

The overarching objective was to develop a cogent plan for the change initiative grounded within the existing fiber of the organization, yet premised on a whole-systems approach. The intent was to address the entire organization at once in a holistic manner. With this objective in mind, the company began to develop plans to align key organizational components with sustainability, including:

- Norms (behavior)
- Processes (how things are carried out)
- Formal systems (performance management processes and rewards)
- Roles and responsibilities (knowledge, skills, and job descriptions)

Overall, change initiatives at Norm Thompson focused on constantly working toward sustainability concurrent with other core corporate goals, such as total customer satisfaction and the provision of high-quality products. In this sense, sustainability—defined as the intersection between a healthy environment, economy, and society—was added to existing business goals. In internally asserting that the company is "working toward sustainability," senior executives highlighted the broader goal that guides the firm, even when it may be necessary to make short-term trade-offs between current business process and more sustainable practice.

Adopting a sustainability focus

The private company of Norm Thompson was nearly 45 years old when the owners first thought about integrating sustainability into the core strategy and operations. Founded in 1949 as a niche outfitter to fly fishers and sportsmen, the company has evolved into a mid-sized industry leader. Traditional ways of doing business had served the company well. However, an evolution in the firm's thinking began in 1993 when company owners John and Jane Emrick began to incorporate into the company's practices their long-held environmental and social values. The Emricks attempts were fueled by the notion that they could make greater contributions by aligning their company with their values.

Building the foundations of organizational change: construction of a "green" headquarters

The Emricks' first attempt at integrating sustainability occurred the following year as they oversaw the design of their new corporate headquarters as a "green" building. Since few contractors had expertise in this emerging area, the Emricks sought to ensure that sustainability factors would serve as a filter through which each decision was made by asking: "Which approach would have the least impact on the environment?" Another obstacle stemmed from non-ownership; the building was leased. This situation added to the decision-making process requirements that the expenses meet an eight-year payback on a conservative lease rate. To finance the incremental expense, the Emricks bundled the "green" costs into one outlay rather than considering each decision as a line item. This holistic view enabled a "true cost" approach to accounting for the building's financial performance.

The building was completed in 1995. Not only did it incorporate daylighting technology, native landscaping, wood certified by the Forest Stewardship Council (FSC), and reclaimed materials but also, within four years, the incremental "green" costs were covered by savings. These continued savings following the payback period, predominantly through energy costs of 35%, now contribute over US$30,000 in annual profit.

As the first physical manifestation of Norm Thompson's sustainability evolution, the building focused attention on the corporate goals related to intertwined environmental, social, and economic performance. The headquarters stands as the literal foundation for the company's commitment to organizational change toward sustainability. The contributions to the bottom line offered the first success story.

Pride in the building was soon tempered as the Emricks became increasingly aware of other, more damaging, aspects of the company's operations, particularly the sourcing of products and of catalog paper. In beginning to plan for broader organizational change, they worked with other senior management team members to ask questions about their business in relation to sustainability, including:

- What happens when employees enter the building? What decisions are they making? Are decisions informed by ecological and social performance concerns?

- Is sustainability being factored into employees' daily work processes?

- What are employees' opportunities to integrate sustainability into product selection, paper usage, and other key aspects of the business?

Senior management realized that the employees had no systematic and science-informed basis for understanding environmental issues and applying ecological and social justice concepts to their work. It became increasingly clear that education and training was the essential foundation from which to truly launch broader-based efforts to bring about organizational change.

Becoming systematic and adopting a framework for sustainability decision-making: The Natural Step training

In search of a way to form a foundational understanding of sustainability principles, John Emrick and Norm Thompson's quality director, Meg Miller, attended a 1997 conference of The Natural Step. With its scientific underpinning and emphasis on systems thinking, The Natural Step framework felt like a good fit for a company that was trying to approach sustainability with a holistic outlook yet little first-hand knowledge.

In order to begin imbedding sustainability concepts fully into operational decision-making, the Emricks agreed that awareness of the issues had to be increased throughout the company. Employees had to understand how sustainability was defined prior to being able to act on the new corporate vision. Therefore, it was decided that the entire workforce would be trained in The Natural Step Framework and approach to making sustainability-informed decisions.

One of the owners, Jane Emrick, and the quality director, Meg Miller, developed a customized, internal training program based on the work of The Natural Step in the field of sustainability. It was unveiled in 1998 with a pilot half-day session presented to a dozen employees. Today, after scores of training sessions and a great deal of employee feedback on content and style, the four-hour training program is now a mandatory component of Norm Thompson's orientation for each of the company's 675 positions. The sessions are interactive, presented through multimedia and consist of:

- Several descriptions of sustainability, including those by the Brundtland Commission ("meeting the needs of the present without compromising the ability of future generations to meet their needs;" see WCED 1987), Mathis Wackernagel ("securing a quality of life within the means of Nature;" see Wackernagel and Rees 1996), and the Native American Iroquois Federation philosophy ("we will consider the impact on the seventh generation"[1])

- An overview of global social and environmental conditions, including global warming, deforestation, water scarcity, and poverty

- An introduction to basic laws of science and systems thinking, based on The Natural Step Framework

- An in-depth presentation on The Natural Step system conditions

- Examples of how Norm Thompson and other companies are acting on these system conditions

- Case studies that demonstrate other companies' commitments to sustainability

The training program, based on The Natural Step, has become indispensable in developing a "shared mental model" of sustainability concepts and its business applications among all Norm Thompson employees. Yet, in and of itself, the training is not enough. Through early challenges, the company learned that communicating a new vision via a training program creates a need for subsequent action.

The first challenge actually stemmed from the success of the training. After attending training sessions, Norm Thompson employees were inspired and excited by the opportunity to contribute on a broader scale. However, when their input was solicited, their views were not always acted on because there were no formal processes or "point people" to ensure follow-through. In addition, some employee suggestions—such as "stop sending catalogs"—were in conflict with the business model, at least in the short term, and were therefore dismissed without comment. As a result, some individuals within the company became somewhat deflated. This effect underscored the importance of taking seriously the need to acknowledge and respond to employee suggestions that arise following training, either through senior management action or by empowering employees to launch new efforts.

---

1   www.seventhgeneration.com

A second obstacle was how to hold employees accountable for achievement of the company's sustainability objectives. Despite appeals during the training sessions, employees rarely took the initiative to make changes that would decrease environmental and social impacts. As in many companies, Norm Thompson employees are assessed according to productivity, measured in terms of sales or some other quantifiable factor. Since sustainability was not explicitly included in performance evaluations, many employees felt that efforts taken to support sustainability might detract from their ability to meet assigned goals against which they were evaluated. Accordingly, employees prioritized sustainability activities lower on lists of things to do. After two years of training, with few examples of voluntary implementation, it became clear that the creation of incentives for action would be an essential component of the company's organizational change and sustainability initiatives.

However, the training did have some benefits. For Norm Thompson, the biggest benefits of the training have been intangible yet essential to core corporate goals. Employees have expressed growing support of and buy-in to the company's mission and values and have shown increased loyalty. In many cases, these employees have also attributed the training sessions to broader-based changes in their homes and lives, describing increased efforts to buy organic produce, use non-toxic cleaners, garden organically, and take other actions that apply sustainability concepts to their personal lives. These actions have linked back to benefit the company positively, as employees regularly report they feel good working for a company that cares about their health and well-being. For example, in a 2000 culture survey, 80% say that Norm Thompson strives to be a company that makes a contribution beyond just bottom-line results. One employee remarked, "I love this company. It stands for the right things—sustainability and work/life balance."[2]

The company believes these elements have contributed to enhanced employee retention, and efforts are under way to assess and quantify whether these results are indeed being realized. However, one clearly quantifiable change has been that the training program has offered a competitive advantage in recruiting efforts. Several qualified candidates for key positions at the company have confirmed that Norm Thompson is now sought out as an employer explicitly because it follows The Natural Step Framework.

Imbedding sustainability into the company: the creation of a corporate sustainability manager position

To ensure follow-through on the sustainability vision, the Emricks determined that they needed to hire someone to manage the process and focus not only on creating internal organizational change but also on accessing helpful external

2   Norm Thompson Culture Survey, 2000.

resources. It was agreed that a businessperson rather than someone from a non-governmental organization (NGO) or governmental background should be selected. The Emricks understood that a core component of organizational change is communication, which is greatly facilitated when the same language is spoken by both parties. With this goal in mind, I was hired in 1999 to focus on fully operationalizing sustainability concepts within Norm Thompson. To demonstrate the importance of the position and ensure that a profitability mind-set would be instilled, John Emrick ensured that the corporate sustainability manager would report to the chief executive officer (CEO).

One of the first actions taken within the new position was to form an internal advisory board for developing an integrated plan that would systematically move the company toward sustainability. The board consisted of representatives from all major departments as well as people in a range of positions, including one of the company owners, several departmental heads and a customer service representative. The team asked, "What is culturally imperative for this company to achieve its expressed goal of sustainability?" The internal barriers and drivers were assessed and six core recommendations were established to overcome the obstacles and to leverage the strengths, as described in Box 6.1.

The key recommendations are to:

1. Set departmental sustainability goals and integrate objectives into departmental fiscal year plans

2. Promote evidence that sustainability can be viable and profitable

3. Develop a strategic action plan and share its vision through clear communication

4. Refine the corporate sustainability manager's position to be an internal advocate and consultant

5. Maintain an open and honest dialog among senior management to ensure an understanding of what sustainability will look like in its application to the company's products and operations

6. Ensure that sustainability is factored into major business decisions

Note: recommendation 4 was made in response to employees concerns that the position would be that of an "environmental cop" rather than that of a partner; recommendation 5 was put forward to ensure ongoing clarification of how to achieve short-term financial goals and long-term social and environmental objectives.

Box 6.1 Key recommendations from Norm Thompson's sustainability cultural integration plan

It is important to note that the recommendations were made after several hours of discussion focused on Norm Thompson's culture and may not be the same for other companies, as every culture is different. Cultural relevance is the most essential ingredient to assess throughout efforts to bring about organizational change. Planning processes and the careful calibration of recommendations so that they work within a company's culture are invaluable.

These recommendations were documented in a cultural integration plan, which was subsequently presented to the CEO and the company president, who accepted all the advisory board's suggestions.

Developing Norm Thompson's Sustainability Action Plan

The first step toward fulfilling the recommendations of the cultural integration plan was to develop a Sustainability Action Plan. This plan is similar to an environmental management system, albeit with a lesser degree of rigor in its internal process mapping. The action plan focuses on a set of objectives and tactics that will enable internal change and the development of internal markets for new ideas. The plan contains annual objectives, such as to undertake negotiations with vendors regarding preference for alternative, more sustainable, materials in products, and the formation of relationships with NGOs that can help in identifying opportunities to purchase more environmentally and socially responsible inputs (e.g. through the use of forest products certified as sustainable and the use of energy from renewable sources). Partners (internal and external), time-lines and budgets are critical components of the plan. The specific recommendations in the action plan are based on a subjective assessment of environmental and social impacts that result from business operations.

Following this assessment process, the internal work group concluded that the core impacts of the company fall within the following categories:

- Products
- Packaging
- Publishing (paper, forestry, printing, Internet migration)
- Transportation
- Influence

"Influence" was chosen as a key impact area in the sense that the company has the potential to have a larger social impact by persuading other companies that sustainability is the smart course of business and by setting a positive, practical example.

Next, the company cross-referenced the above assessment of impact areas with the US Environmental Protection Agency's list of emerging environmental issues to establish five-year goals to track progress (see Table 6.1). Without the company making a deliberate effort to do so, these focal issues relate sequentially to The Natural Step system conditions, offering a clear example of how The Natural Step is imbedded in Norm Thompson's decision-making processes.

Finally, the launching of the Sustainability Action Plan, in early 2000, was carefully considered to ensure maximum attention and to communicate its impor-

US EPA emerging issue	Norm Thompson sustainability-related goal	The Natural Step system condition
Global climate change	The achievement of zero net impact from greenhouse gas emissions	System condition 1: in a sustainable society, Nature is not subject to systematically increasing concentrations of substances extracted from the Earth's crust
Toxic substances	Elimination of identified toxic substances from products and processes	System condition 2: in a sustainable society, Nature is not subject to systematically increasing concentrations of substances produced by society
Habitat destruction	The achievement of zero negative impacts on forests	System condition 3: in a sustainable society, Nature is not subject to systematically increasing degradation by physical means
Waste	The achievement of zero waste in managed facilities	System condition 4: In a sustainable society the ability of humans to meet their needs worldwide is not systematically undermined

Table 6.1 The areas of impact of Norm Thompson, the emerging environmental issues set out by the US Environmental Protection Agency (US EPA 1997) and The Natural Step system conditions

tance. Therefore, to send a signal that the plan was a serious part of the company's overall strategy, the plan was endorsed both by the CEO and by the company president and was presented by all the vice-presidents at an off-site company meeting. All Oregon operations ran on a skeleton crew during the meeting to ensure a high level of attendance.

The action plan remains a central part of corporate planning efforts. Annual goals are negotiated by the corporate sustainability manager and the vice-presidents during fiscal year planning and budgeting processes. The vice-presidents are held accountable for specific components of the action plan. For example, the vice-president of marketing is responsible for increasing the content of recycled paper in catalog pages, in addition to improving customer response rates.

Integrating sustainability into job descriptions and employee recognition programs

In order to officially communicate that sustainability was now being integrated into all jobs, the CEO and president issued a "declaration of sustainability," which states:

> From this day on, sustainability is part of your job. This means you can share in a common mind-set, earn recognition and contribute to the health of the world. Think outside the box, challenge yourself and feel good about your efforts to improve our business and help our planet and future generations. Each of us, no matter what department we're in, can do things—small or large—that will help us achieve our goal of sustainability.

This text was a meaningful symbolic gesture. However, it became increasingly clear that recognition and performance evaluation remained the key factors in ensuring accountability. These issues have slowly begun to be addressed from the bottom up, through work on merchandise.

Concurrently, however, senior management decided that the company culture would be best suited to a combined "carrot and stick" approach to provide incentives for further sustainability work at all levels of the company. The "carrots" are awards given at quarterly associate meetings to those employees who have taken it on themselves to integrate sustainability into their jobs. Since the bulk of the content of these associate meetings is financial, it was decided that it would be most effective to quantify in monetary terms the environmental and economic benefits of employee sustainability activities and to acknowledge these gains.

Sustainability has now become a consistent part of the agenda of the associate meetings. Small and large efforts alike—from switching to online reporting, which saved US$10 per year, to altering a major process, which resulted in a US$100,000 contribution—are given equal recognition. Financial rewards to specific employees were considered but decided against on the grounds that the integration of sustainability should be "part of what we do." This recognition program was useful in highlighting individual efforts. The "stick" remains the accountability measures built into the sustainability action plan, including departmental sustainability goals with associated fiscal year budgets.

Selecting the first high-profile activity

In late 1999, as Norm Thompson executives were trying to work out what the first significant actions to be undertaken should be, the Alliance for Environmental Innovation, a division of Environmental Defense, was completing a report entitled *Greener Catalogs* (AEI 1999). The report offered clear and constructive recommendations on how to improve paper efficiency in the catalog industry. Norm Thompson was featured in the publication as one cataloger that switched some of its paper to recycled content. Therefore, the Alliance offered free technical assistance if Norm Thompson were to commit to attempt and implement more far-reaching changes. Thus, a business–NGO partnership was born.

Norm Thompson management agreed to work with the Alliance because the organization is credible, well-respected, and considered to have significant expertise on the environmental impacts of paper. As Norm Thompson is a major purchaser of paper, the company's management knew that this partnership might provide a unique opportunity to use company buyer power not only to reduce the overall "environmental footprint" of the firm but also to create lasting change in the catalog industry. In addition, Norm Thompson's marketing department was fully staffed and equipped to commit resources to the project.

Through an 18-month partnership, relationships were built with key suppliers. Key personnel learned about the dynamics of the market for coated paper. Empirical studies were performed to assess the way in which customers responded to catalogs printed on recycled paper compared the response to those printed on virgin paper. This research showed that paper with 10% post-consumer recycled content could be used—something that no other major mainstream cataloger was doing—without negatively impacting customer response rates or costs. In addition, the company learned that the environmental savings were not the only benefits that Norm Thompson would realize.

The company could see important "first-mover advantages" to a shift to the use of more recycled content in its catalog paper. Local and national press coverage resulted from the announcement of the switch, and Norm Thompson began to be a considered a thought leader in its industry on environmental issues. Through this exposure, Norm Thompson was able to convince other catalogers to convert to using recycled paper.

Internally, the marketing department became excited about their efforts and asked to make presentations at company meetings. Their pride rubbed off on many throughout the workforce. These demonstrations began proving to people within Norm Thompson that the company could be successful at moving toward its vision and beginning to see real organizational change. These outcomes were perhaps the most important dividends, for they set in motion a level of confidence that is vital to institutionalizing changed behavior. Without a shared belief that results are possible, a bold vision cannot be realized.

Launching a diverse set of sustainability initiatives

Norm Thompson management knew that the Alliance partnership was likely to bolster employee morale, but the company leaders were also clear that results would not occur for more than a year. Therefore, management decided that it was critical to offer tangible proof that every employee had the opportunity to be involved in sustainability, even in a relatively small manner. To underscore this point, several initiatives were launched simultaneously.

For example, the composting of lunchroom food scraps was initiated to fuel a newly built on-site organic garden that is managed by employees. A huge recycling center was constructed, and employees were encouraged to bring in non-curbside recyclables, including batteries, grocery bags, light bulbs, polystyrene, and other items. The company expanded its volunteer match program that offers employees paid time off to serve their community. Also, free passes for public transport were made available to all associates. Special events featuring guest speakers from the Union of Concerned Scientists, members of Congress, and major authors were held and promoted.

It is often reported that these programs, along with The Natural Step training and general work–life balance philosophy, are reasons why employees stay at Norm Thompson. This adds up to enhanced employee productivity and retention, all of which avoid money spent on new employee recruitment and training.

Budgeting and making investments

Given the upfront costs of some sustainability efforts, it is essential to plan at least one to three years ahead and to line up internal support for these activities. All departments in Norm Thompson are instructed to make significant monetary decisions with use of a "sustainability filter."

These philosophies have been implemented through specific actions. For example, every department has a budget line item for direct sustainability expenses. Each fiscal year these expected costs are gathered together into an annual sustainability budget. Another way in which these links are made is that many financial requests incorporate indirect sustainability benefits in their analysis and proposal, which aids in their prioritization. In addition, sustainability has been a key determinant in several major capital outlays and vendor selections.

As Norm Thompson grows and determines where to invest, trade-offs between priorities inevitably occur. Occasionally, sustainability efforts must wait, just as others must. For example, one of the most vivid examples of budgeting for, and investing in, sustainability relates to information technology (IT) to facilitate traditional business operations as well as sustainability efforts. When Norm Thompson launched its sustainability initiatives, the company knew that its IT systems would be crucial for tracking movement toward sustainability. Senior management also knew that existing systems were overwhelmed and therefore not capable of setting out the detailed protocols necessary to report on progress. Therefore, for a variety of reasons the management team decided to upgrade systems, one of which was the company's interest in tracking sustainability indicators more carefully. This process took more than a year because there were many other more urgent needs for bandwidth and IT resources. Therefore, department management initially had to track energy, waste, greenhouse gases, product materials, and other factors manually. Although the reasons for this was understandable, it was very time-consuming and not as accurate as would be achieved with a fully established IT system. However, this approach was the best approach as an interim measure.

The lesson was that patience and working within constraints are essential virtues when creating change, as is perseverance.

Ensuring accountability for continued progress: the essential task

Ensuring accountability for ongoing progress has proven to be the most difficult aspect of creating change on a company-wide scale. When employees are comfortable in their typical, busy routines, they generally respond to their traditional measurements. Therefore, making changes for sustainability—despite interest— will tend to "fall off their full plates." Given this, Norm Thompson discovered that managers must ensure accountability through a variety of mechanisms, each of which may need to be unique to the scenario or even to the employee.

For example, within the company it was clear that merchandizing would be the most difficult area for the transition toward sustainable practices. After two years of success in other areas throughout the company—most notably in paper procurement—product selection remained the "elephant in the living room." Norm Thompson sells thousands of products made by several hundred domestic and international vendors that may change from season to season. As in many other companies, buyers had very little knowledge of the contents and impacts of these products and the production processes under which they were manufactured. Yet the sale of products is how and why the company exists. Staff assigned to overseeing sustainability efforts knew anything that threatened the company's ability to serve its customers with merchandise in which they were interested, at the price they were willing to pay, would be a major risk.

Therefore, initial goals calling for replacement of a couple of specific product materials were set. Based on input from colleagues in other companies, especially Nike and Patagonia, Norm Thompson chose to eliminate polyvinyl chloride (PVC)—a particularly toxic plastic—and to convert the cotton in its products to certified organic cotton. The company set a five-year time-line for these activities— a period that was reasonable given that it might allow vendors to be educated, substitutes to be found and switching costs to decrease. However, the first two years yielded sub-par results and company leaders began to feel the pressure of the self-imposed deadline.

Product buyers were asked why they were having trouble working toward these goals, particularly with organic cotton. The buyers replied that, because their performance was measured largely in terms of customer demand and financial contribution of the products they selected, they needed a clear signal from senior management about how to balance apparent conflicts such as the realization of reduced margins on products with the use of certified sustainable materials. Further, the buyers suggested that they did not have time to be experts in all environmental issues related to their lines but instead needed a tangible way to interpret the benefits of and drawbacks to a range of potential product choices.

In response, senior management commissioned the development of a sustainability scorecard. The scorecard is a method of ranking products based on their environmental impact. Impact is determined by a set of criteria, which were established in partnership with Dr. Michael S. Brown, an independent sustainability consultant. For example, the textile scorecard places certified organic natural fibers at the top and toxic synthetic materials at the bottom.

By using the scorecard, management now holds buyers accountable for improvements toward sustainability by factoring scores into annual performance evaluations. It is incumbent on the buyers to work with their vendors to replace low-scoring materials with high-scoring ones. This approach was chosen because buyer autonomy is a key factor in the company's financial success and is a strong cultural imperative. Accompanying the scorecard is a sustainability toolkit, a user-friendly guide that offers buyers and vendors improvement options, Internet resources and a glossary of social and environmental terms.

As soon as the scorecard was launched, movement began. New materials showed up in product samples, top-selling apparel items were converted to organic cotton and, most importantly, the buyers began to feel empowered and successful. This forward movement arose out of a process that sought buyer involvement. The outcome gave explicit guidance rather than setting lofty goals. The guidelines were concrete and worked within existing norms and procedures. In addition, the performance management component was critical. It was the signal from senior management for which the buyers had asked. Buyers and vendors now understand very tangibly that sustainability has a high enough priority to be factored into performance evaluations.

Going through the scorecard development process proved to the company that creative, collaborative approaches to problem-solving are indispensable. Companies attempting change of the magnitude of moving to corporate sustainability seem to focus mostly on securing buy-in and beginning implementation. However, disregard for longer-term steps that ensure accountability—such as the actions prior to launching the scorecard—is the biggest mistake a company can make in seeking organizational change. Without accountability, change simply will not be maintained. Without appropriate performance management implications, sustainability will remain a dream.

Conclusions: enabling sustainability through change management

Norm Thompson is now four years into its formal attempt to shape a company culture focused on moving toward sustainability. In the first year of the effort, the foundation was literally built and the overall direction set. During year two, Norm Thompson's initiative to make an organizational change to sustainability focused on beginning implementation. In the third year it sought integration. In this fourth year, the process has been guided by efforts at institutionalization.

The company is on track to meet the time-frame of five to seven years for creating a sustainability-oriented company through focused organizational change. Senior management expects to achieve most, if not all, of the major objectives relating to the elimination of impacts from greenhouse gas emissions, use of toxic substances, habitat destruction and waste. Although Norm Thompson still has a lot of hard work ahead, particularly with regard to merchandizing, a solid foundation has been laid and early results have been realized.

In addition to Norm Thompson's paper and merchandise highlights, the company has completed the first round of projects to offset greenhouse gas emissions and has made a major commitment to the use of "green" power. Longer-term efforts will focus on determining how to deliver a sales message by making much less of an impact on natural resources, perhaps without any use at all of catalogs. It is noteworthy that these initiatives are much broader in thoughts than those projects with which the company began its sustainability efforts.

The irony is that starting successfully on a path toward sustainability does not look anything like sustainability. Decision-makers find that loops cannot immediately be closed and that not all products can be converted overnight to non-toxic, non-persistent, non-bioaccumulative, and biodegradable alternatives. In reality, the initial actions may be far less glorious. However, these smaller victories and decisions will ultimately determine a company's success—both in terms of broader organizational change and in terms of movement toward sustainability—as these efforts will create the momentum for driving the change process.

A transformation to a sustainable business enterprise is not likely to occur without consistently implementing effective change-management principles. Establishing a vision and performing a few significant activities is not enough to drive significant change. Although specific activities may vary from company to company, most will be able to turn their dreams into reality by taking the following steps:

- Establish a sustainability vision, mission, and values.

- Articulate sustainability within this existing vision.

- Develop an integrated plan and roadmap to include all departments, and explain how everyone within the organization will be involved in the change process.

- Recognize outstanding employees in moving the initiative forward.

- Hold everyone accountable for progress toward specific objectives.

- Establish systems and procedures to acquire baselines and track progress.

- Weave sustainability-oriented practices into the business plan in a thoughtful, measured way so that cultural elements and profit imperatives are respected and can be maintained.

- Form partnerships with external experts, either from your industry or the NGO community or government in order to validate your actions and leverage your resources.

- Build internal case studies, with quantifiable results, and communicate their success.

- Demand replication and generation of new cases.

- Be persistent yet exercise patience during transition periods when efforts are focused on building the framework for change rather than creating change; these first steps are critical and will pay off.

Norm Thompson's vision is to be a practical model for proving that a company can move toward sustainability in a profitable manner. The core element of the company's approach is to empower employees to question the ways in which everything is done and to identify new avenues for integrating sustainability into all levels of decision-making. Without an appreciation for the nuances of change management, all these efforts would be impossible.

7

Recreating natural-resource-based businesses

Sustaining the land and communities in the US New Northwest

Cecilia Danks
University of Vermont, USA

Martin Goebel and Karen Steer
Sustainable Northwest, Oregon, USA

> Our goal is to . . . provide services and build rural capacity to pro-
> duce and market products that benefit both entrepreneurs and
> forest ecosystems . . . We value and support those who refuse to
> sacrifice the long-term good of the land for the good of the people
> . . . those who seek to find a new path which honors and sustains
> both.
>
> *Healthy Forests, Healthy Communities partnership*

The rural US West has undergone dramatic economic and environmental changes since the late 1980s. While the high-technology industries flourished in some cities, rural communities, built on the region's traditional natural-resource-based industries, have experienced heart-breaking declines in economic and social well-being. The most attractive and accessible of these communities are benefiting from the income brought by new retirees and telecommuters. Most rural communities, however, are left to their own devices to reinvent themselves in the 21st century or lose the places and people they value. A number of community and business leaders scattered among those communities have taken up the challenge of recreating their natural-resource-based industries—with environmental, eco-nomic, and social sustainability as the cornerstones of their efforts.

The precipitous declines in spotted owl and salmon populations are among the legacies of decades of industrial timber extraction, large dams, and chemical-intensive farming. In addition to resource degradation, shifts in land-management policies, increased mechanization, land consolidation, foreign competition, and other structural changes have affected the forest products, farming, and ranching sectors. At the same time, broader macroeconomic and policy shifts have exerted downward pressure on prices for cattle and crops. These economic and environmental changes in turn affect the social conditions of the adjacent rural communities. Local, natural-resource-based businesses have shut down and skilled people have migrated elsewhere to find work. As a result, unemployment has surged in many rural communities of the Pacific Northwest and Interior West, often bringing with it the adverse social impacts of an unraveling social fabric. In January 2003, National Public Radio reported on "the nation's hunger belt," a swath of Western rural counties from New Mexico to Washington State that have the highest rates of hunger in the USA. The state of Oregon topped the list despite having a relatively low poverty rate statewide. The reason why basic needs were unmet in a seemingly prosperous region: the technology-driven economic boom of the 1990s did not reach the working-class rural communities, which experienced only further decline as a result of the convergence of the forces listed above.

Despite these conditions, there remains a deep commitment to place among the rural residents and businesses who have chosen to stay in their communities. Recognizing the need to depart from the boom-and-bust cycles that have characterized the development of the West, they are seeking to rebuild sustainable economies that will allow them and their children to thrive in place. Their challenge pivots on the fundamental question: "What is the most viable way to integrate ecological, economic, and social health in rebuilding their local economies?" Put another way: "What is the pathway toward sustainability?"

Rather than abandon their history of working with the land, many rural entrepreneurs have sought to re-engage with the surrounding resources and build businesses based on restoration rather than extraction. The result has been an emergence of new sustainability-oriented enterprises and community development initiatives throughout the region. These efforts are seen across diverse natural resource sectors. In forestry, jobs are being created to restore forests and to manufacture products out of the wood removed as a by-product of restoration. In ranching, small-scale family ranches committed to sustainability are being maintained by a combination of environmental stewardship and direct marketing. In agriculture, locally owned farms are being managed in ways that protect environmental health while also creating profits.

Yet, despite the "win–win" nature of their endeavors, many of these entrepreneurs face the same challenges that contributed to the decline of their traditional economies. As small businesses they have a difficult time competing in a global commodity market. And, as rurally based operations, they are far from urban-based markets. The leaders among them, however, are turning their rural nature and small size into a marketing advantage. Their strategy is to connect directly with urban markets and share their story of small-town wholesomeness, high-quality products and environmental sustainability. Keys to making those connections have involved working collectively, processing locally, and integrating vertically.

Several such initiatives emerged in the late 1990s. One effort grew from a group of urban and rural businesses that joined with non-profit organizations to establish a collaborative effort supporting rural businesses that perform forest restoration activities through producing and marketing environmentally and socially responsible wood products. The result was the Healthy Forests, Healthy Communities (HFHC) partnership, which helps rural businesses access urban markets for their sustainably produced wood products. Another example of a collective approach is Oregon Country Beef (OCB), a ranching cooperative that sells outside the traditional commodity market and shares a commitment to the principles of sustainability. Also, in the agricultural community, a growing number of farmers have been devising production and marketing methods that focus on sustainability in terms of ecological, economic, and social factors. Stahlbush Island Farms have found ways to put the principles of sustainability into practice by adopting more environmentally friendly farming systems and by processing their high-quality produce at home. These three case studies, described below, illustrate many of the business opportunities and challenges in building new sustainability-focused small rural enterprises that can access urban markets based on a commitment to environmental and social responsibility.

Case studies[1]

In search of ecological restoration and economic resilience: the Healthy Forests, Healthy Communities partnership[2]

Across the US Northwest, rural communities and their surrounding public lands have undergone major environmental and economic transitions: large-scale industrial logging, shifting policies regarding the management of public land, and decades of fire suppression and other management practices have left forests degraded, often with densely packed small-diameter trees at high risk of catastrophic fire and pest infestation. As forest health and the timber industry declined, so too did the economic and social health of many resource-dependent communities adjacent to forest lands. High unemployment, increased poverty, increased reliance on federal assistance, and a loss of working-class jobs and families have affected all facets of community life and well-being. Options seemed limited and, for many residents, hope for the future ebbed.

In 1997, a group of civic leaders and non-profit organizations who had been tackling these issues in their own communities came together to find solutions to the common challenges facing the communities and forests across the Northwest. The participants agreed that their communities' common disadvantages— depleted forests and forestry dependence—could hold a solution for building living-wage jobs within an economy based on forest restoration. Seeking a new role as stewards of the forest, they focused on ways to restore ecological integrity and provide for long-term maintenance of forest ecosystems. They identified new

1   The case studies were adapted from excerpts from Sustainable Northwest 1997, 1998 and van Daalen 2000. See also Rolnick 2001.
2   For more information, see the website of the Healthy Forests, Healthy Communities partnership, at www.hfhcp.org.

opportunities in the excess of small-diameter trees that were a result of logging and fire suppression. Such trees could be more than a mere waste product of restoration and fuel-reduction efforts; they were an undervalued resource that should and could be processed locally to benefit rural residents. Converting this "waste" into marketable products required new forestry practices, new processing techniques, and new markets friendly to an unfamiliar product. The group recognized that success would require more expertise and resources than any community or business could muster on its own. Other challenges to developing new local businesses were also prevalent, including:

● Being located in communities surrounded by public lands, high in poverty, remote from transportation corridors, and limited in infrastructure

● Having limited ability to manufacture products at high enough volumes for the commodity market

● Lacking access to capital to invest in and expand their businesses

However intractable these constraints seemed to be, the group realized that, working collectively, it could begin to overcome them. What coalesced from that initial meeting and the discussions that followed was the HFHC partnership.

A program of the non-profit organization Sustainable Northwest, based in Portland, OR, the HFHC partnership is a regional collaborative dedicated to building capacity in rural communities to perform forest restoration activities and to produce and market the wood by-products of these activities. HFHC businesses convert these by-products—small-diameter suppressed trees and under-utilized species removed to promote forest health—into quality wood products, such as flooring, dimensional lumber, furniture, and crafts. Wood products are marketed under a trademarked brand name that carries the story of social and environmental responsibility.

Products can bear the name and the story of the individual manufacturer, but producers who join the partnership and pledge to meet the HFHC criteria also carry the HFHC label. That label succinctly states their story:

> HFHC is a non-profit network of businesses committed to making the highest quality products from wood sources selected in ways that maintain or restore the health of our forests. HFHC businesses are locally owned and create jobs in small towns throughout the Pacific Northwest. Thank you for buying HFHC products and showing your support for the economic and ecological health of our rural communities.

The HFHC "story" has been important in differentiating these items from other wood products in the marketplace; the commitment to environment, community, job creation, and regional sustainability resonates with urban consumers. However, the true value of the partnership goes beyond this eco-label (or perhaps, more accurately, this "socio-eco-label"). It is truly a partnership in which members engage with each other for mutual benefit. Through its collaborative structure, HFHC provides small, normally isolated rural businesses with the opportunity to share skills and resources to mutually strengthen their businesses. Workshops, open houses, exchanges and a small grants program have helped members to build capacity and combine efforts to promote vertical integration among their manufacturing and marketing operations. One member might produce raw lumber, which another member turns into furniture, which is sold in the showroom of another member, hundreds of miles away.

In addition to fostering mutual support, a core strategy of HFHC is to directly link rural producers and urban consumers based on the common values that they share. HFHC has helped small rural businesses to capture the potential of the rapidly growing niche market for environmentally sound products by providing timely information, new contacts to the urban marketplace, strategic partnerships among producers to guarantee quality and supply, and assistance with marketing. In isolation, these rural community-based businesses were likely to struggle, and in some cases to fail, despite their hard work and commitment to sustainability. As a collaborative, however, they have the potential to leverage common resources, capacities, and marketability in order to create a sustainable future for themselves and the surrounding ecosystems.

In 2002 HFHC was over 50 members strong, including rural manufacturers, non-profit organizations, brokers, and urban-based retailers. One of the members is Jefferson State Forest Products (JSFP), which is featured in Case study 7.1. All the members sign a common "vision and values statement" that affirms their commitment to work individually and together to integrate economic, ecological, and social objectives in all that they do, for the benefit of community and forest health. This vertically integrated network allows rural producers to remain small and at home—and yet thrive. It also gives urban consumers access to products that they can feel good about. By supporting the businesses that help sustain the health of rural communities and the surrounding forest, the Healthy Forest Healthy Communities partnership is living up to its name.

Beefing up sustainable ranching businesses: Oregon Country Beef [3]

The cattle industry is often characterized by dependence on a decreasing number of processors and a limited number of market channels while operating under heavy debt and extremely thin profit margins. These factors contribute to pressure on ranchers and the land, which is already suffering from decades of overgrazing and increasing competition for water. Be it the effects of intensive feedlots or extensive grazing of public land, the environmental impact of cattle production has attracted increasing attention. Add to this mix of stressors the aging of the ranching population and the competition with developers for prime ranchland and it becomes clear that the family-owned cattle ranch—an important cultural feature of the US West as well as a core economic sector—is facing perilous decline. The failure of ranches not only hurts ranching communities but also often leads to the fragmentation of the landscape and a reduction in wildlife habitat.

---

3 For more information, see the website of Oregon Country Beef, at www. oregoncountrybeef.com.

In forests of the Pacific Northwest and Northern California, the history of mining, ranching, and timber booms and busts has produced a scattering of towns and mill sites—some abandoned, some struggling, and others being remade. Towns closest to major transportation routes have shown the greatest ability to revive their economies. Many are now home to new enterprises that are tapping the new economic growth associated with an expanding retirement population, the service sector and/or tourism—the booms of the new century. However, in more remote locations, lacking the amenities that attract tourists and retirees, the social and economic decline is beginning to settle in. In these out-of-the-way places, people and businesses are as likely to move on as be remade. Hayfork, CA, is one such town.

When Jim Jungwirth was growing up in Hayfork in the 1950s, the valley boasted seven sawmills. Six were locally owned. The town was small but thriving and most folks looked back on the 1950s through the 1970s as Hayfork's heyday. But when Jim returned to Hayfork in the early 1990s after being away for a decade, it was to a very different community. Only one large, corporately owned mill was operating, and timber cutting in the national forest that surrounded the town had all but halted. In 1990 a federal injunction on public timber sales—out of consideration for the habitat of the northern spotted owl—effectively removed the primary source of Trinity County timber. In 1996 the last sawmill in the valley closed, choosing to consolidate its manufacturing capacity closer to more reliable timber supplies and cheaper labor. Within a few short weeks, 160 jobs were lost—a tremendous blow to a town of 2,000 people. Within a few years, over 40% of the payroll in Hayfork had disappeared. By the end of the decade, almost 80% of Hayfork children relied on the school's "Free and Reduced Lunch Program," an indication of how many families were struggling to make ends meet.

When Jim and his wife Lynn returned to Hayfork, they did not want to get involved in the politics of land management, but they did want to strengthen the struggling community and hoped to inspire a renewed connection between the local economy and an ethic of land stewardship. With these goals in mind, they were instrumental in establishing the Watershed Research and Training Center, a non-profit organization that has worked since 1993 to "promote healthy communities and sustainable forests through research, education, training and economic development."*

Though an original board member of the Watershed Center, Jim moved away from the non-profit sector and set about to address the challenge in a new way. With the eye of an entrepreneur, he believed he could make a living and create jobs in his community by making products that are beneficial to forest health. Jim founded Jefferson State Forest Products (JSFP) in 1996 with the vision of utilizing "responsibly harvested" material in quality designed products that allow workers to make a decent living in rural communities. His partner, Greg Wilson, provided design craftsmanship.

At JFSP, the term "responsibly harvested" implied a concern both for ecosystem health and for social well-being. Consistent with this approach, Jim purchases wood that is the by-product of restoration thinning prescribed to improve forest health and reduce the threat of forest fires. The historically under-utilized wood from these sources required experimentation in how best to mill, dry, manufacture, and introduce them to the market. JSFP also prioritizes the purchase of waste material and lumber from small independent mills that process low volumes of wood from well-managed forests. JSFP became "chain-of-custody" certified by the Forest Stewardship Council in order to handle certified wood for special orders.

*   www.thewatershedcenter.org

Case study 7.1   **Healthy Forests, Healthy Communities partnership profile: Jefferson State Forest Products** (continued opposite)

Source: adapted from McKinley 2002

Knowing that he could not compete in the commodity lumber market, Jim decided to focus on secondary manufacturing. He found that creating a successful wood-product manufacturing business in the vacuum of a failed industry to be a major challenge. The cascading effects of the closure of Hayfork's last mill included a growing number of failed businesses and an increasing reluctance of banks and lenders to support enterprises in the community. Many workers moved away. The workers who remained in the area often did not possess the diversity of skills needed. Equally important, the community spirit was broken, and optimism undermined. Jim explained that the net result was "a lack of willingness to share the risks inherent in creating a new business, to make the investments in training, machinery, and capitalization necessary to try something new in wood products" (McKinley 2002).

With perseverance, however, he built the business. The county fairgrounds rented space to JSFP on the provision that everything would be moved out for a few weeks during the annual county fair to make room for displays, livestock, and fair-goers. JSFP's first big order was with the alumni society of a major university. It proved a perfect way to grow the business in stages. The university supplied recycled wood from a remodeled building, JSFP designed and built quality furniture from that historic wood and the alumni society marketed the products to its members. Because they did not have to secure raw material and market the outputs, Jim and Greg could invest their limited capital and time on developing a product line, acquiring and constructing manufacturing equipment, and training employees. They also identified a fruitful market niche: mid-sized custom orders for businesses that expect high-quality products and service and that also like the idea of doing business with a company committed to environmental and social responsibility. Their biggest customer has been Whole Food Markets, which uses JSFP fixtures and other accessories in over 70 stores nationwide. Retail fixtures, flooring, and furniture have become JSFP mainstays. In addition, Jim and Greg continue to experiment with new ways to utilize beautiful pieces of "waste wood," eventually diversifying their product line into kitchen accessories, cider presses, and even cremation urns.

Marketing has been critical to JSFP's success. Jim asserts, however, that he could not have successfully undertaken marketing on his own. Rather, he explains, "the key to rural manufacturing is an urban–rural partnership. We can't succeed selling to ourselves [in the Hayfork area or even in Trinity County]" (McKinley 2002). This need for broader market reach led JSFP to become one of the first business partners of the HFHC partnership. Through this partnership, Jim not only accesses distant markets but also shares entrepreneurial lessons with like-minded rural manufacturers across the northwestern USA.

By 2002, JSFP had 16 full-time employees and the company no longer fitted in the three buildings it occupied at the fairground. However, they had already demonstrated a model to the community—that a home-grown, sustainability-oriented, forest products company could succeed at a community scale, even where a big corporation had closed its doors. With encouragement from Jim and others, the County government secured California State funding to build a forest products business incubator, and the Watershed Center, working with other agencies, secured private funding for equipment and capacity building for other start-up companies. In the summer of 2002, JSFP moved out of the fairground into the new business incubator as the anchor tenant. Jim has his sights set on his next challenge: encouraging new entrepreneurs to fill the incubator in order to help remake the wood products industry and to reinvigorate Hayfork's local economy. "What we are really in need of are new risk takers," Jim says; "Know any?"*

* For more information on Jefferson State Forest Products, see its website, at www.jeffersonstateproducts.com.

Case study 7.1 (continued)

Like the residents of forest communities, many ranching families do not want to give up their way of life without a fight. That "fight," some ranchers have found, is best won through cooperation.

In the late 1980s a group of Oregon ranchers formed a new, cooperative enterprise which they called Oregon Country Beef (OCB). OCB began as a handful of families dedicated to preserving the family ranch, improving their rangeland's environmental health, and serving the customer directly. The families have all signed OCB's "graze well" principles, which set the cooperative's standards and cover a wide range of issues, such as long-term productivity, biological diversity, maintenance of predators, and watershed management.

Doc Hatfield, one of the co-founders of OCB, further elaborates on their decision-making philosophy: "All our decisions are based on making the program profitable for the next generation, and also in the next 4 weeks" (van Daalen 2000). Therefore, he and his wife, Connie, as well as other OCB ranchers, assert that they advise one another:

> Keep your eye on that long-term goal, but keep it working in the short term while you are going there. With a defined goal and strong core values, we can routinely change what we are doing to meet the needs of the customer. Change is the only absolute we have (van Daalen 2000).

Their point-of-purchase marketing materials eloquently explain their values:

> Our roots extend a century and a half deep to a time when most of our ranch families' ancestors were crossing the Oregon Trail. We have a passion to communicate our beliefs about the land through a beef product you can savor and trust. As part of our commitment to growing cattle in harmony and balance with Nature, we have chosen not to use growth hormones or feed antibiotics. We feel our beef grown this "old fashioned" way has better flavor and texture and we invite you to taste the Oregon Country difference.[4]

Their website (www.oregoncountrybeef.com) also presents marketing messages for the romantic as well as the discriminating consumer who cares about the land, the animals, and human health (see Quote 7.1). This construction of image and issues is central to OCB's marketing,

By 2002 OCB had more than 40 member ranches, with 2.5 million acres under management by cooperative members, most of which have become more economically viable because of their adherence to environmental, social, and economic principles and to customer satisfaction. Furthermore, by directly marketing their product to health-conscious grocery stores and restaurants, OCB has successfully reduced the dramatic price fluctuations that commodity beef producers have been forced to tolerate for decades. Enjoying 20% annual growth in sales, OCB reached US$15 million in sales by 2002.

If OCB beef is a value-added product, the greatest value they add to their meat are the values held by its members. According to Doc, OCB's business success has been based on reaching a "growing group of people who are concerned about the

4   OCB marketing materials.

Story 1 (the Image)

Our product is more than beef.
It's the smell of sage after a summer thunderstorm,
the cool shade of a Ponderosa Pine forest.
It's 80 year old weathered hands
saddling a horse in the Blue Mountains,
the future of a 6 year old
in a one room school on the High Desert.
It's a trout in a beaver built pond,
haystacks on an Aspen framed meadow.
It's the hardy quail running to join the cattle for a meal,
the welcome ring of a dinner bell at dusk.

Story 2 (the Issues)

Oregon Country Beef assures quality

All Oregon Country Beef [OCB] cattle are under the direct ownership and stewardship of our individual coop member ranchers. OCB does not buy cattle from traders or outside sources to supplement our production commitments.

We are committed to the sustainability and health of the land, the health of our animals and ultimately the health of our customers.

OCB cattle are vegetarian fed from calf to processing and do not receive, at any time in their life, feed, antibiotics, or hormone and steroid implants for added weight gain. Our cattle are grown naturally for maximum taste and tenderness, within a well-defined quality assurance program.

Quote 7.1 The Oregon Country Beef stories

Source: www.oregoncountrybeef.com

quality of their food—both the health of the land and animals it was produced with, and the health of the people working to produce it" (van Daalen 2000). He further asserts:

> In general, agriculture doesn't do marketing. [Agriculturalists] produce what they want to produce, and then try to find someone to peddle it to. As we like to say, our product is more than just beef. We live in a society of strip malls and discount chains that are totally removed from the community and the producers of food. You can only sit in a traffic jam for so long before you start wanting something real. People want to know that somewhere it's still wild, honest, and free. We put these things together to create a quality eating experience for a consumer who wants a quality beef product in their diet. Those are the things that give it value. We focus on consumers who share our values.

One of OCB's first customers was Kyotaru, a Japanese company whose dealings with the cooperative suggested an alternative to the traditional competitive model. Doc explains:

> We use the Japanese concept of *shin-rai*, where several companies work together for the benefit of everyone, including the consumer.

> We have a *shin-rai* partnership with a feedlot, packing house, five distribution companies, and about 50 retail outlets (van Daalen 2000).

OCB's partnership with their meat-packing house exemplifies the *shin-rai* concept. Doc's wife Connie asserts that:

> Washington Beef was already successful, and had everything in place—the state-of-the-art equipment . . . If we had to own that facility, and deal with all the rules and regulations . . . [there is] no way [that we could afford it]. Instead, we utilize their facilities, and they do a fantastic job getting our beef into the food stores. We are in daily communication with them and the five distributors. This allows us to sell direct to the consumer and get out of the commodity-pricing of current markets (van Daalen 2000).

Thus, through their cooperative, members can vertically integrate some of the processing and marketing.

Connie bears primary responsibility for marketing to natural food stores. OCB has sought to effectively communicate its approach, often through visits to the land. One such visit occurs annually and is focused on retail buyers, as Connie explains:

> Once a year in August, we invite all the meat cutters, store owners, and meat distributors to our ranches for a big barbecue. Last year we got a whole posse of meat cutters on horses and took their picture—the "Whole Foods Buckaroos." Those guys will never be the same. We are all learning from each other (van Daalen 2000).

Knowing the power of this exchange, all OCB's ranch owners spend one weekend a year in an urban retail store doing an in-store demonstration, cooking their meat and sharing samples and stories. This gives the rancher the chance to get to know the meat cutter and the consumers, and vice versa.

Among the most important lessons learned by OCB are:

- A cooperative is strongest if its members share a common vision, values, and commitments.

- Market your story, not just your product.

- Establish direct relationships with consumers and clients—and listen to them.

- Change and adapt constantly.

- Bucking the establishment "system" is possible.

- A third-party certifier is necessary, especially when competitors begin to appear; however, certification standards must be developed both by the certifying group and by the ranchers, and adoption must be beneficial to all.

- Make decisions by consensus.

● Involve all family members, especially women.

● Seek assistance from uncommon places and organizations.

The success of OCB is attributed to the broad, long-term vision and flexible cooperation that governs the decisions of the business. The cooperative proves that a resource-intensive industry such as beef farming can be well managed and financially lucrative because of—not in spite of—commitments to more environmentally friendly, community-centered, and health-conscious practices.

Growing a sustainable farming system: Stahlbush Island Farms[5]

As the fourth generation on the land, Karla and her husband, Bill, have transformed the 2,000 acre Stahlbush Island Farms from a chemically intensive operation into a farming system that seeks to integrate sustainability concepts and practices. The change has been good for more than just the local ecosystems. The farm is more profitable today than it ever was under the former "conventional" farming system. In addition, Stahlbush Island Farms has enjoyed steady double-digit growth annually by applying its sustainability-focused production methods to over two dozen varieties of fruits and vegetables sold to 40 states and in 14 countries (Sustainable Northwest 1998).

For over a decade Karla and Bill Chambers have been developing a sustainability-focused farming system through their mid-sized agricultural operation that is economically profitable and minimally harmful, and even beneficial, to the environment. The Chambers are at the vanguard of a new agricultural movement that combines the best practices from organic and conventional agriculture. As a result, crop yields at Stahlbush Island Farms have increased, the safety and quality of food products have been enhanced, soil quality has improved, and chemical and water use have decreased. Their farm was the first to be endorsed by The Food Alliance, a Portland-based non-profit organization that has developed a "seal of approval" for sustainable agriculture producers. In addition, Stahlbush produce also carries the Salmon Safe seal, recognizing their efforts to protect water quality. The Chambers have received national recognition for their striving to integrate sustainability concepts into their farming systems, including a Founders of a New Northwest Award in 1998 from Sustainable Northwest (van Daalen 2000).

Karla believes that America's chemical-intensive agricultural system is a direct outcome of the Great Depression, when producing vast amounts of cheap food was the focus. "We're now one of the wealthiest countries on the planet and should be able to correct this. But now we don't know any better," says Karla. "Why do we buy these huge, awful-tasting, white-centered strawberries? We think we're getting a good deal because they're cheap and they're big." She further asserts:

> The vision of agriculture that we've been working under is not working for farmers. The cheap food policy we set course on 40 years

5 For more information on Stahlbush Island Farms, see its website at www.stahlbush. com.

ago, with its price controls and commodity markets, has forced farms
to grow ever larger to keep up with rising input costs. Most of us are
going broke. We're already down to less than 1% of the US population
living on farms, and how many more farmers will we lose during the
current economic cycle? (van Daalen 2000).

In response to these issues, Karla and Bill have been developing an alternative
vision for agriculture. Karla describes their approach as follows:

> Rather than relying on a tool chest of herbicides, insecticides, and
> fungicides, we have focused on using natural systems to their fullest.
> At the core of this approach is using cover crops to naturally grow
> nitrogen, and rotating crops to naturally break disease and insect
> cycles. We have taken some of the best methods from the organic
> community, as well as advanced science from the [conventional]
> agriculture community, and combined them . . . We are focused on
> a safe and sustainable farming system, and on growing produce that
> is more affordable to consumers than the high cost of organic pro-
> duction allows (van Daalen 2000).

In order to overcome increased labor costs associated with sustainable practices,
the Chambers have focused on using innovative technologies from other industries to re-engineer and retool their equipment. The farm is moving away from
capital-intensive, large heavy equipment and substituting lighter, lower-impact
equipment.

All these approaches represent distinct breaks from the family's past practices,
which in Bill's family spans 86 years in Oregon and for Karla's family 113 years.
However, they are consonant with a deep desire to stay on the land. She grew up
on a ranch that has been home to her family for five generations. "I come from a
rich agricultural heritage," affirms Karla, "That's why, when I think of my family,
I'm not thinking about the next five to ten years. I'm thinking about the next 25,
50 and 100 years. That's the cycle we should be thinking about for the natural
resources we manage" (Sustainable Northwest 1998).

The Chambers bought their own farm in 1985: 353 acres blessed with river-
bottom soil on the banks of the Willamette River near Corvallis, OR. Karla remembers coming down the driveway for the first time as owner:

> We had just signed the paper. We had just put our name on an enor-
> mous amount of debt. Enormous. Bill and I were driving down the
> driveway thinking "What did we just do?" That's a lot of risk when
> you're 26 and 27 years old. That could have been a lifetime of debt or
> bankruptcy (Sustainable Northwest 1998).

The farm they had acquired was producing sugar beet for seed, and soft white
wheat. Within a 60 mile radius of the farm, however, over 210 different agricultural
crops were being grown. "We can grow almost anything in the world," explains
Karla, "These are beautiful, rich, productive, river bottom soils" (Sustainable
Northwest 1998). The farm now grows and processes broccoli, corn, green beans,
peas, pumpkins and other members of the squash family, spinach, strawberries,
and bell peppers, as well as grass seed and wheat. Only a portion of the farming

operation is certified organic, but all is "nearly chemical-free." Since they started, they have reduced their chemical use by 85%.

Their pathway toward sustainability, over the 14 years of operation, has not always been easy. Farmers often see their profits eaten up by swings in the commodity market. Karla vividly recalls the usual pricing dynamic:

> The way I was raised in production agriculture, we grew wheat and cattle and alfalfa and at the end of a 365 days' tremendous labor input somebody told you what your commodity was worth. And that somebody was sitting in Chicago or New York (Sustainable Northwest 1998).

This situation inspired them in 1990 to integrate their operation vertically by building a food-processing plant that allowed them to add value to their raw produce, taking it one step closer to the consumer. Whereas, typically, a farmer, a broker, a processor and a customer would be linked in the chain of custody, this decision removed several players, thereby eliminating overheads and increasing the margins. Today, the farm grows and processes all the pumpkin for Mrs. Smith's pumpkin pies, a popular US brand of prepared desserts (Sustainable Northwest 1998).

These decisions have allowed Stahlbush Island Farms to pay its employees more and to offer benefits, including medical, dental, and retirement plans and informal profit sharing. It has also allowed the business to grow smart and remain profitable during times when US agriculture has been very unprofitable. Chambers comments:

> Commodity prices have reached a 40-year low in the past 3 years, while energy, chemical, and equipment costs have increased significantly. There has been massive consolidation among those entities that farmers buy and sell to, and farmers have lost control of agriculture in the process. In addition, cheap imports have made it impossible for farmers to compete with [farms in other] nations that pay labor $0.35 per hour . . . As a result, we face a choice: we can import the food or import the labor. Currently, farmers are doing both and US agriculture depends on an illegal labor force, with 60–70% of Hispanic workers in the country illegally. The direction agriculture took 40 years ago has also put it in conflict with environmental concerns (van Daalen 2000).

The goal of Stahlbush Island Farms remains to grow and process the highest-quality food products available while at the same time improving their most important natural resources: soil and water. The Chambers are committed to improving soil health and soil and water quality. "You start with the soil and end with the food product—we look at the whole system," says Karla (Sustainable Northwest 1998). Karla explains that broccoli grown conventionally will probably have between 15 and 20 chemical applications. At Stahlbush, broccoli is grown with three or fewer. The treatments they do apply are approved as certified organic. At the same time, Stahlbush employs many other methods in growing broccoli, including in-row planting of cilantro and the use of cover crops. "It's not any one tool, but a whole combination of tools," adds Karla:

> We've received clear signals from consumers that they want fewer chemical inputs in their food supply. Our focus is to hand our customers a certificate and say, "yes, this has been residue-tested for 36 or 40 different chemical pesticide residues through a third party, and here are the results." We concentrate on growing food that is residue-free (Sustainable Northwest 1998).

To start, the Chambers replaced chemically intensive operations with a labor-intensive system. Now they are using a system that is management-, technology- and labor-intensive. "We are taking technology that is readily available in other industries and applying it to farming. It is really that progressiveness that is allowing us to move even farther away from chemically intensive agriculture," asserts Karla.

To accomplish their goals, specific practices have been established at Stahlbush. They include:

- Rotating crops annually to help break disease and insect cycles, control weeds and improve soil health

- Growing cover crops to enrich soil organic matter, generate natural nitrogen and promote cleaner groundwater by reducing soil erosion and nitrogen leaching

- Reducing and eliminating pesticide use through advanced technology, coupled with intensive management (if pesticides are necessary, the organically approved pesticides are looked at first)

- Testing for soil and product chemical residues at independent third-party laboratories; Stahlbush Island Farms employs one of the strictest pesticide testing procedures in farming today, testing in parts per billion for over 20 chemical residues

- Conserving water through irrigation practices that use water efficiently and minimize run-off

- Recycling and composting of inputs; for example, all water is used a minimum of three times in the food processing plant, all cardboard and wood are recycled, and organic plant waste is composted

Worldwide the need for agricultural products continues to rise as the population grows. In addition, consumers are becoming increasingly concerned about how their food is produced. Karla asserts (Sustainable Northwest 1998) that this reality leads to new questions and energizing possibilities:

> How do we continue to improve these natural resources while the demand is greater today than ever before? That to me is what's so exciting about sustainable agriculture.
>
> At Stahlbush, I see us taking a national leadership role in defining a new farming system—one that does not sacrifice yields for profits. And one that can continue to feed more and more people and at the same time improve the natural resource base that we inherited, and that we're responsible for.

What these cases can teach us

In each of the three cases described here, local entrepreneurs chose to reinvent traditional natural-resource-based industries rather than to abandon them. Their commitment to place—to the communities and landscapes they call home— stands in marked contrast to the leaders of the boom-and-bust enterprises that preceded them. That commitment to place made the goal of ecological and socioeconomic sustainability a natural choice, even as they maintained their roots in what may be typically viewed as exploitative industries. The value they place on sustaining rural landscapes and livelihoods resonates with an urban market increasingly interested in environmental and social responsibility. The challenge each group faced was how to get their products and their message to those markets.

Although developed independently in different sectors, these cases show some striking similarities from which lessons can be drawn. HFHC members, OCB ranchers and Stahlbush Island Farms each deliberately chose not to continue in commodity production despite its dominance in the timber and agricultural sectors. Not only did small size and transportation costs make them uncompetitive in commodity markets, but also they felt that the commodity model had failed rural communities, families, and the environment. The way to social and ecological sustainability required the forging of a different path.

They each chose a "value-added" path, and added value in multiple ways. Value-added businesses are typically understood as those that process raw materials into intermediate or finished products. Each group developed (or, in the case of OCB, contracted for) processing capacity that added value to their products in this traditional sense. In addition, each group added environmental value by choosing production or procurement practices that contribute to the ecological health of the ecosystems on which their businesses depend. Likewise they contributed value to their communities through local job creation, through the positive models they demonstrated, and through civic engagement. Finally, by sharing their ethical values and sustainability objectives, they added qualities to the products that the consumers valued. Their stories could add value just as additional processing did. High-quality products and personalized service made possible by the relatively small scale of the operations can also be considered value-added aspects of these businesses.

For HFHC and OCB, getting their goods and message to market required that they work collectively with small businesses that might otherwise be their competitors. By pooling resources devoted to marketing and/or by combining products for larger orders they were collectively able to reach urban markets that their individual members could not have accessed. Moreover, their networks enabled them to share expertise and build individual capacity. Even Stahlbush Island Farms, which grew fairly large and managed its own marketing, benefited from participating in sustainable agriculture networks and certification programs such as the Food Alliance and Salmon Safe.

Of course, there are many producer networks and cooperatives, especially in agricultural sectors. The rural producers in these cases, however, also forged strong ties with urban-based non-profit organizations, clients, and consumers. These new relationships have been critical to the success of these groups. HFHC, the most integrated of the groups, has a mix of members that includes rural manufacturers and urban retailers as well as rural and urban non-profit organizations that assist in capacity-building. This diverse membership meets together at retreats and workshops, where they develop mutual understanding, new friendships, and fruitful business relationships. HCFC, OCB, and Stahlbush Island Farms all put effort into reaching outside their organizations to host visitors and hold events that help form direct personal relationships with the people who buy their products.

Although the conscientious consumer is an important source of demand, these groups had their greatest marketing success with intermediary businesses and retailers that shared a commitment to environmental and social responsibility. Examples include Whole Foods, which was an important customer of both OCB and JSFP, and Mrs. Smith's, which purchased Stahlbush purees. Whole Foods was not selling its store fixtures to its customers, so JSFP's products were not chosen because its "story" would appeal to consumers. Rather, JSFP's story appealed to Whole Foods itself, because the story reflected the values Whole Foods shared. Likewise, Mrs. Smith's does not buy Stahlbush's pumpkin puree so that it can advertise its pies as "certified sustainable" or "chemical residue-free;" it buys the puree because the company itself values a high-quality product that is sustainably produced.

The story may be the hook that gets a buyer to make the first order, but service and quality are what make them steady customers. In each of these cases, the producers not only have a good story but also have great products and reliable service to back them up. Repeat customers, making regular medium-sized orders, were essential to the sustainability of these businesses.

Story is important, and common values can unite—but small businesses based in remote communities need more than a good story. They need to build capacity to overcome structural disadvantages and, in many cases, they need help in building that capacity. In each of these cases, entrepreneurs sought ways to achieve vertical integration—from raw products of the land to the final consumer—while growing only as large as was comfortable for them. Through local or shared processing and shortened marketing chains, more of the revenue generated from sales of final products went to the producers. That flow, in turn, enhanced their ability to invest in the sustainability elements of their businesses.

Thus, the value of partnerships—for capacity-building, vertical integration, marketing, and information-sharing—is perhaps the most salient lesson from these cases. The importance of the relationships built on shared values among rural producers and between rural and urban entities is clearly evident in each case. Less visible is their reliance on scientists and environmentalists who can point to the new practices that help heal ecosystems. These businesses want to do right by the land but often rely on the expertise of researchers and others who are at the cutting edge of understanding ecosystems and developing land-management alternatives that can promote ecological health. Small businesses are ready to experiment and innovate but they cannot support a basic research program. Policies that support sustainability need to support research and extension for sustainable practices as well as capital and capacity-building for sustainability-oriented businesses.

Together, these cases highlight some of the factors that can help small businesses to succeed—despite formidable challenges—and contribute to economic vitality in a way that promotes both environmental health and community well-being. These individuals, businesses, and organizations are at the leading edge of translating sustainability concepts into practice in rural communities. They are working to imagine, define, and refine the tools and techniques to make the sustainable world a reality.

8

Growing a sustainable business
Establishing and financing new ecologically and socially restorative ventures

Matthew A. Klein
Verdant Power, Washington, DC, USA

Among established industries, the phrase "sustainable business" is being introduced into the corporate lexicon and is beginning to take a slight hold in the marketplace. Ford Motor Company is moving toward fuel-efficient vehicles more aggressively than is mandated. BP is exploring the viability of biodegradable products and renewable energy. This movement will be successful when the practice is so ubiquitous that one again refers only to "business," because the designation "sustainable" is understood and fully integrated into all aspects of strategy, operations, practices, and products.

Although shifts currently under way may still fall far short of what is required to slow or reverse global environmental degradation, big business is generally applauded by the public for even token attempts at "reform." Emerging ventures, however, often are not taken seriously as they struggle to integrate sustainability into their core operations.

Without validation from the larger marketplace that comes from substantial sales, brand identity, or corporate longevity, social entrepreneurs are often dismissed as irrelevant or "fringe" thinkers. Thus, new companies whose products and internal processes are consistent with growing rather than depleting the principal value of natural systems, ironically, face special obstacles to their own growth. However, non-mainstream thinking is precisely what is needed now to change the course of ecological and social disharmony set in place by mainstream economic systems.

In this chapter, I explore the obstacles stemming from building sustainability into the core of new ventures. Specifically, I outline strategies for growth based on the case of Verdant Power, a renewable energy start-up. In the next section, I begin by describing characteristics of sustainable companies. In the following section, a few of the challenges that new sustainability-focused businesses must face are discussed, with the assertion that, even within the current policy and economic climate, opportunities exist for sustainability-focused businesses that offer a net competitive advantage over their non-sustainable counterparts.

Specific opportunities and funding strategies are laid out in the third section, with attention to new options for private, socially minded "angel investors" and government and foundation grant opportunities. This alternative pathway for launching a new business is then illustrated in the subsequent section through the case of Verdant Power. The chapter concludes with an overview of this range of alternative funding options as well as some thoughts on scale and growth of new sustainability-focused businesses.

What makes a company sustainable? Characteristics of sustainability-focused businesses

Sustainability is most usefully thought of as a process rather than as an end goal. A company may use an empirical framework, such as that provided by The Natural Step, as a guide on the path toward sustainability (Nattrass and Altomare 1999). Three criteria may be used to assess a company's progress along this path. First, the end service or product must reduce, or at least not increase, a company's overall social and ecological footprint (Wackernagel and Rees 1996). One way of defining this end goal is to say that the company's output must conform to The Natural Step system conditions (see Chapter 4). Second, the internal processes of the company must comply with this same imperative. A vendor of organically produced clothing that sources its labor to sweatshops does not qualify. Finally, the company must be internally financially sustainable. It must provide a service or product that is competitive with traditional unsustainable methodologies.

Figure 8.1 describes the dynamic tension between economics and sustainability. A truly sustainable company would achieve financial success and provide ecological and social returns. There certainly is a place for organizations that achieve high social returns but are not able to compete within the existing constraints of a hardline capital market system. Organizations providing essential social services must then be funded publicly or through non-governmental organizations (NGOs), otherwise they would not exist. It is problematic to name these companies or industries, because a smart entrepreneur will one day find a way to bring these businesses into the realm of market success. One can tell which they are, though, by examining those that are selected out by an unforgiving private funding system.

There is an ongoing debate about the appropriate mix of social and financial return. What are people willing to sacrifice financially to gain socially? In Figure 8.1, a sustainability-focused company would be plotted somewhere in the upper right-hand quadrant—that is, above the x-axis (in profit) and to the right of the y-axis (contributing positively to sustainability)—with the precise coordinates in

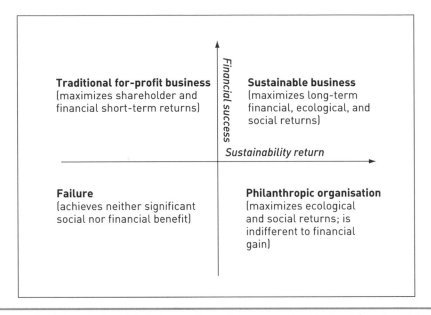

Figure 8.1 The relationship between financial success (vertical axis) and social (or sustainability) business return (horizontal axis)

question. The company must, with each strategic decision and capital investment, balance potential sustainability benefits with financial obligations to stakeholders.

A sustainable company must flourish in the marketplace and have the potential to compete effectively. A business may design the product that will single-handedly reverse environmental degradation, but if it does not propagate it cannot achieve its desired effect. Some industries, such as those producing renewable energy, have an easier time with this twofold goal because a component of sustainability is "baked into" the final product. Independent of the socially responsible intentions of the corporate decision-makers, the products of a company may also be considered somewhat neutral; for example, Ben & Jerry's ice cream may be seen as fatty and unhealthy but also as a fun, psychologically nourishing part of the human diet.

Perhaps the most remarkable example of the other end of the spectrum is the story of Ray Anderson, founder and former chief executive officer (CEO) of Interface, Inc. As described in Chapter 1, Anderson started a wildly economically successful commercial carpet business that had, in the past, transformed fossil fuel resources (the principal input into synthetic carpet threads) into landfill in a most expedient and noxious way. Through a variety of technology, process, and business paradigm shifts, Interface, Inc. is now on the path to sustainability (Anderson 1999). At the same time, Interface, Inc. does over US$1 billion in annual sales and, even in the current depressed market cycle, commands a US$300 million capitalization.

The Interface, Inc. example challenges the (mis)perception that sustainability is synonymous with lower-quality output. It may be easier to discharge the effluvia from manufacturing processes without a thought as to what happens next or to plunder natural ecosystem capital rather than live off of the abundant income that arrives daily to our planet from the energy of the Sun. Ironically, this happens by course through a mind-set that a truly successful business would never entertain regarding its financial capital.

Sustainably developed products have been shown repeatedly to match or exceed the quality of the output of the traditional "take–make–waste" system. Interface's floor-covering service receives greater accolades than does competing carpet purchased in the usual way. As illustrated by Gretchen Daily and Katherine Ellison in Chapter 2, natural reservoir systems such as the one that flows to New York City purify and transport clean water better and more cheaply than do human-made filtration plants. Janine Benyus (1998) provides numerous examples of materials made naturally with speed, strength, durability, and minimal energy input that outstrips humans' capabilities.

We are only now beginning to hear from the biggest player in this market, the strongest force: that of natural systems. As a financial analyst on Wall Street, I witnessed again and again a whole trading floor (and thousands like it across the world) hold its breath in anticipation of the latest non-farm payroll numbers, or the Federal Reserve's impending decision on whether or not to lower the Fed Funds rate by 0.25%, and then collapse into frenzy in reaction to these relatively trivial data.

In contrast, floods, hurricanes, and droughts have staggering impacts not only on health and social equity but also on the global economy. Catastrophic events may stifle productivity and cause immediate distress to insurance and other industries,[1] yet the broad financial system includes no effective mechanism to address these losses. Longer-term, degradation of ecosystem services has negative wealth effects, such as reduced availability of medication and healthcare, nourishing food, and even leisure activities, such as tourism or travel.

As humans approach the boundary of what natural systems can sustainably provide, interconnected social, ecological, and financial systems are impacted. Businesses seeking to put investment capital to work at its "highest and best use" given the risk associated with a particular project will find less attractive uses—as with a lumber company facing accelerating marginal costs for each new unit of

---

1   According to the *E/The Environmental Magazine* (*E/TEM* 2002): "With global climate change . . . in the United States during the last three decades, the number of weather-related natural disasters has increased five-fold . . . The industry to be hardest hit by these careening catastrophes is insurance. According to the Department of Energy, insurance losses from natural disasters have increased 15-fold since 1960, even when corrected for inflation. Carlos Joly, the chairman of the United Nations Environment Program's insurance industry initiative, says, 'The threats to our economies and lifestyles from climate change are no less consequential than terrorism.' In the 1960s the average was 16 'large' weather-related disasters annually in the world. Now, the average is 72. The combined insured losses, corrected for inflation, have jumped from $7 billion to more than $90 billion . . . Insurance industry profit has narrowed nearly six-fold in the last decade, sending the $2 trillion industry into shock."

timber harvested—as well as greater risks. When natural forces truly have their say in shaping our economic and social systems, their voice will be impossible to disregard.

How sustainability-oriented companies can become established in a non-sustainable system: challenges for new sustainability-driven businesses

Consider innovation in the technology sector and Moore's Law, which states on Intel's own website that computer processing speed will double every 18 months.[2] Imagine the obstacles that a company would face in advancing the idea of increasing chip speed at such a rate while simultaneously reducing the environmental impact from manufacturing processes and concurrently sourcing labor to disenfranchized populations in ways that expand their opportunities.

This example begins to illustrate how emerging sustainable companies face many of the same barriers that large, proven businesses encounter in trying to retrofit their operations. Yet, these start-up companies have neither the resources nor the influence necessary to buck well-established trends.

Thus, emerging sustainability-focused companies face two challenges. First, they do not represent the incumbent approach. This holds true for any new business, as an entrepreneur is someone who introduces a concept, technology, or product that is revolutionary in some way. Yet a new sustainable business faces additional restrictions. The challenge is not only to compete against an incumbent methodology or technology but also to replace the incumbent paradigm. This may be understood in the context of the dual, potentially opposing mandates that require the entrepreneur to make decisions that simultaneously benefit the company's short-term financial condition and protect the value of natural capital for future generations.

The current paradigm in business has to do with linear processes. Analysis of the linear system in comparison with cyclical natural processes has been addressed intelligently and at length by others, such as Paul Hawken, Amory Lovins and L. Hunter Lovins (Hawken 1993; Hawken et al. 1999), Lester Brown (2001) and William McDonough and Michael Braungart (McDonough and Braungart 2002). However, as with the cycle of re-use that allows natural systems to function quite successfully, sustainability-oriented businesses may similarly reject the current standard to their benefit. This may happen most obviously by recycling physical resources. A more complex adaptation would consider the long-term impact of harvesting physical resources and how to change practices to decrease impacts. A sustainable economy would also give similar consideration to its human capital. For example, by providing an equitable, safe and nurturing working environment a company may increase productivity and efficiency and thus achieve greater financial as well as social success.

2 www.intel.com/research/silicon/mooreslaw.htm

Sustainability-minded businesses have certain advantages that traditional businesses do not enjoy. These benefits derive from the true model of a sustainable company, which is successful because of, not in spite of, its social mission. If, for example, outgoing delivery trucks that would normally return empty for another sortie are instead used to bring back supplies of raw materials, then cost savings are achieved and fossil fuel emissions are reduced by cutting in half the total time that these trucks are on the road.

In another arena, energy lost to heat, as with an automobile's brakes, can be (and now is) used to recharge batteries. A small company in Benedict, MD, called Solomon Technologies (www.solomontechnologies.com) has developed an elegant motor–generator that has been installed in several dozen sailing boats. In contrast to polluting, high-maintenance diesel engines, the electric motor propels the boat with greater efficiency. When sailing, the propeller that would normally act only as a drag on the boat can instead power a generator and charge batteries. Ultimately, the system will be able to electrolyze hydrogen to power an on-board fuel cell.

Development of this process of electrolysis is already under way through cooperation between Solomon Technologies and another start-up company, called HaveBlue (www.haveblue.com), which is pioneering the use of fuel cells on sailing boats. By combining this technology with a solar array in lieu of a backup diesel generator, these companies have enabled the creation of a mobile, self-contained, ultra-low-emission vessel. This technology is widely applicable beyond the recreational maritime industry and, importantly, proffers financial benefits proportionate to its lesser environmental impact. Companies that attempt conscientiously to deliver their products in sustainable ways have only to work out strategies for business growth in order to be held out as models of businesses that are moving towards sustainability.

The important point is not that it is possible to find one-off examples of the attractiveness of renewable products and sustainability-driven services, because, undoubtedly, it is even easier to illustrate by example the opposite. It is important that humans come to accept the notion that they exist within natural systems and that they cannot innovate better systems than those that Nature has evolved over millennia (Quinn 1992). People have come to believe that they have gained efficiency, "produced" energy even, through linear processes that begin with extraction, treatment, transportation, and limited productive use, and end, in short order, with disposal. These assumptions are deeply flawed.

A convenient euphemism is used to describe and justify the way that capital markets are allowed to operate without regard for sustainability and can be summed up by the concept of "externalities." Externalities describe everything that the powerful business and political incumbency does not want to acknowledge or pay for. It is deemed that the effects of invading the principal value of Nature are negligible because of the scale of natural systems and their ability to absorb this mistreatment. Unfortunately, this limitless ability no longer exists. Once businesspeople and policy-makers recognize this reality—once the full costs of environmental degradation through manufacturing, transportation, and disposal are made explicit in financial cost–benefit analyses—sustainable business will become the norm. The term "sustainable business" will become redundant.

How can a new sustainability-driven business grow? A consideration of financing

Until sustainability-oriented ventures become more accepted, what is the path for a new sustainable company in today's market environment? As a real-time case study, I will describe an alternative-energy company from my role as CEO of Verdant Power. Verdant Power, a renewable-energy company begun in 1998, acts as a systems integrator and designer of proprietary turbine systems that generate electricity from free-flowing river or tidal currents without need of dams, impoundments, or civil works. In addition to delivering affordable and safe electrical energy, the systems will be used to develop other social and ecological services, such as irrigation, water purification, and hydrogen production. As with any new company, the fuel for Verdant Power's growth is financial capital.

Early-stage sustainability-focused businesses are generally not attractive to traditional sources of investment capital. Venture capitalists are, for the most part, focused on financial investment criteria and returns. They are not incented to care about the social rate of return. Furthermore, despite the recent economic downturn and market collapse, institutional funders are arguably the best-capitalized group still.

Further complicating the start-up funding landscape, a new breed of intermediaries has emerged, offering "strategic advice" and "access to capital." These groups do not have the blind pool of money to invest at their discretion. They have turned the traditional flow of funds and strategic guidance—from the venture capitalist to the entrepreneur—on its end, and actually charge a fee-for-service for help with business plans, strategic relationships, and access to funding (for which they take a finder's fee). Given the expectations of reduced returns that follow from the recent market decline, straight equity is a riskier proposition than it used to be.

These services, however, do little good to a new business with scarce cash and with more immediate needs than a desire for strategic partnering or a make-over of its business plan. This is not to say that these people have no value to add; rather, they are an artifact of the asymmetrical relationship that a sustainable start-up is likely to find with traditional institutional capital—the leverage rests solidly with the latter group.

The challenge is that a new business such as Verdant Power is not ready for the traditional markets at any ameliorative terms. For social entrepreneurs, however, other options exist, including:

- Mission-driven private capital (i.e. led by values and focused on the double or triple bottom line)

- Public funding (i.e. regional, national, and international sources)

- Collaboration with non-governmental organizations (NGOs) to share grant allocations for mutually beneficial projects

Thus, despite the obstacles, and within the existing capital market structure, there can be a net competitive advantage to being a sustainability-focused company. This benefit is manifest in the social entrepreneurs' ability to tap into new sources of financing not available to other businesses. These opportunities are emblematic of real change: the convergence of the non-profit, for-profit, and public worlds in creating new business models. Mission-driven for-profit organizations are collaborating with business-minded non-profit organizations. These partnerships will help provide the financial fuel to launch new sustainable businesses and will result in the most efficacious model for advancing sustainability.

Verdant Power has taken advantage of this trend in an explicit, concrete manner. The company has signed a memorandum of understanding with Environmental Resources Trust, a non-profit organization based in Washington, DC, whereby the two groups will jointly pursue projects of mutual interest and advantage. Also, in the US, in addition to various federal allocations to sustainability in the private sector, state and local governments also have financial support available. For example, Verdant Power received US$500,000 out of a combined total of US$10 million in specific series of grants from New York State. Scott Sklar, president of the energy consulting firm Stella Group, estimates that there is US$4.9 billion available from state clean-energy funds and the Clean Air Act in the first decade of the 21st century.

Accessing seed money

Angel investors

As with most new businesses, initial seed money generally comes from the founders themselves, to the extent that they have the necessary resources. Next, with a well-formed concept of the relevant market and the specific business plan— but with delivery of an actual service or product still months or years away—the founders turn to "friends and family." These people invest because they believe in the entrepreneur and the business opportunity. Friends and family are more likely to invest with a social entrepreneur because they can justify the investment as part of their social giving program.

The same is true with the next target audience: "angel" investors. Angels are wealthy individuals, partnerships, or families with the resources available to make relatively high-risk investments in early-stage businesses. These investors have a good deal of financial sophistication and experience, as well as both the patience and the wherewithal to endure the long corporate cycle from blackboard idea to cash-back. Ideally, these individuals also have the knowledge, insight, or contacts to provide the new business with strategic resources in addition to money. In return, angels are rewarded with outsized returns; they commonly seek between 10 and 50 times their initial investment.

In many cases, angels maintain a portfolio of private investments, with the assumption that less than 20% of them will be successful. Unlike an investment in a broadly diversified fund of large public companies, failure here, probable on 80% or more of the portfolio, means losing every dollar invested. Since angels often do not know the entrepreneurs outside of their nascent relationship to the company, and because they are often financially savvy and conditioned to be skeptical (chances favor any given company being one of the 8 in 10 that fails, not one of the 2 that succeeds), this group is tough to access. These difficulties have increased since 2000, when what was "funny money" has turned into the nest egg that people rely on for retirement or emergencies. Today, angels are less willing to put these funds at risk.

Angel investors can, however, still be found. The first avenue is, of course, intense networking through earlier investors, colleagues, trade journals, or professional associations. There are also a number of existing and developing networks of people looking for mission-driven deal flow who are interested in connecting with social entrepreneurs. Many networks and forums exist to help put the social entrepreneur in front of mission-driven angels.

For the most part, these groups act as brokers rather than as dealers. The field is not sufficiently established to attract blind pools of capital from individuals who would be limited partners to be invested at the discretion of the fund's general partner. Instead, the angel networks introduce the company to the investor and may broker a transaction.

Often, these groups offer more than just deal flow; they host recognized speakers, they sponsor round-table discussions and they provide a venue for investors, entrepreneurs, and other interested parties to network with each other. They themselves may be structured as either non-profit or for-profit organizations. Revenue is harvested from grant financing, membership dues, conference attendances, company presentation fees, and, sometimes, from a finder's fee or other method of taking a small percentage of the financial return that they helped to precipitate.

One effective early-adopter organization in this space is the Investors' Circle, located near Boston, MA. In addition to connecting social entrepreneurs with potential investors, this group sponsors educational forums and provides venues for the discussion of the advancement of social profit investing. Interestingly, Investors' Circle gave rise to one of the few exceptions to the broker versus dealer rule.

Commons Capital, which arose from Investors' Circle, is a small fund set up in the spirit of traditional venture capital. Funds are raised from individual or institutional investors, and each investment decision is made by the fund managers, not the original investor. The fund sponsors are compensated through a combination of a small annual percentage of assets under management and a carried interest— a percentage of profits earned. Some larger social venture funds exist, such as Calvert and Domini, and traditional institutional venture groups often have an arm dedicated to social investing in private companies.

In the case of an individual mission-driven investor, the angel may or may not be willing to sacrifice potential financial return for a social return. The majority of angels seek out companies in the upper left-hand quadrant of Figure 8.1—the deals with the real potential for high financial return. These are often people who have made their own money or preserved family money through disciplined business practices.

In all probability, angels will decide individually what return—if any—they expect from their investments, perhaps deal by deal. These angels will mentally allocate this differential to their program of social giving. Thus, an individual investor may consider the capitalized difference between an expected return for a traditional business and that from a sustainability-focused business as part of their personal philanthropy. However, they often have an explicit or implicit financial allocation to charitable giving that is separate from their investable pool of assets. Many of these people are actual philanthropists as well and they tend to establish private or community foundations to carry out their charitable goals.

In my experience, values-led angels are a sharp-minded group, often experienced or even professional investors. Unlike friends and family, these people care deeply about your business model, its market and its ability to flourish there. In fact, since these are often new markets, they want to see that the proposed business can not only succeed in a market but dominate it. Finally, but perhaps most importantly, they want to see a management team that is experienced, innovative, committed, and financially incented. They want management to have a large equity stake in the company. They want management to have values related to the business in question that are compatible with their own and that are made explicit in the company's mission statement.

To profile the ideal mission-driven angel investor, consider as an example Robert Tishman. Tish, as he is known to friends and colleagues, is a rare combination of a hyperenergetic, intelligent, successful businessman and a conscientious human being, nearly to a fault. His business is and has been investing, from private equity to his own public equity limited partnership where he is a founder and managing partner. A dedicated family man, he is concerned about the future of the world that he leaves for his four children. Tish is an ideal angel investor because he has the investment experience required to evaluate an early-stage deal and to validate the terms and valuation to other investors. He has the connections and the knowledge to be of strategic importance, and he cares enough about the mission of the company to want to support a profitable sustainable business. Finally, he is smart enough to see that demographic and policy shifts combined with the coming clash between available ecosystem resources and the pace at which people are consuming them will create an environment that favors sustainability-driven businesses.

A social entrepreneur must believe that his or her company is making some contribution to the restoration of natural and social systems, and that acting on this belief intelligently is the surest path to ultimate financial success. The company must seek out like-minded angel investors or face the daunting task of convincing investors of the merit of these hypotheses. For example, federal and state mandates require increasing percentages of renewable energy production. California law-makers approved a bill in August 2002 mandating that 20% of energy come from renewable sources by 2017, a more stringent requirement than any other state (*SJMN* 2002). A smart investor will recognize in this policy the foundation of an investment thesis.

Angels are not the only source of values-led capital, although, being unencumbered by responsibility to outside stakeholders, they tend to be the logical place to start. Angel financing should propel a company through early research and development (R&D), test marketing, prototype development, and, often, initial revenue generation. The next course of action is institutional funding and, in the case of sustainability-driven businesses, public and grant money.

Institutional funding and grants

Typically, a growing business turns next to some form of institutional capital. This may come in the form of investment partnerships, private equity groups, or venture capitalists. Ideally there will be a "step-up" in valuation between each new round of financing. This change in valuation is recognition of the value that the business has added to the previous capital input through advanced R&D, brand proliferation, revenue growth, or other tangible manifestations of progress. The "step-up" is reflected in a higher price per share at the beginning of a new financing round—known as the "pre-money" phase of that round—relative to the end of the previous round—known as that round's "post-money" phase.

Importantly, social entrepreneurs have the opportunity to take an extra step before knocking on the (heavy, varnished maple) doors of the venture capitalists. Sustainability-focused businesses have obstacles to overcome relative to their non-sustainable competitors, but some of the offsetting advantages are available in the early stages of growth. The advantages that they have lie in their exclusive access to alternative sources of financing and their ability to forge alliances with the public-sector and NGO community. These resources should be thoroughly explored before a sustainability-driven business continues down the traditional financing path to private institutional funders.

For example, in the USA regarding renewable energy space, local, state, and the federal government—even conservative administrations—recognize the need to reduce reliance on fossil fuels. Their reasoning ranges from providing environmental benefits through improving on political relations with petroleum-exporting nations. The result of these different rationales is the allocation of—in terms relative to a start-up business that thinks in units of thousands, or perhaps millions, of dollars—enormous pools of money. State funds alone, earmarked for some form of clean energy, total US$4.2 billion. Federal budgets are constantly being rewritten to include more funding for sustainability-driven businesses.

The private sector recognizes this shift—in fact, often leads the charge—and perpetuates what is near the beginning of an admittedly slow cycle of acceptance of a new model for business. In this model, companies focused on environmental or social justice are taken seriously and are eligible for serious financing. One example of a company successfully accessing state grant funding is Plug Power, headquartered in Latham, NY, a publicly traded company that develops proton-exchange membrane (PEM) fuel cells. Funding from public clean-energy funds allowed Plug Power to grow to the extent that it was able to orchestrate a successful initial public offering (IPO) and, at one point, to attain a multi-billion-dollar market capitalization.

This funding model provides advantages for a sustainable start-up. Although producers of non-sustainable energy are not made to internalize the costs of the detrimental social and health byproducts of their systems, they also do not have the same access to this public capital. Perhaps more appealing, this money, generally awarded to sustainability-driven businesses in the form of grants, is not "dilutive." More often than not, the company does not have to give up ownership or incur debt to receive these grants.

Case study for a new financing model: Verdant Power

Verdant Power provides a real-time, in-process example of the above financing model. Verdant Power intends to close an angel financing round shortly. The company has a substantial R&D history and extensive relationships with vendors, partners, policy organizations, industry associations, and clients. The company has a prototype model of its turbine and an agreement to deploy its systems in a marquis site in New York City. However, Verdant Power has received negligible revenue to date and little, though increasing, acceptance of its market niche; furthermore, the company's systems are more than two years from commercialization.

The company is on track to raise US$2 million from angel investors—including retirement of obligations and capital restructuring—at a US$10 million valuation. That is, Verdant Power is in the midst of selling 20% of the company for US$2 million. Outside investors will purchase 20% of the company, there will be no debt, and the entire enterprise will be valued at US$10 million. In current market conditions,[3] for a company at Verdant Power's stage of development, the terms described may represent a slightly rich valuation. Three years ago, perhaps, 20% of the company could have been sold for US$10 million, resulting in a US$50 million valuation. Two questions arise: why is it important to set these terms, and under what conditions will Verdant Power be able to do so?

An angel round at favorable terms to the company means, of course, that the principals will own a greater amount of the company and will thus have greater ability to benefit from its appreciation in value. However, more is involved. This angel round will not provide the total capital required to grow the company. Also, the next group of funders, typically institutions such as venture capitalists, will want to see several things in a potential portfolio company before giving it financial support.

These institutional investors will want to see that the management is incented, that it has "skin in the game" (i.e. that it has something to lose). A management team that does not own significant equity in its own company does not have the necessary motivation required to see the company succeed. Also, to sell more of the company to venture capitalists it will be essential to have something to sell. For example, if 85% of a company is owned by outside investors, not enough is left to interest institutional funders.

Finally, by determining a valuation, the company is creating a currency. In a public company this currency is "liquid;" it is easily converted to cash. The equity currency of a start-up company, although illiquid, does have relevance in ways that can be immediately attractive to the company. It can be used as partial compensation to engineers or salespeople, or even to acquire a competing company in its very early stages. In short, it can be used at least partially in lieu of scarce cash to

---

3   At time of writing (Fall 2002), the Dow Jones Industrial Average hit 7,500 points; the NASDAQ has fallen from 5,400 to under 1,200 in the past few years, and stands near its seven-year low.

attract talent, even at this stage of illiquidity and risk. For Verdant Power's demonstration at New York City's East River, the company is literally using small portions of equity to compensate the additional laborers that are needed and even to "rent" a safety chase boat. Better terms set on the valuation mean more currency is available for these purposes.

How can an alternative energy company or other sustainable business command more attractive terms than the less revolutionary (which may be perceived to be less risky) competitor? The angel investor must be indifferent to the new valuation, or better off for it. This comes about from the effect of non-dilutive grant money and from mutually beneficial collaborations with public and foundation entities. A company with the ability to access this kind of funding and these partnerships, all other things being equal, is more attractive to the angel.

Verdant Power, for example, intends to raise at least US$3 million in grants in connection with this angel round. In effect, then, since the company will give up no equity for this money, investors are buying in at a US$7 million valuation rather than at a US$10 million valuation. Another way to look at it is that for every dollar of equity purchased the investor gets back US$0.30 in cash in addition to the business that the management team can build from the original dollar. The company is, in effect, pre-selling this benefit in the angel round.

One way to make this work, while ensuring that the terms of the deal are fair both to the company and to the investor, is to identify an amount that a non-sustainable business might fetch in an open market. Let us say, hypothetically, that the true worth of the company post-money (including the new capital raised) is US$8.5 million. In such a case, the investor hopes that at least US$1.5 million can be raised through grants.

However, this new model raises other complications. Perhaps investors are not convinced by this logic. A company may overcome this skepticism in several ways. First, as mentioned before, the target population has some predisposition to seek out values-led companies for their investment dollars. Also, angels make their decisions based on a binary outcome: either the company fails and they lose their investment, or it is successful and they reap sizable rewards. In the case of Verdant Power, the company was able to prove that it had a viable concept before asking investors to believe the thesis blindly.

The company was awarded a US$500,000 grant from the New York State Energy Research and Development Authority (NYSERDA) to deploy a test-and-demonstration unit in the East River off Manhattan. The company's successful grant proposal has opened the door for further funding from NYSERDA and others; Verdant Power expects to receive additional monies, as well as support with permitting and licensing issues, as the company develops this into a 10 MW site.

NYSERDA has given Verdant Power the grant so that the company will help to provide reliable, safe, and clean energy to the city, create jobs and source manufacturing in the state. New York State will take no equity interest in Verdant Power, and it is paying the company to do necessary research that will increase the value of the company. Finally, and perhaps most importantly, Verdant Power intends to offer investors an explicit guarantee to protect their ownership interest in the company.

There are myriad ways to structure an anti-dilution provision, from an esoteric "full ratchet" provision to a simple award of warrants—options to attain additional shares of stock—on the issuance of new shares. The important items to consider are that the terms are simple and just and that they set the company in the proper place to maximize the likelihood of success at the next financing round under expected, better, or worse conditions. One way to do this is to include in a subscription agreement a clause that says that the investors' percentage ownership in the company is guaranteed until, in Verdant Power's case, US$3 million of grant money has been raised. The company believes that it can raise considerably more than US$3 million in grants. However, a guarantee on this amount was deemed sufficient as a show of good faith that would still give the company flexibility to entertain future financing options.

If the company's strategy proves wrong, and Verdant Power needs to find additional money by selling more equity, the company will issue warrants to the angel investors in proportion to the issuance of shares to the new investors. The net effect of these actions will be to transfer corporate ownership back to the original angels, which brings the company closer to the dynamic that would have been established in the absence of this strategy. The company will make the event that triggers the expiration of this anti-dilution clause the raising of a certain level of grant money. It could also be tied to a particular time-frame, to a percentage or dollar gain from the original investment, or to reaching a prescribed overall company valuation.

The reasoning behind the decision made is twofold. First, it makes sense to target the benefit that a sustainability-driven business has—access to non-dilutive public and foundation funding and collaborations—not to protect investors from general market, policy, or political risk nor even from overall management performance. Second, this provision must expire before a serious approach is made to institutional funders. Even if venture capitalists ultimately embrace this strategy, its explicit existence may be enough of a complication that institutions would rather turn away from this deal and toward one of many other funding opportunities. It should be noted that, even if the termination conditions have been met in advance of the venture capital round, the extra complication of investigating the terms of a provision that once existed may be a drawback, or the new institutional funders may be motivated to seek out for themselves similar protection.

If Verdant Power is successful at raising this grant money—which means surviving on the founder, friends and family, angel funding, and organically generated revenue in the meantime—both the company and the investor are happy. If the company needs to raise additional capital by selling additional equity, it simply (and rightfully) gives back some of the advantage that has been in effect pre-sold. The investor is mostly indifferent, but not entirely if the company does not properly manage the sense of failure that could incorrectly be associated with such an event. Also, in a down round (i.e. at a subsequent lower valuation), the investors' percentage ownership will not be diluted as it would normally, but the dollar value of their investment will be lower. This is the case, though, with any deal. Again, the company specifically does not want to protect early investors against losses of all kinds, because a sustainable business has no particular advantage that would allow it to do that.

This strategy does affect subsequent financing rounds as the company is competing successfully in its marketplace for sales and is similarly ready to position itself for private institutional funding. If the public or grant financing is not successful, the company will in all likelihood not be able to appeal to private funders. Under particularly poor circumstances, these strategies could leverage the downside risk and make the company worse off than if it had followed the traditional path. For example, it could be argued that a down round is more likely to occur when one starts from a "higher" valuation.

However, if done properly, this risk is minimal but the potential reward is large. That reward is, first, the attraction of private capital and, second, the attraction of that capital at terms favorable to the company and fair to investors. There will always be subsequent financings to engage in: IPO, follow-on offerings, mergers or acquisitions, debt, convertible notes, or other more esoteric options. In each case, the more of the company that is owned internally and the "cleaner" the balance sheet, the better off the company will be going into the next deal.

Finding grant funding and non-traditional collaborators

Finally, given that it is so important to the company's growth and to its ability to successfully complete an angel financing round, how does a sustainable-minded start-up find this grant money? There are literally billions of dollars out there; one must be an entrepreneur. At Verdant Power, management developed the requisite skills and contacts internally. The company has also contracted with independent consultants to broker relationships with potential funders, where their skill sets exceed or complement those of Verdant Power management.

In addition, Verdant Power has formed an understanding with Environmental Resources Trust (ERT), a non-profit organization that pioneers the use of market forces to protect and improve the global environment. ERT focuses in part on development and propagation of new clean-energy technologies. The organization also seeks to catalyze the renewable-energy market by substantiating and marketing blocks of power that have significantly reduced environmental impacts.

In the collaborative relationship between Verdant Power and ERT, Verdant Power is able to leverage ERT's knowledge and relationships while also partnering with ERT on specific projects of common interest. In addition, ERT gains similar access to Verdant Power's resources. Of equal importance, this relationship has the advantage of giving the company access to foundation grant money dedicated to 501(c)3 organizations as well as to project financing or program-related investments (PRIs) from the foundations. Typically, this type of financial support is not available to for-profit companies. A third-party grant made to ERT has allowed it to hire a full-time development officer. This person will research potential funders and write proposals for joint projects benefiting both ERT and Verdant Power. It is vitally important, both ethically and legally, not to abuse such a relationship nor to use the non-profit tax-exempt status simply as a conduit from the foundations to the for-profit company.[4]

4 In a related model, organizations may have non-profit and for-profit arms associated with them so that grant money received by the non-profit arm may work to the benefit

ERT itself could be used to illustrate an altogether different way for a sustainable organization to grow in its early stages, a path that will be explored only briefly here. In the course of its business, the organization is able to generate earned revenue that is substantial relative to its operating budget. Having grown largely through foundation grant money, ERT, and many other non-profit organizations like it, could convert to a for-profit status or, more likely, spin out profitable portions of the organization as new businesses. There are examples of success from taking this pathway as well, such as Stonyfield Farm.

New models for structuring sustainability-focused companies and allowing them to proliferate within a new (sustainable) economy must involve new ways of thinking about the organization of and interrelationships between the public and private sectors. Shared missions between corporations, public entities, and NGOs exist more often than they are recognized. A closer collaboration between these groups can lead to more efficient processes and more effective efforts. At the same time, it is important to recognize potential abuses of a new system and to consider how these are to be defined and by whom they are to be arbitrated. Although there is a real danger of having the pendulum swing too far the other way, it is the case that the current policy is too restrictive; it does not encourage or often allow potentially beneficial cooperation.

Concluding thoughts: launching and financing a sustainability-driven business

Overall, for sustainability-oriented businesses, the financing path is clear and unique. It begins with mission-driven founders, friends, and family, and angel money to build a business to the point where it is attractive to public funders. Once the company has developed sufficiently, it may pursue government and foundation grants and mutually beneficial collaborative relationships and use this "free equity" to continue executing on the business plan. When this money dries up or shifts from grants to government contracts,[5] then the company may be attractive to traditional sources of private investment capital—the venture capitalists that had been avoided until now, though diligently courted all along.[6]

of the for-profit arm. As Verdant Power is not of the scale required to pull this off, it has decided against this approach because one of two things may happen: the two entities will remain close, with shared directors or officers, and will risk self-dealing, or they drift apart as a result of checks and balances designed to prevent self-dealing and will lose their ability to benefit each other.

5   A gray area exists here—all funds received come with some expected deliverables. One could define as a grant those monies that expect less in return than would be expected by a normal client in the marketplace. In Verdant Power's case, the threshold becomes the company's stated goal of installing power at US$1,500 per kilowatt.

6   One does not walk into a venture capitalist's office and walk out with a check. It is never too early to build relationships with these people, and one of the best ways to do that is to approach them before you need money from them. I have seen several eyebrows rise

As with a game of chess, the funding strategy should be integrated along its entire range and it should be thoughtful with regard to indeterminate future scenarios. It is necessary to have a store of different plays in reserve to counter the competing moves of the marketplace, general economy, and shifting public policy. This implies being mindful of the interaction of one funding stage with another and of the impact on each segment of the finance plan in various versions of the future. For example, the purpose and significance of the angel financing opportunity described has everything to do with the preceding and following rounds; it allows a company to structure a round in terms more favorable to both parties than otherwise possible and it sets the company up for successful institutional funding.

Although there will generally not be enough seed money available to start-up companies to allow them to achieve "escape velocity," sustainability-oriented companies now have a growing set of options. Nonetheless, to stay in orbit—to be successful long-term and thereby promulgate that success among the company's supply chain, among newer companies wishing to replicate the success and among the established businesses which are open to new ideas—a company must ultimately become profitable in financial as well as in environmental and social terms.

Regarding the issue of scale, these approaches are most directly relevant to the traditional start-up that begins with a handful of people and an idea. In contrast, Cargill Dow, which manufactures with renewable materials and processes products formerly made from petroleum-based substances, is an illustration of a large start-up. It was seeded with US$750 million from its two parent companies, motivated, at least in part, by the values of the Cargill family. However, this chapter does not focus on how to become an enormous conglomerate, nor even advocate that as a goal.

A preferred course of action that Verdant Power intends to pursue is to spin off new, complementary businesses as the core technology matures. For example, in addition to delivering affordable and safe electrical energy, Verdant Power's systems will be used to develop other community-based services, such as irrigation, desalinization, the creation of potable water, the oxygenation of anoxic waters, and the production of hydrogen through electrolysis. Each of these modular technologies may be created as new, smaller businesses and, importantly, be cycled again through the mission-driven, grant financing path described above. These approaches provide a pathway for sustainability-focused businesses—which should always be understood as businesses that continuously strive to be sustainable—that can grow in the current, flawed market and policy setting.

and heads turn up from notepads when I answer the question "How much are you looking to raise from us?" with "Nothing."

Part 3
Case studies from the financial services sector

It is not enough to be industrious; so are the ants.

What are you industrious about?

Henry David Thoreau

New institutions in the financial sector represent another component of the emerging "ant colony." Part 3 illustrates how efforts to rethink investment returns and value are occurring. The examples of the Dow Jones Sustainability Index (Chapter 9) and Shorebank Enterprise Pacific (Chapter 10) show how innovative ideas are changing the ways in which resources are used and supporting a shift toward sustainability.

9
Screening for sustainability
A case study of the Dow Jones Sustainability Index*

*Alois Flatz***

SAM Sustainable Asset Management, Switzerland

The confluence of several distinct trends is rapidly increasing the relevance of sustainability to mainstream companies. First, investors increasingly see forward-looking non-financial metrics as key to understanding a company's true value. Second, a wide range of stakeholders demand ever-greater transparency from multinationals on impacts and management of responsibilities to society at large and the environment. For example, a few years ago, Nike's reputation was already at stake when the CEO realized that labor conditions in Asia actually mattered to its consumers in New York.

Concurrent with these shifts are relatively new developments that enable analysts to combine macroeconomic decisions informed by socioenvironmental issues—which has been possible with available data for many years—with a new ability to make similarly informed microeconomic decisions based on data related to sustainability. The net result of these changes is that not only is sustainability-focused assessment increasingly relevant to businesses and shareholders alike, but it is also now possible. The time has come for sustainability-screened indexes.

This chapter presents a case study of one of the most prominent efforts to assess the sustainability performance of the world's leading companies and integrate the results into an index tracking the financial performance. Following a definition of corporate sustainability, the chapter describes the characteristics of traditional indexes and draws out the implications for indexing the performance of companies that embrace sustainability. The development of the Dow Jones Sustainability

* This chapter is a slightly adapted version of a previously published chapter, in: D. Esty and P.K. Cornelius (eds.), *Environmental Performance Measurement: The Global Report 2001–2002* (New York: OUP, 2002): 66-81.

** With assistance from Erica Tucker-Bassin and Colin le Duc.

World Index (DJSI World) is described, with particular attention to how challenges in assessing corporate sustainability have been addressed. Finally, the risk and performance attributes of the DJSI World are explored to determine the value and validity of tracking the performance of corporate sustainability leaders in general. The bottom line is that companies embracing sustainability do not underperform the wider market in the longer run, but add value financially as well as to natural and social capital.

Sustainability and financial markets

Trends reshaping financial markets

Since its launch in 1999, the Dow Jones Sustainability World Index (DJSI World)[1] has benchmarked the performance of the world's leading companies embracing corporate sustainability. The Index enables investors to track and adapt their products along sustainability guidelines.

As of August 2001, 33 licensees have created financial products based on the DJSI World, with total assets under management amounting to more than €2.2 billion. These investors are offering sustainability-driven mutual funds, equity baskets, certificates, and segregated accounts.

Concurrently, several other indexes have been established in the field of socially responsible investment both in the USA and in Europe. For example, since 1990, KLD (KinderLydenbergDomini) has managed the Domini 400 Social Index,[2] with particular emphasis on the societal contribution of North American companies. In July 2001, UK-based index provider FTSE (Financial Times Stock Exchange) launched the FTSE4Good[3] series of indexes to provide a benchmark to the SRI (socially responsible investment) community. The DJSI differs from these indexes significantly, as its methodology is based on a best-in-class approach. While both the FTSE4Good and the Domini 400 Social Index pursue ethical approaches and do exclude a number of industry sectors, the DJSI aims at identifying the top 10% of companies embracing corporate sustainability in each industry sector.

Recent legislative changes in Europe and Australia have also confirmed the trend toward incorporating sustainability criteria in investment decision-making. For example, both the United Kingdom[4] and Germany[5] have passed laws obliging pension funds to disclose their investment policy with regard to environmental and social criteria. In August 2001, Australia's Senate (ASTO 2001) passed an amendment to the Financial Services Reform Bill to require superfunds and investment managers to disclose their policy on ethical investment. Significantly,

---

1 See www.sustainability-index.com.
2 See www.kld.com/benchmarks/dsi.html.
3 See www.ftse4good.com.
4 Under the terms of Pensions Act amendments that took effect on July 3rd, 2000, Britain's pension funds will be required to disclose whether they take full account of the environmental, social, and ethical impact of their investments.
5 As promulgated in the *Federal Law Gazette* (FLG 2001: 1,310).

the Swiss Federal Social Security Fund awarded State Street Global Advisors, the investment management arm of State Street Corporation, a €320 million global equity index mandate based on the DJSI World in May 2001, the largest mandate of its kind (SsgA 2001).

Relevance of Corporate Sustainability Performance Indexes to the investment community

An index tracking the performance of companies embracing corporate sustainability is valuable in providing insight into the future financial prospects of a company or industry. It is of particular importance as future financial performance is increasingly affected by a business environment continuously reshaped by intertwined social, environmental, and economic issues.

Traditional valuation metrics increasingly consider future-oriented, forward-looking indicators of the health of a company. Given the fundamentally forward-looking nature of sustainability—premised on ensuring the future of ecological and social systems—these new indexes provide investors with essential and highly relevant insights (Funk 2001). In addition, however, to truly offer investment insights, sustainability-oriented equity research must be not only forward-looking but also based on industry-specific value drivers (as opposed to generic data), transparent and easily understood, and capable of adding value to existing valuation methods. Corporate sustainability indexes incorporate all of these characteristics.

Sustainability indexes are based on the hypothesis that a portfolio of stocks that are characterized by a superior sustainability performance is expected to outperform comparable portfolios, at least in the long run (e.g. 5–10 years). The reasoning for this expectation is sound. Companies actively managing scarcities resulting from global sustainability trends such as climate change are likely to achieve a higher return on equity (ROE) and/or a lower required rate of return (RRR) than companies that ignore these trends. In the automotive industry, sustainability trends such as climate change affect the core product. The current discussion around a law to curb greenhouse gas emissions from cars in California clearly shows that companies that manage to reduce the carbon intensity of their product portfolio can be expected to be in a better competitive position in the future. Higher ROE in the automotive industry may result from a better understanding of investment opportunities or from lower non-operating cost, because of a better understanding of risks associated with, for example, climate change. Higher ROE in the automotive industry may also result from social pressure groups channeling demand into cleaner vehicles such as highly fuel-efficient hybrid cars.

A lower RRR may result from a better understanding and management of risks. The RRR is a function of both operating and financial risks. For instance, a carmaker actively managing the challenges of climate change may reduce its operating risks and thereby lower its equity costs. It presumably would also result in lower borrowing costs, leading to lower costs of capital and, again, to higher ROE. Lower borrowing costs may also be the result of investors considering other parameters than just risk and return. High ROE and low RRR result in free cash flow that can be invested profitably when embracing sustainability trends. A portfolio, or an index composed of this type of company, thus will appreciate faster than a portfolio or an index of companies not embracing theoretically profitable investment opportunities. Investments in companies embracing sustainability thus promise higher returns and, due to lower business risk, better risk–return ratios. Based on this hypothesis, better performance can also be expected on a risk-adjusted basis.

In response to increasing recognition of the investor advantages to screening for sustainability, a number of indexes were established in the 1990s. The DJSI reflects changes in valuation of a universe of companies that are leaders in terms of corporate sustainability. While the universe of companies embracing sustainability is broader than the DJSI, the DJSI focused on the leaders among the companies embracing corporate sustainability in each industry. Thus, the DJSI not only traces, but also represents, a universe of leading companies pursuing sustainability strategies.

Index characteristics and challenges for sustainability

Characteristics of an index

Security market indexes are designed to reflect valuation and changes in a specific set, or universe (Reilly and Brown 1997). Movements of the index's performance are supposed to allow inference to movements in the performance of the securities in the underlying universe. The universe targeted, together with the purpose of the indicator, determines which factors need to be considered in designing the index. Sample size, sampling method, and the weighting scheme are prominent examples of design elements. The targeted universe can cover as much of the broad domestic economy or as little of some subset of a particular niche security market.

Indexes are based on statistical information and calculation and, in general, have the following characteristics (www.stoxx.com):

- Accurate and reliable data
- Clear, transparent, and replicable methodology
- Rules-based processes
- Objective and bias-free
- Component data freely available

An index tracking the performance of corporate sustainability leaders must have all the above-mentioned characteristics of a traditional index. In addition, it must be flexible enough to meet changing indexing trends and investor demands, such as the demand for broader benchmarks.

Challenges for an index tracking corporate sustainability

The fact that, since inception in 1999, the DJSI alone attracted about 40 institutional licensees representing around €2.2.billion clearly shows that increasing numbers of investors are aligning their investment strategies along sustainability criteria. This growing number of new financial products integrating sustainability in their core investment strategy provided the impetus for a neutral, rigorous, transparent, and easily replicable measurement of corporate sustainability. The challenge facing the indexing industry has been how to measure and quantify corporate sustainability and how to integrate the results into an investable index that meets the needs of the investment industry.

With specific regard to incorporation of this type of equity research into an index, very specific new challenges arise, including:

- Development of relevant assessment criteria (generic and industry-specific). An index tracking the performance of corporate sustainability leaders first needs to define corporate sustainability and relevant assessment criteria. Criteria representing the challenges deriving from sustainability trends have to be developed and quantified in such a way that the best-positioned companies can be measured and identified.

- Gathering of corporate information. The next important challenge facing an assessor of corporate sustainability is how to gather the correct information to measure economic, environmental, and social performance dimensions. While some global companies publish corporate sustainability reports, the majority of companies are only beginning to understand and, hence, report on the concept behind corporate sustainability. More important, not all data are consistent, relevant, or comparable.

- Quantification of corporate sustainability. A key challenge in developing an index tracking corporate sustainability is how to quantify corporate sustainability. In most cases, sustainability developments are qualitative in nature, so they may lack easy quantification. While assessing companies' environmental performance and emission targets seems relatively straightforward, a consistent and equally quantifiable method is not readily available for many aspects of social and economic developments.

- Identification of sustainability leaders in each industry group. Given that sustainability trends affect each industry differently, industry-specific challenges arise. As a result, industry leaders need to be identified for each industry group, known as a "best-in-class" approach. Sustainability leaders within each industry group need to be ranked according to their corporate sustainability performance relative to one another. Individual industry groups should not be excluded based on the perceived sustainability of the particular sector.

- Constructing an index with appropriate selection rules. A further challenge is how to construct the index. While most indexes represent a group of stocks with a specific goal, it is imperative to define clear selection rules reflecting the particular focus of an index. The number of companies considered corporate sustainability leaders and how their stock should be weighted is the critical consideration and challenge when selecting final components. When identifying leaders for each industry group, minimum sustainability standards need to be set to clarify at what threshold a company should no longer be considered a sustainability leader.

● Fulfilling traditional index requirements. Last, a corporate sustainability index needs to fulfill all the characteristics of a traditional index—it should be accurate, reliable, transparent, and consistent.

The Dow Jones Sustainability Indexes, a collaboration of Dow Jones Indexes and SAM Sustainable Asset Management,[6] were developed as a response to these needs and challenges and, since their launch in 1999, have grown in number of licensees and assets under management.

Construction of the Dow Jones Sustainability Index

As can be seen in Figure 9.1, the construction of the DJSI follows a clearly defined, rule-based process. This process allows for identification and selection of the 10% of leading companies that embrace corporate sustainability in each industry (out of a universe of 2,500 companies). The following section provides more details on key elements of the index construction process.

Investable universe and industry allocations

In determining the initial investable universe of the index, several key issues are considered, including:

● The core purpose of the index

● What the index should represent

● The acceptable level of liquidity of the stocks

● The acceptable level of tradability

● The optimal level of convergence of the currencies represented

The Dow Jones World Index of the 2,500 largest companies in market capitalization, of the total universe of more than 5,000 companies, is used as a basis for the DJSI World investable universe. The targeted universe can cover as much as the broad domestic economy or as little as some subset of a niche security market.

---

6 The DJSI World is produced by SAM Indexes GmbH, a collaboration between SAM Sustainable Asset Management and Dow Jones Indexes. The main function of SAM is to provide the research, while Dow Jones Indexes conducts the calculation and distribution functions for the DJSI.

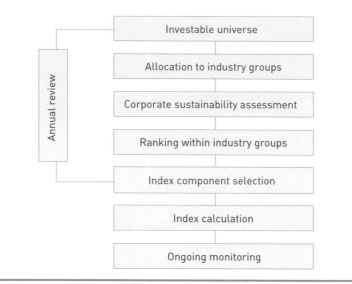

Figure 9.1 Overview of the Dow Jones Sustainability Index construction process

A critical further step is determining the allocation of industry groups for the investable universe. The homogeneity of the stocks allocated to each industry group must be fairly high because dependence on similar sustainability trends allows comparison among the relative performance of industry components, which are based on the 64 industry groups of the DJSI World.

Component selection

Several challenges exist in the actual construction process, and various key decisions have to be made. First, the purpose of the index must be unambiguously stated. That is, decisions must be made about whether the index should provide an investment universe and benchmark for active asset managers or the direct basis for a financial product (such as an investment certificate). These determinations will be then reflected in the specific composition and weighting of the index, which are relevant to target investor groups. For example, an active asset manager usually prefers to have a wide investment universe to have the possibility of choice in stock selections; however, a passive investor prefers a smaller universe to keep transaction costs low (e.g. about 30 stocks for a certificate).

Moreover, the number of components has a major impact on the risk attribution of the index as a whole because the risk correlates negatively with the number of companies due to diversification. The DJSI decided to provide both a benchmark and an investment universe (DJSI in 2001–2002 contains approximately 300 components) as qualitative criteria play a major role in the index construction process.

Setting the right threshold distinguishing the best-positioned companies from the others, and setting minimum standards to be applied should the overall level of quality within an industry be poor, is also of critical consideration regarding component selection. The threshold depends on the number of components needed per industry grouping because the "best-in-class" approach is not always applicable, given that there are industries in which few companies react to sustainability trends.

Component selection can be based on one of three possible approaches:

- Market capitalization

- Numeric

- A mixture of both

Selection based on market capitalization has the major disadvantage of possibly being dominated by a single company with a very high market capitalization. If the top-ranked company in terms of sustainability has a high market capitalization, no other companies embracing sustainability in that industry sector could qualify because the allocation of allowable market capitalization will already have been taken up by very highly capitalized stocks.

Selection based on the numeric approach, for example, would hone in on the top 10% of companies based on the number of companies in the specific industry group. This method would select 250 companies from an industry group comprising 2,500 companies. This approach has the disadvantage of often not providing an ideal asset allocation per sector and, hence, a possibly limited risk spread.

In light of the issues related to the various methods, the DJSI World pursues a mixed approach incorporating both numeric and market capitalization weighted elements,[7] which allows for a good representation of an industry's market capitalization while also assuring that the leading sustainability companies are included.

A further step in the selection of components is how the selected components should be weighted. With regard to traditional indexes, three methods are used to weight the components within indexes:

- Market value weighted (e.g. NYSE Composite Index, Standard & Poor's 500 Index, Nasdaq Composite Index, Wilshire 5,000, London FTSE, MSCI Indexes)

- Price weighted (e.g. Dow Jones Industrial Average, DAX 100)

- Equal weighted

Regional and sector allocation, currencies, and the method of stock weightings need to be similar. In the case of the DJSI World, free-float price-weighted market capitalization (i.e. the portion of shares that are freely tradable) was selected to reflect the DJGI's move to a similar basis.

---

7 See www.sustainability-indexes.com.

Challenges of measuring (assessing) corporate sustainability and developing an index

In general, assessment criteria should be easy to measure, understandable, clear, and precise. The challenge for DJSI was that corporate sustainability is widely based on qualitative criteria, so the most significant challenge was to develop quantitative proxies for qualitative data and to integrate the factors into a system that meets the major requirements of indexing (e.g. the need for replicability and objectivity).

However, even quantitative data related to corporate sustainability efforts are very difficult to access for many reasons. First, as there are no standards for sustainability accounting (of environmental and sociocultural issues) no legal obligation exists for issuing reports on these issues, and, therefore, often data are not readily available. Second, in the cases in which data are available, comparing companies based on environmental and social information is difficult because companies are active in very different business lines, even within one industry group. For example, IBM and Dell are not comparable because they pursue different business models. Third, the "boundaries of analysis"—including what factors are included in reports and how extensively through the supply chain data are gathered—may be defined differently by companies. Most firms use production sites as their "system borders," although some companies may include transport and storage sites as well. In line with current thinking of the major research institutes in the field of sustainable development, the DJSI determined that the only viable approach to defining corporate borders is to consider the whole life-cycle of a product. However, companies often do not have the data since they do not control the whole value chain. Fourth, there are no specific clear indicators from the investment community, and only very divergent standards for normalization (emissions aggregated to global warming potential). Finally, many companies simply do not have any data to report on many of the issues that corporate sustainability assessments must cover, and, when they do, there is very little historical information.

In the case of qualitative criteria, the most common assessment approach to quantification is to precisely define parameters through closed-end or multiple-choice questions to which a score is attributed. However, a major challenge is defining the criteria parameters. For example, how many environmental policies/charters are considered the ideal number to be signed—two, five, or ten—when the real issue is the quality of the implementation of these charters?

Moreover, maintaining relevance of the criteria is another important challenge. Trends and industry challenges are in constant flux, which means that criteria must be updated constantly. Furthermore, criteria should represent not only challenges deriving from global trends but also regional challenges where possible.

These two issues are addressed by annual updates and an approach based on the hypothesis that large-cap companies face similar challenges based on global social, environmental, and economic trends. The same rigorous approach applied worldwide for the DJSI World allows for clear comparisons despite geographic spread and worldwide relevance of criteria.

Given the wide range of sustainability trends and driving forces, criteria must be selected geared to distinguishing between sustainability leaders and laggards. In addition, criteria need to be interdependent to represent the fact that companies are imbedded in a broader societal context. Studies have shown that companies that are leaders in one criterion are usually leaders in others as well.[8]

Defining corporate sustainability criteria for the Dow Jones Sustainability Index

Table 9.1 provides an overview of the criteria used in the SAM Corporate Sustainability Assessment, which forms the basis for the DJSI World. This approach has been developed with the intention of addressing the challenges indicated above. In addition, criteria are derived from the sustainability trends highlighted in earlier sections and focus on factors such as industry value drivers and success factors in relation to managing the challenges of a changing environment. Each criterion listed is divided further into sub-criteria that are not listed.

In essence, assessing a company by specific criteria incorporates evaluation of a number of issues, specifically:

- Exposure of a company to a specific criterion (the challenge the company faces with regard to a particular criterion)

- A company's policies/strategies to cope with specific criteria

- The management systems in place to implement policy/strategy

- Internal review processes to check progress in relation to specific criteria

- A company's track record—quantifiable if released and qualitative: documents/interviews/media/stakeholders

Criteria used in the DJSI World corporate sustainability assessment are reviewed annually, and external experts are asked to provide insight and recommendations to improve criteria and the entire assessment methodology. Moreover, efforts such as the Global Reporting Initiative (GRI) are taken into account to ensure that the criteria used are fully aligned with efforts to standardize corporate sustainability reporting and assessment.

Gathering corporate sustainability information

Many sources of information exist, including company reports, questionnaires, industry studies, interviews with companies, third-party opinions (stakeholder inputs), and various media. A wide range of sources are used, some to access basic information and insight (e.g. NGOs, academia), while others are used to check the validity and truthfulness of company responses to questionnaires and interviews (e.g. global and regional newspapers, industry watchdogs).

---

8   Source: SAM internal studies to assess the efficiency of the corporate sustainability assessment methodology.

Opportunities	*Risks*
Economic criteria	
● Strategic planning ● Investor relations ● Scorecards and measurement systems ● Customer relationship management *Industry-specific example:* ● Brand management	● Corporate governance ● Risk and crisis management ● Corporate codes of conduct ● Supply-chain management ● Financial robustness *Industry-specific example:* ● Specific risk management issues
Environmental criteria	
● Strategic planning ● Environmental, health, and safety reporting *Industry-specific examples:* ● Environmental reporting ● Eco-efficient products	● Environmental management systems ● Eco-efficiency performance *Industry-specific examples:* ● Fuel consumption ● Greenhouse gas strategy
Social criteria	
● Strategic planning ● Management attention to human resources ● Workforce capabilities ● Engagement with external stakeholders ● Social reporting ● Employee benefits and remuneration systems ● Employee satisfaction *Industry-specific example:* ● Social impact on communities	● Labor-practice indicators *Industry-specific example:* ● Occupational health and safety

Table 9.1 SAM Corporate Sustainability Assessment criteria

Source: www.sustainability-indexes.com

Owing to the wide range of corporate approaches to reporting on sustainability performance, many environmental, social, and/or sustainability rating agencies have created questionnaires to fill this void. The challenge remains in response bias, as individuals may read and understand questions in an assessment questionnaire differently because of language barriers, lack of guidelines, or cultural and regional differences. For example, there may be significant room for differing interpretations of questions by individuals within the company, and some companies may take an exaggerated approach to answering questions. This room for interpretation could be significantly reduced in the new DJSI methodology as it avoids open questions. Moreover, questionnaires are expensive for both parties, and feedback rates are usually low, leading to an inadequate assessment universe and information base. Therefore, DJSI continues to optimize the scope of the questionnaire and provides the unique opportunity to complete the questionnaire online.

Regarding documentation provided by the companies, language issues exist given the global coverage of the assessment. This issue is particularly acute with regard to Japanese companies, which often require the assessor to have all documentation translated from Japanese to English. Analysis of company documentation is also open to misinterpretation, and there is a high risk of error, exemplified by the fact that this part of the corporate sustainability assessment for the DJSI World has the highest potential for errors according to external reviews and auditor reports (PwC 2001). In addition, there are cultural differences in how much information is actually recorded in company documentation.

Conducting company interviews is very costly, and their effectiveness depends heavily on the availability and seniority of the interviewee. Thus, replicating this approach across different companies is very challenging.

The wider media and the opinions of stakeholders are used primarily to verify the truthfulness of feedback provided by companies. This process is highly efficient, given the use of modern databases and the Internet. For example, for the DJSI World, the Dow Jones Interactive database, which covers more than 45,000 media sources worldwide, is tracked daily. An important consideration for the assessment is to avoid one-sided interpretations of data.

A further challenge in gathering company information for corporate sustainability assessments is the issue of fair disclosure to all shareholders. Companies are required by law to provide all shareholders with exactly the same information so as not to give one shareholder an advantage over another. Many corporate sustainability assessments ask companies for information that they are not willing to provide to the wider financial markets, and this creates gaps in much of the feedback provided to assessors and rating agencies.

For each company in the DJSI World assessment, the input sources of information consist of the responses to an online corporate sustainability assessment questionnaire, submitted documentation, publicly available information, analysts' direct contact with companies, and/or their main clients and the media.

Questionnaires specific to each DJSI World industry group are distributed via the World Wide Web (www.sam-group.com) to companies in the DJSI World investable stocks universe. The questionnaire is designed to ensure objectivity by limiting qualitative answers through predefined multiple-choice questions. The completed company questionnaire, signed by two senior company representatives to ensure truthfulness, is the most important source of information for the assessment which is done by a sustainability analyst with distinctive expertise in the respective industry sector.

For the DJSI World, the questionnaire process has been streamlined to enable companies to answer the questions online. This interactive tool enables a company to update and change its most recent updates in the existing questionnaire and, in turn, facilitates efficient and accurate assessment by the analyst. The feedback rate of the corporate sustainability assessment questionnaire has improved from 15% in 1999 to 25% in 2001. Furthermore, the process helps to reduce the error margin of data input and interpretation by analysts.

Analyzed documents include sustainability reports, environmental, health, and safety, social and annual financial reports, and all other sources of company information—for example, internal documentation, brochures, and websites. Analysts also review media, press releases, articles, and stakeholder commentary written about a company over the past year. Finally, each analyst personally contacts individual companies to clarify questions arising from analysis of the questionnaire and company documents.

Although corporate sustainability assessment information-gathering depends heavily on a company's willingness to participate in the process (which is often determined by the incentive of being part of the index), the trend toward greater transparency in corporate reporting eventually will allow for more streamlined access to information and, hence, greater efficiency in the assessment process.

Quantifying corporate sustainability assessment results

Quantification is clearly a core issue in corporate sustainability assessment, given that the overall objective is to aggregate the performance of a company in terms of specific criteria into an overall sustainability performance score. Challenges exist regarding quantification of qualitative data, management of large volumes of company data, and consistent objective application of the assessment methodology

Qualitative criteria are measured via an ordinal metrics scheme, which allows the differences between companies' performances to be expressed where one company can be identified as better or worse than the next, rather than in absolute score terms. Subsequently, aggregation of the performance scores is done via the weighting of the criteria answers, the challenge being to bring the criteria into a meaningful relationship that represents the correct importance of a criterion relative to the overall system. Regarding the potential for subjectivity in this quantification, this is addressed by adopting the Delphi approach of accessing expert input.

Moreover, the increased use of information technologies may increase the quality of data management handling, capacity, and efficiency. For the DJSI World, approximately 1,000 companies are assessed yearly and monitored constantly, which requires massive data management skill to ensure effective data capture and analysis to ensure, in turn, effective quantification of corporate sustainability performance scores. Use of an extensive database and introduction of an online questionnaire enhances data security and helps to increase accuracy and data replicability and comparability.

Corporate sustainability assessment data is open to wide misinterpretation from both the company being assessed and the assessor. It is vital to ensure that subjectivity is minimized while developing a company's quantified score. Using the same analyst for an entire industry group facilitates a coherent application of views, constant internal assessor training and clear working procedures, and cross-checking by different analysts enables objectivity and accuracy of results. External audit reviews also may be used to ensure objectivity and replicability, both of which are critical factors for an index.

The corporate sustainability assessment enables calculation of a sustainability performance score for each company. Reviewing, assessing, and scoring all available information in line with corporate sustainability criteria determines the overall sustainability score for each company in the DJSI World investable universe and, subsequently, allows comparison of performance and identification of leading companies to be included in the index.

In the DJSI World, corporate sustainability assessment and subsequent quantification and scoring is conducted in three stages: questionnaire assessment, quality and public availability of information, and verification of information. This process is described briefly below.

- Stage 1: questionnaire assessment. All answers provided in the questionnaire receive a score. Each question has a predetermined weight for the answer, the question, and the theme and class within the question.[9] The total score for the question is the combination of these weights (e.g. see Table 9.2). The weighting of each answer is automatically calculated by the SAM Information Management System and totaled to give a score for the questionnaire. The weight of the questionnaire as an information source depends on whether the questionnaire and answers provided have been approved—in other words, signed by at least one senior management member of the company. If the questionnaire is not signed, less weight is given to the questionnaire and, accordingly, more weight is assigned to Stage 2.

- Stage 2: quality and public availability of information. Company documents and publicly available information about a company are scored according to their scope, coverage, and ease of access.
  - The scope and coverage of a company's documentation are evaluated for each dimension: economic, environmental, and social. In this stage, the analyst assesses how well implementation of policies and management systems is documented across the entire company. The evaluation is scored based on the scale portrayed in Table 9.3.
  - The ease of access to a company's publicly available information and documentation is evaluated for economic, social, and environmental dimensions (see Table 9.4). This evaluation covers all publicly available documentation as well as information provided to SAM Research for the assessment.

- Stage 3: verification of information. Information provided in the corporate sustainability assessment questionnaire is verified to ensure that quantification of a company's sustainability performance reflects reality. The verification process assesses whether a company implements and commits to its stated policies and management practices.

9 For full disclosure of questions and weightings in the assessment process, go to www.sustainability-indexes.com.

	Weight of answer	Weight of question[a]	Weight of theme[b]	Weight of class[c]
Question				

Question 45: Has your company signed environmental charters, or is it committed to principles of sustainability councils/coalitions?
  • Yes (please specify)
  • No charters signed				

Answer				
Member of more than 3 accepted charters	100	0.40	0.25	0.15
Member of 2–3 accepted charters	0.66			
Member of 1 accepted charter	0.33			
No charters signed	0			
No answer	0			

[a]   In this case, question 45
[b]   In this case, environmental charters
[c]   In this case, strategic sustainability opportunities

Table 9.2 Sample question and individual criteria weightings

Level of scope and coverage	Score	Criteria
Low	0	No documentation *or* only a few case studies without context or lack of worldwide coverage.
Medium	1	Acceptable quality of documentation. Description policy/management system/activity and information about coverage in a systematic way.
High	2	Good quality of documentation. Strategy, implementation of management systems, performance against targets described in detail.

Table 9.3 Scope and coverage of corporate sustainability information

Level of public availability	Score	Criteria
Low	0	No public information.
Medium	1	Most information is for internal use; some public information exists.
High	2	Most information is publicly available.

Table 9.4 Public availability of corporate sustainability information

  – The process begins with cross-checking a company's answered questionnaire with documents provided by the company and publicly available documents. In addition, the company's record is verified by reviewing media and stakeholder reports. If necessary, direct interaction and clarification with the company are also undertaken by the analyst to verify selected parts of the assessment.

  – For each dimension, a sample of company answers is analyzed in depth to verify truthfulness. If the answers provided by the company cannot be validated or are contradicted by information found in company documents or other publicly available documents, this is reflected in a lower truthfulness factor, which results in a lower allocation of performance scores.

Within this context, the consistency of a company's behavior and management of crisis situations is reviewed in line with its stated principles and policies. A wide range of issues are included in this part of the corporate sustainability assessment, such as:

● Commercial practices (e.g. tax fraud, money laundering, anti-trust issues, balance sheet fraud, and corruption cases)

● Human rights abuses (e.g. cases involving discrimination, forced resettlements, child labor, and discrimination against indigenous people)

● Workforce conflicts (e.g. extensive lay-offs and strikes)

● Catastrophic events or accidents (e.g. fatalities, workplace safety issues, technical failures, ecological disasters, and product recalls)

In the internal review, SAM Research weighs the severity of the crisis in relation to the company's reputation and crisis management quality. If the company fails to meet its stated policies and management practices as found through the review, scores may be reduced or deleted entirely for whole criteria or specific individual questions. In extreme cases, the verification process may exclude companies from the eligibility list, as determined by the DJSI Index Design Committee.[10]

10 The Index Design Committee consists of the representatives from Dow Jones Indexes and SAM (each company having two seats).

Following the three stages outlined above, a company's total corporate sustainability score is calculated. According to predefined scoring and weighting structures, answers provided on the questionnaire by the company are weighted against scores for quality and public availability and for truthfulness of information. The resulting corporate sustainability score is verified through review of a company's involvement in critical issues. A company's total corporate sustainability score at the highest aggregated level is then calculated (see Box 9.1).

For all questions:

$$TS = \sum(CLW \times CRW \times QUW \times \sum AS \times [QAW + DAW \times DAS]) - QVS$$

where:

TS = total score
CLW = class weight
CRW = criteria weight
QUW = question weight
AS = answer score
QAW = questionnaire assessment weight
DAW = weight of quality/public availability and truthfulness of information
DAS = score for quality/public availability and truthfulness of information
QVS = questionnaire verification score

Box 9.1 Corporate sustainability assessment score formula

The results of the calculation outlined above are based on ordinal metrics, which means that the scores can only be used for comparison and ranking purposes, not to determine a company's absolute performance score. Plus it is not possible to use the scoring for weighting purposes of the components (via under- or overweightings factors representing the sustainability score) in the index construction. The DJSI remains an index weighted based on market capitalization.

Calculating the score for corporate sustainability assessment provides the basis for selection of components for the DJSI World. A key focus in the future will be on how to reconcile this score with shareholder value creation or destruction.

Meeting requirements of traditional indexes

An index tracking the performance of companies embracing sustainability has to meet the requirements of traditional financial indexes as far as possible, especially with regard to accuracy and reliability of data; transparency and replicability of the methodology; and processing based on rules, objectivity, and independence. To ensure accurate and reliable data, the DJSI World is reviewed quarterly and annually to ensure that the index composition accurately represents the top 10% of leading sustainability companies in each of the DJSI World industry groups. Various IT (information technology) systems help to increase data quality, verification systems are used as described earlier, and quantified proxies of qualitative information are designed to enable data accuracy and reliability.

Moreover, to ensure quality and objectivity, an external audit and internal quality assurance procedures, such as cross-checking information sources, are used to monitor and maintain the accuracy of the input data, assessment procedures, and results. In addition to quarterly and annual reviews, the DJSI World is continually reviewed for changes to the index composition necessitated by extraordinary corporate actions—for example, mergers, take-overs, spin-offs, initial public offerings, delistings, and bankruptcy—affecting the component companies and their corporate sustainability performance. Finally, corporate sustainability monitoring is part of the ongoing review process. Once a company is selected as a member of the DJSI World, its corporate sustainability performance is monitored continuously.

With regard to transparency and replicability of the methodology, each of the Dow Jones Sustainability Indexes is accompanied by publication of a guidebook[11] outlining all of the decisions that have been made in development of the DJSI, especially in terms of meeting all of the challenges mentioned in this chapter. It includes the corporate sustainability methodology, index features and data dissemination, periodic and ongoing review, the calculation model, and the management and responsibilities of all parties involved. In addition, the primary research of the DJSI World is based on a consistent rule-based methodology, the details of which are transparent via web publication.

To ensure objectivity and freedom of bias toward companies and investors for an independent and accurate corporate sustainability assessment and index construction, all processes are reviewed by an external, independent auditor for the DJSI World. An average error margin for the corporate sustainability performance assessment is determined by reviewing a representative random sample of 25 companies among the upper half of the companies that were not selected because of relatively low corporate sustainability performance scores and the lower half of companies selected for the DJSI World. The average error margin in 1999 was 0.55%; 0.72% in 2000, and 0.74% in 2001.

Free availability of data is assured by publication of all details related to the corporate sustainability questionnaires, criteria groups, weightings used for scoring aggregation purposes, overall results, and index components.

Finally, to ensure that the index assessment is independent and objective, the DJSI World has established two important committees. First, the DJSI World Index Design Committee is solely responsible for all decisions on the composition and accuracy of the DJSI World. In particular, the DJSI World Index Design Committee is solely responsible for all changes to the index methodology, which is detailed in the current DJSI World Index Guide. Second, the DJSI World Advisory Committee is composed of independent, third-party professionals from the financial sector and corporate sustainability performance experts. The Advisory Committee advises the DJSI World Index Design Committee on index composition, accuracy, transparency, methodology, and the corporate sustainability performance assessment in line with the latest DJSI World Index Guide.

Thus, there are many challenges in assessing, measuring, and quantifying corporate sustainability, and the DJSI World approach has been devised expressly to address these challenges.

---

11   See www.sustainability-index.com/htmle/publications/guidebooks.html

In the next section, we examine the risk and performance attributes of the DJSI World to determine the value and viability of developing an index tracking the financial performance of sustainability leaders a whole.

Risk and performance attribution of the Dow Jones Sustainability World Index[12]

As could have been expected, the sustainability leaders thus were not immune to the general downturn in equity prices the world has experienced since mid-2000. According to the DJSI World, an investment in the companies that lead in corporate sustainability would have yielded a cumulative negative return of –6.9%, or –2.7% per year in US dollars. Volatility hovered at around 18% for the first 14 months, before dropping to some 16% for the last 10 months.

Figure 9.2 indicates how the two indexes have fared in comparison. From inception of the DJSI World until the end of July 2001, the Dow Jones Global (DJ Global) has fared better than the DJSI, losing all, but not more than, its interim gains. Reasons for this disparity are many common factors that affect all indexes including aspects such as country allocation. Owing to its specific composition, the DJSI is under a particular influence of the euro.

Relative performance needs to be compared on an all-things-being-equal basis, if any specific claim is to be judged. Portfolio theory answers the question of what makes such comparisons by adjusting historic returns for the risks incurred. Since 1999, the DJSI World has displayed an annual volatility of 17.12%, while the DJ Global has had an annual volatility of 15.27% (see Table 9.5). The DJSI World has thus been more volatile. If this volatility is an unbiased reflection of the risks incurred, then the difference in volatility is big enough to warrant risk-adjusted return measurement. One risk-adjusted measure of performance is the Sharpe ratio, which relates the return a portfolio earned, above what an appropriate risk-free alternative could have earned, to the volatility experienced. Since 1999, the annual returns of the DJSI World and the DJ Global have been –2.7% and 0.0%, respectively. We assume the average risk-free rate to have been 4%, which yields a Sharpe ratio of –0.39 for the DJSI World and of –0.26 for the DJ Global.

Yet, calculating Sharpe ratios alone does not provide for a true all-things-being-equal basis. Nor is a comparison of Sharpe ratios sufficient to draw conclusions about the sustainability case. Three aspects need to be considered when dealing with relative performance. They are differences in exposure to common factors, differences in exposure to specific factors, and pure chance.

Exposure to common factors

Over any period, two indexes will be influenced to different degrees by common factors unless their composition is completely equal. Comparison of the compo-

12   This section has been contributed by Mr. Thilo Goodall.

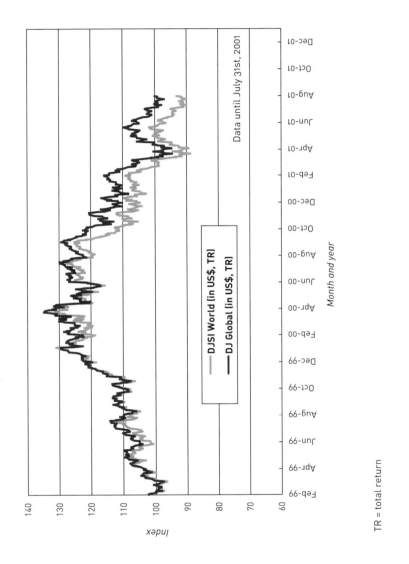

Figure 9.2 Performance of the Dow Jones Sustainability World Index (DJSI World)
and the Dow Jones Global (DJ Global), 1999–2001

	DJSI World	*DJ Global*	*Difference*
Volatility (%)	17.1	15.3	1.8
Return (%)	−2.7	0.0	−2.7
Risk-free rate (%)*	4.0	4.0	–
Excess return (%)	−6.7	−4.0	−2.7
Sharpe ratio	−3.9	−2.6	−0.3

* The risk-free rate is the average of global euro-currency rates.

Table 9.5 Return and risk comparison of the Dow Jones Sustainability World Index (DJSI World) and the Dow Jones Global (DJ Global), February 1999 to July 2001, total returns in US dollars

sition of DJSI World with that of the DJ Global as of 31 July 2001 reveals that they were far from equal (see Table 9.6). First, companies in the Euroland make up 23% of the DJSI World, compared with some 13% in the DJ Global. UK companies account for 19% of the DJSI World, but less than 10% of the DJ Global. In turn, Japanese companies account for only 6% in the DJSI World, while they account for 10% in the DJ Global. US companies account for less than 40% in the DJSI World, but 60% in the DJ Global. There is thus a strong representation of European companies in the DJSI World, at the expense of Japanese and US companies.[13]

The excess weight of some 10% in Euroland companies implies that the euro has greater influence on DJSI World's return than on the DJ Global's return. Indeed, some 2% of the DJSI World's cumulative underperformance of 6.9% can be attributed to the euro's 25% decline during that period.

Currency impacts can be controlled for, in part, by calculating indexes on a hedged basis. Other unequal impacts of common factors are much more difficult to control for. One example is the overweight in large-cap companies. The DJSI World has a much higher percentage of companies with large market capitalization than does the DJ Global. This difference in composition can hardly be controlled for. The significant overweight of large-cap stocks is caused by the assessment process, which starts from a universe of the 2,500 largest companies worldwide. Some 2,500 small caps that are members of the DJ Global are not assessed. Over periods during which large-cap companies do relatively better than small caps, the DJSI World does relatively better than the DJ Global. The opposite is true as well: there are periods where small caps do relatively better than large caps,

---

13   It is unlikely, however, that US companies lag others in sustainability to the degree indicated by these figures. Indeed, the construction process may account for part of the US underweight. The "best-in-class" approach, with "class" defined as an industry or industry group, is one of the characteristics distinguishing sustainability from other approaches. The approach clearly stresses industry specifics, allowing for a fair comparison within industries, while acknowledging the difficulties of comparing companies across industries. Focusing on industry strata can have an impact on country strata, if sustainability is distributed unevenly across industries within a country. Therefore, no direct inference should be made to the regional distribution of leading companies embracing sustainability.

Country or region	DJSI World (%)	DJ Global (%)	Difference (%)
AUS/NZ	1.03	1.40	−0.37
Canada	2.24	2.19	0.05
Denmark	0.38	0.27	0.11
Euroland	22.78	12.83	9.95
HK/SG	0.51	1.14	−0.63
Japan	6.42	10.02	−3.60
Norway	0.23	0.13	0.10
Sweden	0.98	0.83	0.15
Switzerland	8.13	2.53	5.60
United Kingdom	18.91	9.81	9.10
USA	38.38	58.85	−20.47

AUS/NZ = Australia and New Zealand

Euroland = countries that are members of the euro currency system; European countries that are not members are listed separately

HK/SG = Honk Kong and Singapore

Table 9.6 **Country allocation of Dow Jones Sustainability World Index (DJSI World) and Dow Jones Global (DJ Global), as of July 31st, 2001; country/currency allocation without Emerging Markets**

as has been the case since January 1999, so the DJSI World will do worse than the DJ Global. At least 1.8% of the cumulative underperformance of the DJSI World since its inception can be attributed to this difference in composition.

The DJSI World also has an above-average number of "growth" companies—that is, companies that tend to reimburse investors in capital gains rather than in dividends (see Table 9.7). Whether "growth" is a true characteristic of the sustainability universe is hard to assess. It is tempting to attribute the overweight in "growth" companies to the notion that sustainability companies are embracing global change and seeking opportunities to profit from it, so they find investment opportunities where companies not integrating sustainability considerations do not. This would justify an above-average number of "growth" companies. Yet this explanation is not necessarily the only one possible. In any case, in times when "value" companies outperform "growth" companies, the DJSI World will lag the DJ Global. The small overweight in growth stocks has caused another 20 bps (basis points) of cumulative underperformance since inception.

Exposure to specific factors

The "best-in-class" approach applied to the sustainability universe leads to a small number of companies comprising the index. On July 31st, 2001, the DJSI World comprised 225 companies, while the DJ Global comprised 5,029. Thus, each company included in the DJSI World carries considerably more weight than in the DJ Global. This makes the DJSI World a less diversified universe and, thus, more vulnerable to specific factors.

	DJSI World (%)	DJ Global (%)	Difference (%)
Size	19.80	−39.80	59.60
Success	0.00	5.20	−5.20
Value	2.60	4.10	−1.50
Variability in markets	9.80	14.60	−4.80

Note: allocation according to the Aegis Global Equity Risk Model™, Barra Inc.

Table 9.7 Risk factors in the Dow Jones Sustainability World Index (DJSI World) and Dow Jones Global (DJ Global): allocation according to Barra™ factors (without Emerging Markets); figures shown are the percentage of standard deviation of developed markets universe, as of July 31st, 2001

Mispricing of companies and corrections of their mispricing is one such factor. The DJSI World is composed as a price index, as equity indexes usually are. Value-based indexes are rare because of the difficulty of assessing intrinsic value. Examples of value-based indexes are trade-weighted currency indexes based on purchasing power parities. Price indexes by definition cannot consider valuation. In addition, the DJSI World selects the leading companies with regard to their market capitalization. If the market capitalization is affected by severe mispricings, and there is no reason why leading companies embracing sustainability should be shielded from mispricings, the DJSI World will tend to include the more severely mispriced companies within an industry, as long as the sustainability rating is comparable. The impact of a correction of the mispricing of these companies on the DJSI World, therefore, is larger than the impact of the industry-wide correction on the broader index.

Mispricings and their subsequent corrections on the stock level have indeed been affecting the DJSI World. Lucent Technologies and EMC Corp. are two examples. In the 22 months of its membership in the DJSI World, Lucent alone accounted for a cumulative underperformance of 1.9%. EMC Corp. accounted for 2.9% of the relative underperformance during its nine months of membership alone. The performance of Lucent Technologies and EMC Corp. was not related to their sustainability rating, but to the recent IT bubble, so the DJSI World had no means of excluding them, regardless of their mispricing.[14]

14   Relative price movement across strata can thus shift the composition of the index if the relative movements are more pronounced in the index than in the entire universe. This has been the case and experience to date with the DJSI World. Large caps have corrected more than small caps since August 2000, and information technology and telecommunication companies have seen their prices slashed much more than those of companies from other sectors. US companies provide large percentages of both large caps and of technology companies, so that about 6% of the current underweight in US companies can be attributed to relative price movements since inception of the DJSI.

Chance

As an unbiased measure of valuation and performance of the sustainability sector, the DJSI World is inevitably prone to be taken as "evidence" for or against the hypothesis of a sustainability business case. Interpreted as a portfolio, it will be expected to outperform comparable portfolios, at least in the long run. The reasoning behind this expectation is sound, as mentioned earlier. A portfolio or index of leading companies that embrace sustainability can be expected to appreciate faster than a portfolio or an index of companies that do not address profitable investment opportunities. Investments in such companies promise higher returns and, due to lower business risk, better risk return ratios. Better performance can thus be expected on a risk-adjusted basis.

Unfortunately, the DJSI World will never be able to prove this reasonable expectation in relation to a comparable index. First, the issue of comparability will remain unsolvable. Different exposures to common factors can never be fully controlled for, and the influences exerted can take many years to even out. Second, specific factors come into play when index membership is restricted to the leaders within a universe. Third, the impact of pure chance, inherent in any investment, can override a sound investment case. A soon as chance has to be taken into account, statistical methods have to be used to decide for or against a case. The usual expectation is that the underlying value-added will persist sooner or later and will override all adverse chance influences, and perhaps even different exposures to common factors. Little consideration is given to the amount of time and the number of observations needed to make statistical methods applicable and enable them to detect significant differences in performance.

In fact, the number of observations needed for supporting any claim of "value added" is uncomfortably large. For the moment at least, the index cannot help to determine whether investing in companies embracing sustainability is worthwhile. It may never do so. Nevertheless, the overall rationale behind this investment thesis is sound. Sustainability may be claimed to produce higher-than-average returns on a risk-adjusted basis. On a before-the-fact basis, portfolios comprising sustainable companies thus may be labeled "better" investments, with "better" defined in risk–return space, even when the index or the portfolio fails to deliver on the promise after a relatively short period of time.

Conclusions

To assess the importance and success or failure of sustainability indexing and investing, it is crucial to remind ourselves of the mechanism of sustainability investing: that its primary goal is to identify companies that are best positioned to profit from trends that are redefining the basis for business success. Clearly, the competitive rules affecting industries and businesses are shifting to the company's management of risk and opportunity derived from economic, social, and ecological trends. Leading companies addressing sustainability therefore derive competitive advantage while also reinforcing the likelihood of these trends becoming reality. Sustainability investing and indexing's "best-in-class" approach aim to identify the leaders. Promoting the fact that competition, in the Schumpeterian sense, is healthy and a driver for continuous innovation shows that this approach addresses one of the basic tenets of our market economy. Therefore, sustainability investing and indexes tracking the performance of leading companies in terms of sustainability are particularly appropriate as an investment hypothesis, compared with negative screening approaches designed to allow investors a direct expression of their personal ethical values.

Concerning the methodology for assessing corporate sustainability, there are a number of key challenges. Assessment of corporate sustainability is a very new concept; a lengthy history on which to base judgments is lacking. The assessment methodology described in this chapter is a work in progress, and improvements must be made to orienting the content toward criteria that better reflect companies' performance and risk attributions. Furthermore, regional particularities will be given increasing prominence as specialized regional and emerging market assessment approaches are developed.

Moreover, there is a distinct dearth of scientific backup to many of the tenets of the sustainability investing hypothesis and approach. Increased collaboration among academia, science, and business should be promoted to close this gap. This cooperation between the sciences and the private sector will also provide the background for the much-needed standardization of corporate sustainability reporting.

Finally, it is premature to suggest definitive conclusions regarding the business case for sustainability. As discussed, a much longer time-frame is needed to attribute index or fund performance to particular sustainability criteria or strategies. Evidence regarding a positive impact of sustainability on outperformance of an index is not conclusive. However, available empirical evidence supports the view that sustainability investing has not led to a long-run-adjusted underperformance versus a conventional approach. Measured over shorter periods, risk-adjusted sustainability performance deviates from a conventional approach. Currently, investment biases (such as a regional bias or a slight growth tilt) are potentially the dominating driver of risk-performance differences. Therefore, it is possible to attest that companies that pursue sustainability do not underperform the wider market in the longer run, although they very clearly deliver major benefits to society and the environment as well as contributing positively to the vibrancy of the overall economic system. That an index incorporating companies that lead in their approach to sustainability has no negative effects on risk performance and, in fact, adds social, ecological, and economic value may explain the dramatic increase in interest with regard to sustainability investing in recent years. The DJSI has thus evolved into a compelling example for the message that adding value to natural, economic, and social capital simultaneously does not compromise investors' expectations regarding risk performance.

10
Banking on sustainability
A case study of Shorebank Enterprise Pacific

Jennifer Sokolove
University of California at Berkeley, USA

> Working along with natural principles of development, expansion,
> sustainability, and correction, people can create economies that
> are more reliably prosperous than those we have now and that are
> also more harmonious with the rest of Nature.
>
> *Jane Jacobs*[1]

When the northern Oregon Astoria Plywood Company was dissolved in 1992, a 16 acre toxic waste site was all that remained of the waterfront industrial property that had marked the eastern edge of the town since the 1870s.[2] Although Astoria's hillside perch above the Columbia River limits the flat land available for new construction, the environmental liabilities and economic costs of cleaning up the site precluded re-use of the mill's former location. This lingering residue of industrial processing is not unusual. In the coastal Pacific Northwest, boom–bust cycles in natural resource industries have left a legacy that continues to shape the economic, environmental and social context of the region.

In the case of Astoria, however, a situation that would have normally resulted in an abandoned and polluted industrial site took a different turn. A sustainability-focused lending institution, Shorebank Enterprise Pacific, provided key short-term financing that allowed the city to work with the state Department of Environmental Quality to clean up the property. The clean-up attracted a private developer who purchased the site and partnered with the city to build compact river-view homes. Astoria residents hoped that the businesses and homes in the new

---

1 Jacobs 2000: 12. This quote formerly appeared prominently on the Ecotrust website (www.ecotrust.org) in the section describing how Ecotrust (and its affiliates) work to promote the conservation economy.
2 The plywood company actually halted operations in 1989, but was not formally dissolved until 1992.

development, Mill Pond Village, would spark revitalization of the blocks beyond. Without the loan from Enterprise Pacific, the city would not have been able to raise sufficient capital to turn the industrial site, or "brownfield," into a new gateway to the community.[3] In addition, the development did more than reclaim the land. Enterprise Pacific strongly encouraged "green building guidelines" and a "smart growth" approach to the new development, so Mill Pond Village also offered an environmentally friendly development on the riverfront property.[4]

Since it was established in 1995, Enterprise Pacific has invested more than US$13 million in projects such as Astoria's Mill Pond Village. Its capital has gone primarily to support innovative, small businesses and distressed, rural communities in the coastal temperate rainforests of the Pacific Northwest.[5] The institution

3   Astoria was lucky in their timing on this project. Previously, Oregon law had required complete clean-up of any toxic site, but the law was made more flexible in 1995. By agreeing to ban recreational use of the mill pond and capping some of the sediments on the site, Astoria brought the clean-up costs down from US$5 million to US$1.4 million. The city planned to clean up the site and then sell it to a private developer, but it first had to fund the clean-up. Toxic waste is typically the responsibility of the current owner of a property, no matter whether or not he or she caused the contamination, so there was a general wariness about owning the site before it was certified as clean. In addition, the property was assessed at only US$1.1 million (expected value post-clean-up). The US Environmental Protection Agency (EPA) provided a brownfields pilot grant to help defray the costs, and the state's Department of Environmental Quality granted Astoria half the cost of the clean-up if the city would take title to the property, but even then the city had trouble raising sufficient funds. A local bank was willing to make the city a loan, but only if Astoria would guarantee the loan with its General Fund. The bank was not interested in the waste site as collateral. In Astoria, the General Fund is used to pay the firefighters, the police, and many of the most important public employees, so that condition was deemed unacceptable. Shorebank Enterprise Pacific, as a non-profit organization, was willing to front the costs of significant research on the risks of lending on the mill site property, spending more on research than it was likely to receive in interest. Enterprise Pacific's research convinced them that the property itself was adequate collateral, and, with that additional assurance, the Bank of Astoria was willing to come in on the loan as an equal partner. While Enterprise Pacific and the Bank of Astoria worked out the financing, city staff worked to convince the private and public creditors (ranging from Weyerhaeuser to the Small Business Administration) to assign their liens to Astoria. All of the pieces finally fell into place, and the clean-up started, in 1996.
4   The development was planned as a high-density use of infill space, consistent with smart growth principles. Builders also commit to at least 10 of 30 "green development guidelines" in six categories such as landscaping, pavement and drainage, electrical and mechanical choices, and building materials. The lists were commissioned by the developer, Venerable Properties, and encourage native plant landscaping, the use of recycled materials wherever possible and no use of pesticides or herbicides (personal communication from Art Demuro, President, Venerable Properties Inc., June 14th, 2000). This approach is meant to allow flexibility while ensuring that the development will be environmentally benign.
5   The Northwest is often understood to include much of Montana, Idaho, Oregon, Washington, and British Columbia; the additional modifier "Pacific" generally limits the referent to the coastal states. The coastal temperate rainforest imagined by Enterprise Pacific founder Ecotrust covers a broad swath of the North American coastal plain and mountain range from northern California to southeast Alaska. It is largely distinguished by proximity to cool, moist ocean air, a moderate range of temperature, and frequent precipitation, clouds, and fog (Ecotrust and Conservation International 1991).

promotes the concept of conservation entrepreneurship—principled business practices that strengthen local communities and maintain or restore local ecosystems. Structured primarily as a revolving loan fund, Enterprise Pacific's target investment region ranges from southeast Alaska to northern California, and it is headquartered near the southern end of that region, in Ilwaco, WA, between the mouth of the Columbia River and the shore of the Willapa Bay (see Fig. 10.1)

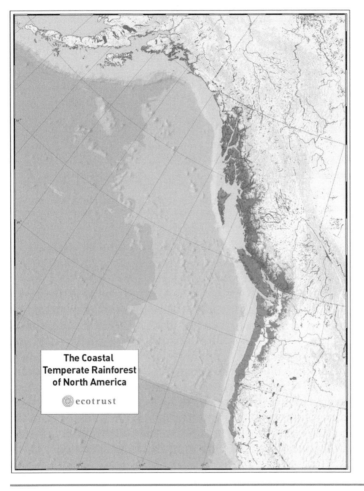

The Coastal
Temperate Rainforest
of North America

ⓐecotrust

Figure 10.1 The coastal temperate rainforest of North America

Source: www.ecotrust.org/imagearchive/bioregionmaps.html. Map reprinted by permission of Ecotrust.

Enterprise Pacific was incorporated as a non-profit organization and not as a commercial bank, because it aims to provide risky credit and significant marketing assistance to its clients, services difficult to support on the profit margin of a conventional bank. The organization seeks the nexus of rational economic self-interest and conservation while remaining attentive to the relationships between social equity, economic enhancement, and ecological integrity.

This chapter introduces the work of Enterprise Pacific. It explores when and how the provision of credit can catalyze increasingly sustainable business practices, economic development and environmental stewardship. In so doing it also details the challenges and opportunities of working toward environmental conservation within broader conventional capital markets.

Environmental and social histories shape the kinds of actions that are possible in the present. Therefore, I begin the chapter by describing the historical conditions that gave rise to the premise that guides the work of Shorebank Enterprise Pacific—that sustaining natural environments is tied to sustaining the human populations that depend on them.[6] In order to illustrate the specific context in which Enterprise Pacific began operations, I next describe the economic, ecological, and social conditions in the coastal Pacific Northwest. I continue by sketching the history of Enterprise Pacific, outlining its initial goals and the evolution of its programs. Finally, in the conclusion I provide an analysis of the difficulties inherent in the provision of sustainability-focused credit programs and offer suggestions for solutions based on the experience of Shorebank Enterprise Pacific.

Leveraging capital for sustainability: convergence of community development and environmental concerns

The US National Community Capital Association (NCCA) held its 2002 annual training conference in late October at the downtown Marriott Hotel in Oakland, CA.[7] Shorebank Enterprise Pacific, as a community development lending institution and NCCA member, attended the meeting, as it had in preceding years. Although the conference retained the feel of any industry gathering—binders, name tags and anonymous hotel coffee urns—this meeting differed from prior events in one significant way. At previous conferences, attendees interested in the environmental impacts of their loans were likely to have met only informally, often over lunch. This conference placed environmental considerations on the official program.

A new 2002 panel—Is there a Sustainability Bottomline?—examined the question of whether it is possible to "add sustainability to the capital equation." Panel organizer Rosalie Cates, of the Montana Community Development Corporation,

---

6 Although ideas that fall under the broad rubric of sustainable development are common the world over, in this chapter I focus specifically on the ways in which a particular version of sustainable development emerged in the coastal Pacific Northwest.

7 The NCCA is a nationwide organization of American community development financial institutions. Member organizations provide capital, technical assistance, and development services to economically disadvantaged communities.

wanted to explore how to measure and underwrite for sustainability. She also wanted to hear ideas about how to claim sustainability as a loan outcome and how to assess whether or not there was a market for sustainable loans. Her three panelists were engaged in efforts to answer these questions within the contexts of Shorebank Enterprise Pacific (Ilwaco, WA), Coastal Enterprises Inc. (Wiscasset, ME), and the Sustainable Jobs Fund, LP (Philadelphia, PA, and Durham, NC).

This trio of presenters represented a group of institutions at the forefront of a new trend in banking, capital management, and community development. Almost none of the approximately 40 people gathered in that room had any experience with integrating environmental sustainability into their community development programs. In addition, the audience was a small percentage of the nearly 600 conference participants. One frustrated lender left the room after 20 minutes, whispering on his way out, "I thought this was about financial sustainability." But the mere existence of the 2002 panel indicates that interest in combining environmental considerations with community development is growing. Community developers are beginning to entertain the idea that local economic development will be more durable if environmental concerns and community development issues are addressed simultaneously. If this dual approach is more successful in catalyzing economic revitalization, it has the potential to increase the success of individual businesses in the community, making it easier for loan clients to leverage additional working capital and to repay their loans. If this happens, and loan capital circulates back to the community developers more quickly, then there will be more opportunities to reinvest in new entrepreneurs and developing businesses (although this faster capital circulation may also have the effect of decreasing interest income to these same institutions).

Just as community development organizations are finding convergence between poverty and environmental degradation and are perceiving the need to address the two concurrently, conservation organizations are increasingly discovering that they must address the economic and social concerns associated with environmental problems. The Environmental Defense Fund (EDF) made this linkage explicitly in the late 1970s by arguing that there was "economic common ground between industry and environmentalists" (Gottlieb 1993: 140). However, it was not until the 1990s that the argument began to gain widespread support across a broad range of environmental groups. The change occurred in two ways. First, established environmental organizations began to develop programs explicitly focused on financial incentives for conservation. Second, new organizations emerged, often (but not always) mimicking the structure and strategy of successful institutions working in other regions. Both efforts aimed to catalyze change in private land use or production practices by leveraging changes in government policy or altered consumer preferences. For example, land trusts used changes in tax policy to facilitate landowner compensation for the conservation value of property; sustainable agriculture organizations attempted to expand demand for organic products by helping growers in making the transition to organic growing and in marketing their produce.

These shifts—within the community development and environmental fields—represent an important broader trend. Despite radically different histories and aims, individuals and organizations working on community development issues and environmental concerns have moved toward one another in terms of both ultimate goals and in terms of everyday practices. Community development and environmentalism both emerged as major social movements in the late 1960s and early 1970s. Each focused on a problem relating to the human condition. One addressed poverty and economic injustice; the other took on environmental destruction. Community developers embraced capital as a potent force for driving social change; environmentalists emphasized litigation, education, and advocacy, often eschewing the capitalist system as part, if not all, of the problem. However, in the contemporary moment of "market triumphalism" (Peet and Watts 1996), a growing number of environmentalists are exploring the positive potential of capital. Simultaneously, community development financial institutions are beginning to consider that financial and social sustainability might be related to environmental sustainability.

The emergence of Enterprise Pacific marks this growing recognition of convergence between environmental and economic well-being. By combining the traditional tools of community development—lending, market assessment, product development, and technical and research assistance—with the science and policy analysis of environmentalism, Enterprise Pacific joins the two movements. Enterprise Pacific envisions a new future for communities, one marked by economic, social, and ecological vibrancy and resilience.

Identifying the context for economic, social, and ecological investment: the Pacific Northwestern coastal temperate rainforest

> The shoals are covered with shellfish, among which the oyster is the most abundant, and constitutes the principal article of export . . . The waters of the Bay, and all the streams that enter into it, are well stocked with fish . . . The peninsula is a flat, marshy and sandy plain, elevated but a few feet from the water level, and covered, as is the whole region around the Bay, with a dense growth of gigantic forest trees, principally spruce, fir and cedar.
>
> *James Swan, 1857*[8]

Enterprise Pacific's headquarters sit on the edge of the Port of Ilwaco, overlooking the entrance to the mouth of the Columbia River. Its new "green" building, constructed with massive timbers salvaged from an old Astoria port building, draws visitors and clients to the town's industrial waterfront. The structure was designed and built by more than 30 local artisans and contractors. In addition to re-using salvaged lumber, the building adheres to a set of "green" specifications. Construction waste from the site was sorted and resold when markets could be located. Only native plants were used in the building's landscaping, and the permeable surfaces

8 Swan 1972: 25-27.

in the sidewalks and parking lot were designed to work with bioswales to manage stormwater run-off naturally. Metalwork in the building was constructed from recycled scrap, wide windows provide passive solar heating and light, and the stains and finishes that were used to color the interior and exterior wood are water-soluble.[9] The edifice provides a tangible demonstration that environmentally sensitive construction is both possible and economically viable in coastal communities.

Just north of the town, a spit of land extends 26 miles north, protecting the vast shallows of the Willapa Bay from the full force of the Pacific Ocean. Approximately 70% of Enterprise Pacific lending through 1999 focused on the two counties—one in Oregon, one in Washington—that bound this estuarine section of the coast. Along the coastal plain, wind and rain fall on long flat beaches before the prevailing winds drive them towards uplands covered with Douglas fir plantations.[10] In Washington, Pacific County makes up most of the watershed for the Willapa Bay. Just across the Astoria–Megler Bridge, on the Oregon side of the river, the tidelands and forests fall under the jurisdiction of Clatsop County. The coastal areas of both counties are dependent on fishing and the largesse of Portland and Seattle vacationers, whereas the economies just inland, but still on the west side of the Cascade Mountains, are more reliant on timber and agriculture. Both counties, like many rural places in the US West, are experiencing a decline in the percentage of personal income derived from natural resource industries and an increase in the amount coming from services, government, and non-labor income.[11]

The history of this region is one of plenty and prosperity, in terms of culture, trade, and ecological systems. For thousands of years, the relatively mild climate and abundant food sources along the coast made it a regular stopping point for Native American tribes. Most European-American settlement on the Pacific Northwestern coast occurred after the 1850s. Resource extraction—primarily of furs, logs, seafood, and agricultural products—for urban markets around the world and in the western portion of what is now the US provided the initial impetus for most of those settlements (although extraction of the region's natural resource commodities for European markets began as early as the 1780s). For the coastal communities closer to the developing northwestern cities, tourism also played a significant role in local economies, at least intermittently, beginning in the 1870s. For over 100 years, these natural-resource-based industries remained central to coastal economies. In the 1980s, as these industries declined in economic importance measured in terms of dollar values, they often still shaped how coastal

9 Most observers are impressed by the attention to efficient and environmentally benign construction in the new building and to the focus on local craftsmanship, but a few have questioned the decision to build at all, arguing that Enterprise Pacific should have redeveloped an empty space in downtown Ilwaco.

10 Commercial forests account for 70% of Oregon and Washington land west of the Cascades (Schwantes 1996: 12). Douglas fir (*Pseudotsuga menziesii*), western hemlock (*Tsuga heterophylla*), western red cedar (*Thuja plicata*), Sitka spruce (*Picea sitchensis*), and red alder (*Alnus rubra*) provide the majority of the local industrial harvest.

11 This trend has been noted in many locations. For convincing data, see the statistics, by county, on the per capita earned income and unearned income over time, compiled by the Bureau of Economic Analysis at the US Department of Commerce Estimates (www.bea.gov). Radtke and Davis (1999: xi) estimate that in 1995 55% of personal income in Pacific County came from transfer and investment income.

communities identified themselves and described their histories and futures. Natural resources, and thus ecological issues, were intertwined with perceptions of identity, place, and economic opportunity.

Not only does much of the region share a common economic history, but a significant portion of the Pacific Northwest also shares a familiar landscape. The geography of concern for Enterprise Pacific maps closely onto an area identified as "Cascadia"—the region directly influenced by the Cascade Mountains, including the mountain range itself and the maritime lands to its west. The region can be identified by characteristic soils, patterns of precipitation and water flow, climate, flora, and fauna. The striking beauty of the Cascade Mountains meeting the ocean, the unceasing rain, vast forests of enormous trees, and legendary salmon runs— these images appear repeatedly in accounts of Pacific Northwestern history, in advertisements for coastal tourism, in the rhetoric of the region's contemporary corporations, and in the stories told by and about people who live in the region. The particularity of the land and climate play an active role in shaping under-standings of what it means to live in the US Pacific Northwest.

The coastal counties where Enterprise Pacific is headquartered have had signif-icant booms in natural-resource-based industry over the years, but, by the early 1990s, most industries were in decline. Technological changes in the timber industry had decreased the amount of labor required per unit of output. Old-growth trees were almost entirely depleted in the region. Northwestern forestry also faced growing competition from the southeastern USA, as well as increasing federal regulation regarding endangered species in response to declining popula-tions of species such as salmon and spotted owls. Salmon fishing was bringing in a fraction of the income it had in previous decades because of seasonal closures, declining populations of fish, dwindling consumer demand, and increasing global aquacultural supplies. For the region's ranches and dairy farms, environmental regulations made it more and more difficult to run a cattle ranch on diked tidelands in a high-precipitation climate, and it has been decades since milk prices have increased significantly. Although prices for locally grown cranberries were strong in the early 1990s, they could not support an entire economy.[12] Govern-ment and service-sector jobs played an increasingly large role in the local economy as resource-based industries diminished. Both high unemployment and low per capita income characterized the depressed economy of the area. In many of the rural, small towns along the coast, residents grew increasingly frustrated with the reduced economic options available locally.

The specific environment and history of the Willapa and the Lower Columbia provided an ecological and economic context in which both a conservation organ-ization and a bank could visualize profitable businesses premised on environ-mental stewardship. Therefore, Ecotrust and the Shorebank Corporation, the founders of Shorebank Enterprise Pacific, chose the Willapa Bay and Lower Columbia as the first places within the coastal temperate rainforest to test their

---

12   Cranberry prices have risen more or less consistently over the past 20 years, and the cranberry acreage in the US has undergone a massive expansion over the past decade. Over-production from all the new acreage led to a substantial decrease in cranberry prices in the fall of 2000.

vision. The area offered a functional ecosystem, well used by local residents, which should be both productive and profitable if managed and marketed appropriately.

Intertwining conservation, communities, and capital: the emergence of Shorebank Enterprise Pacific

Shorebank Enterprise Pacific is the product of two parent organizations—the Shorebank Corporation, a community development bank holding company head-quartered in Chicago, IL, and Ecotrust, an environmental organization located in Portland, OR. Both parent organizations had an interest in conservation and development, but their institutional histories were radically different. Shorebank Corporation grew out of the community development and civil rights movements. Ecotrust traces its history through the environmental movement. These unusual partners worked together to structure a new non-profit organization that could benefit from both areas of expertise. The Shorebank Corporation operates on the assumption that providing underserved communities with access to credit can drive economic development and neighborhood revitalization. Ecotrust believes that environmental stewardship is more likely to take place within a functional and prosperous local and regional economy. Their partnership links credit, economic development and environmental stewardship to aim for what they term a "conservation economy."[13] In this conservation economy, economic activity is harnessed for environmental and social good, reversing conventional patterns in which financial capital transforms natural resources and interpersonal relations into money.

   The overarching goal in the creation of Shorebank Enterprise Pacific was to harness the positive potential of capital to effect both socioeconomic and environmental change. Like the Shorebank Corporation, Enterprise Pacific believes that "rational economic self-interest" is a driver for economic development, and that credit is one way to harness and direct that interest. But its philosophy carries that logic one step further—if credit and economic self-interest can drive economic development, then, by improving economic situations, Enterprise Pacific can also expect to induce positive environmental change. The institution is committed to "putting its money where its mouth is," making its organizational economic success dependent on the economic success of its clients. Accomplishing this goal hinges on the willingness of (urban) consumers to put their money into "green" products authenticated through stories of the environmental and socioeconomic sustainability of their production and the natural, rural, communities where they were harvested and produced.

13   "Conservation economy" is a term Ecotrust developed to guide its vision of capital as a positive agent for social and environmental change. Such an economy integrates concepts of efficiency, resiliency, and diversification with considerations of social, natural, and financial systems (for more information, see Ecotrust 2001).

The idea for Shorebank Enterprise Pacific initially emerged from broadly circulating conversations within the environmental movement. Environmentalists were interested in the possibility of an economic development that could aid rural communities in conserving, and simultaneously profiting from, their natural resources. Ecotrust's founder, Spencer Beebe, had worked overseas in developing countries connecting environmental stewardship to economic development in resource-dependent communities. Beebe learned to look for communities that were located close to ecosystems or spectacular natural scenery that attracted national or international attention. Not surprisingly, the founders of Enterprise Pacific looked for a similar set of features when they attempted to apply this approach to the US. Their first step was to find the right kind of ecological context. Tropical rainforests and their associated rich biodiversity had enjoyed the environmental spotlight for almost 20 years. It seemed entirely possible to redefine the coastal Pacific Northwest by highlighting its ecological features, "creating" a temperate rainforest.[14] The job was made easier by the fact that Northwest regional identity has historically been very much tied to the massive trees of the coastal forest, so the idea of a temperate rainforest made sense in the context of typical Northwest imagery and narrative (e.g. see Dillard 1992; Robbins 1983, 2001; Schwantes 1996).

Ecotrust had been interested in environmental conservation in the Willapa Bay area of the coastal temperate rainforest even before it incorporated as a non-profit organization in 1991. Beebe believed that Willapa conservation would be best served by a program to promote sustainable economic development.[15] The program, Ecotrust imagined, would support and develop environmentally sensitive

14 This is not meant to imply that the coast is not a rainforest according to a set of specific ecological characteristics, nor to suggest that Ecotrust and Shorebank Enterprise Pacific are the only organizations that promote a vision of the Pacific Northwest as a unified region. It is meant to draw attention to the fact that the coast was much less frequently referred to as a temperate rainforest prior to the establishment of the Portland-based Ecotrust. The idea of a temperate rainforest was also evaluated as a potential marketing tool for precisely the reason that the tropical version had been so successful in raising public attention and financial support for environmental work (Shorebank Corporation and Ecotrust 1992a, 1992b, 1992c).

15 Ecotrust was also interested in the trend toward community-based resource management. As it began developing a framework for conservation-oriented economic development in the Willapa, it also started working with the The Nature Conservancy to build a collaborative community-based group to discuss, and develop solutions for, environmental problems and conflicts in the Willapa basin. Initially, it seemed possible to combine both goals in one organization; however, banking and its necessary access to private financial information did not prove to be a good fit with open, community-wide discussion, so Enterprise Pacific incorporated as a separate entity. The collaborative group, under the name of the Willapa Alliance, continued to play an independent role in environmental conservations in the Willapa, bringing together a wide range of Willapa interests, compiling a huge resource base of ecological data on the local area and forging new partnerships on place-based education and salmon-stock restoration. However, it also stirred up local suspicions about environmentalist outsiders, and that image limited its overall effectiveness in catalyzing social and environmental change. It eventually closed its doors in 2000.

local businesses. After hiring the successful founder of a rural import substitution program for small businesses, work began to explore the potential for a similar kind of project in the Willapa. The research of the new program manager indicated that what Willapa businesses really needed was access to capital and to marketing, product development, and technical assistance.[16] However, as an environmental organization, Ecotrust had little in-house experience with capital, lending, and business development. Therefore, it began looking for a partner that could provide the core competencies it lacked.

One of Ecotrust's board members was a founding president of the Shorebank Corporation in Chicago, an institution with just the kind of economic expertise Ecotrust needed from its partner in this endeavor. The Shorebank Corporation was established based on the idea that a lack of economic development could be rectified with access to capital. In 1973, its founders bought an inner-city bank in the South Shore neighborhood of Chicago, with the goal of using the bank to catalyze economic development and community revitalization. They aimed to reverse the disinvestment processes that were causing deterioration of what had been a relatively prosperous and comfortable neighborhood into a minority ghetto. The argument was simple. If the bank could collect deposits from individuals, corporations, and other institutions that cared about alleviating poverty and economic depression in Chicago's South Shore neighborhoods, then it could make that money available to entrepreneurs within these communities, sparking economic revitalization from the inside out.

Shorebank refined this vision of social change in 1974, initiating a direct-mail campaign to solicit "development deposits" from people outside the South Shore communities who had a record of contributing to liberal causes (Taub 1994: 63). Depositors would get services and benefits that they might gain with any other bank, but they would have the additional satisfaction of knowing that their deposits were "doing good." Most contemporary banks have only limited ties to any particular geographic area. If an institution is associated with a specific city or community, it often accepts local deposits and disperses that money throughout a wide area through its loans and investments. Shorebank's strategy reversed this pattern, which was also common in the early 1970s. Shorebank accepted deposits, maintained check accounts, and offered assorted financial services to people located across the country. Shorebank then directed those funds into geographically concentrated investment in South Shore entrepreneurs and communities. These deposits played a major role in South Shore Bank's profitability.

However, Shorebank management soon noticed that it was still impossible for the bank to provide all the services needed by small-scale entrepreneurs, first-time homebuyers or even South Shore residents who had little experience with saving or budgeting. It was simply not viable for a for-profit bank to provide services such as mini-courses on how to balance a checkbook, or on basic accounting, to its customers free of charge, but those kinds of services were important to the bank's overall development mission. With that in mind, between 1978 and 1980, the

16   She assessed the needs of 50 businesses and followed 13 businesses in the Willapa over the course of an entire year (personal communication with former program manager, Ecotrust, October 2nd, 2000). All but one of those 13 businesses have since failed (personal communication with former Ecotrust staff member, November 22nd, 2000).

founders created several non-profit affiliates of the Shorebank holding company that could provide South Shore customers and communities with additional services, that could work toward organizing those communities, and that could seek out grant support to fund its supplementary activities.

Over the next two decades, with mixed success, the Shorebank Corporation adapted this structural model of for-profit lending associated with non-profit support to other rural and urban areas where it seemed that the provision of credit to low-income people might help foster economic development.[17] By 1990, when the incipient Ecotrust initially approached the Shorebank Corporation with its idea to develop a rural source of environmentally friendly capital, Shorebank had invested approximately US$600 million in low-income and moderate-income communities and had gained national recognition in the field of community economic development.[18] Ecotrust wanted to know whether Shorebank's model of for-profit and non-profit banking affiliates could be adapted to address environmental conservation as well as integrated economic development within communities bypassed by conventional capital.

For the Shorebank Corporation, Ecotrust's idea presented an economic opportunity by opening new markets for capital and identifying an entirely new source of deposits. Environmental causes might lure depositors who wanted their money to "do good" but who did not have poverty and "race" at the top of their priority lists. In the 1990s it seemed likely that the environment would be as attractive to depositors with substantial discretionary income as poverty alleviation and racial equity had been in the 1970s. The 1970s had been the era of development deposits. Perhaps the 1990s would be the era of "eco-deposits," drawing a new community of depositors to the Shorebank Corporation's family of institutions. Place-based eco-deposits that could guarantee environmental and economic investment in a particular region appeared particularly exciting. Ecotrust and Shorebank imagined a bank that would invest deposits from across the nation in "green" development in the coastal temperate rainforest. The creation of a new bank that would rely on eco-deposits to bring additional capital into the Willapa Bay region seemed

---

17 Shorebank now has operations in Chicago, Cleveland, Detroit, and the upper peninsula of Michigan. It also has consulting staff who reside in Eastern Europe and others who undertake short-term assignments in Asia and Africa.

18 President Clinton's government updated and refined the Community Reinvestment Act in 1995, and he drew special attention to the work of the Shorebank Corporation as exemplifying the goals of the new legislation (after drawing heavily on their expertise in its rewriting). Congress initially enacted the Community Reinvestment Act in 1977 (12 USC 2901) to encourage federally insured banks and thrifts to meet the credit needs of low-income and moderate-income residents in the communities in which they operate. Since then, the Community Reinvestment Act has required all banks to help meet credit needs in the communities where they are physically located. This community reinvestment lending can involve many small loans, which can be expensive and time-consuming to process and manage. Therefore, many banks lend to community-based non-profit relenders at a very low interest rate (1% or 2% is common) so that they can dispense with administering the actual loans themselves.

plausible, and it could give Shorebank a competitive advantage in the now crowded field of mission-driven lending and investing.[19]

Even so, the partnership between Shorebank and Ecotrust was not a particularly easy fit. The Shorebank Corporation began the first meeting by questioning Ecotrust's commitment to social and economic equity, asking whether Ecotrust cared more about trees than about people. Although Shorebank's leadership was interested in the new partnership, the Shorebank Corporation as a whole had no frame of reference for concern with environmental issues and had little interest in adding yet another idealistic and difficult mission to those already on its plate.[20] In addition, the two organizations had radically different organizational cultures and expectations for how work should be accomplished. Several observers emphasized the careful, thrifty approach Shorebank took to daily transactions, while noting that Ecotrust—with its reliance on grant funding, not on its own profit margins—tended to work in a less-disciplined, creative manner, often getting frustrated by the apparently over-zealous Shorebank concern about risk. However, after three years of regular meetings, conversations, planning, and assessment, the two organizations finally developed a plan to start a new business together. Ecotrust and the Shorebank Corporation jointly founded the ShoreTrust Trading Group in 1995.[21] ShoreTrust was set up as a 501(c)(3) corporation[22]—the first of a suite of for-profit and non-profit affiliates Ecotrust and Shorebank envisioned in the Willapa.[23]

In addition to founding ShoreTrust, which was renamed Shorebank Enterprise Group, Pacific, in 1997, Ecotrust and the Shorebank Corporation developed an

19 Ron Grzywinski, Chairman, Shorebank Corporation, personal communication, December 8th, 2000; Mary Houghton, President, Shorebank Corporation, personal communication, December 7th, 2000.

20 Both Mary Houghton (President) and Ron Grzywinski (Chairman) insist that environmental issues were just not on the Chicago Shorebank radar screen at all. Grzywinski argued that, "In Chicago, there are coho salmon in Lake Michigan, but you don't think about them. Here [on the Northwest coast], everyone thinks about salmon. In an urban area, you tend to have other priorities" (personal communication, December 8th, 2000). Houghton was very specific about those priorities: "In an inner city, ghetto area, you really see racism, poverty, drugs—these things are actively in your face, and you feel like those are the priorities. People in Portland can think of a zillion ways that economic and social issues are also resource-based. But people in Chicago don't think like that" (personal communication, December 7th, 2000).

21 ShoreTrust, an amalgamation of Shorebank and Ecotrust, became Shorebank Enterprise Group, Pacific, in a 1997 effort to make all Shorebank Corporation subsidiaries and affiliates immediately identifiable. Names have been rather a problem for Enterprise Pacific over its history. It was first imagined as the Willapa Development Institution, then became the Pacific Marketing Group, was incorporated as ShoreTrust, and finally reached its current incarnation as Shorebank Enterprise Group, Pacific, which is increasingly being shortened to Shorebank Enterprise Pacific.

22 In the US, 510(c)3 corporations are voluntary, self-governing organizations that serve public purposes and do not distribute profit. They are exempt from federal taxes by virtue of being organized for one or more of the charitable purposes described in the 501(c)3 revenue code.

23 Although Shorebank Enterprise Pacific is, by name, more formally affiliated with the Shorebank Corporation, Ecotrust raised all of the initial operating capital for the organization.

entire suite of organizations devoted to supporting this conservation economy. The affiliates include: Shorebank Pacific, a commercial bank also headquartered in the Willapa; Ecotrust Canada, a non-profit organization committed to extending Ecotrust's ideas along the coast across the Canadian border; and the Natural Capital Fund, a Portland-based green venture capital investment fund. These institutions, Ecotrust and the Shorebank Corporation share common board members, fundraising and project implementation.[24] Their activities are coordinated through regular "team meetings," held every few months, attended by the leadership of each organization.[25] In general, Enterprise Pacific collaborates closely with three of these partner organizations—Ecotrust, Ecotrust Canada, and Shorebank Pacific.[26] Figures 10.2(a) and 10.2(b) illustrate these intertwined institutional arrangements.

At the outset, Enterprise Pacific was organized to lend to small "green" businesses, from a revolving loan fund.[27] That loan fund was established with a US$1

24 A board of directors governs Enterprise Pacific. Initially, board appointments were divided evenly between Ecotrust and the Shorebank Corporation. Recent reorganization, granting Enterprise Pacific the independent authority to develop and appoint its board, recognizes the institution's autonomous development and recasts it more as a partner to its founders. The board of directors began with eight members. It grew to ten members with the addition of Ecotrust Canada to the family of Ecotrust/Shorebank organizations in 1995 and Shorebank Pacific (the for-profit bank affiliate of Shorebank Enterprise Pacific) in 1997. Each of these new organizations gained one seat on the board. Membership on the board has typically been heavily weighted towards leadership in the Ecotrust/Shorebank organizations but it has also always included two residents of the target coastal geography. For the first five years of Enterprise Pacific's existence, although the specific people changed, those two individuals were consistently residents of the Willapa area. In 2001, a resident of the mid-south coast of Oregon, where Enterprise Pacific is expanding its programs, was invited to sit on the board. In addition, the board has usually included a business owner who is engaged in the "green" marketplace in some capacity. Stan Amy, for example, the founder of a chain of natural food grocery stores in Portland, OR, has served on the board for several years.
25 In addition, Enterprise Pacific partnered with Ecotrust Canada to open an office granting Enterprise loans in Ucluelet, extending its lending capabilities into the region of Vancouver Island. That office is now officially a part of Ecotrust Canada.
26 Initially, Ecotrust and the Shorebank companies also expected the Willapa Alliance to play a large role in community projects in Pacific County in conjunction with Enterprise Pacific. However, the Willapa Alliance had generated so much local animosity that it was never able to serve as the forum for consensus decisions about Willapa resource management it had aimed to be.
27 Although there was actually a fair amount of local capital available in the Willapa already, community banks there were primarily staffed by long-term local residents, and application for a loan from one of those banks ensured that at least some people in one's town would know the intimate particulars of one's economic situation. When Ecotrust and Shorebank first considered bringing a revolving loan fund to the Willapa, they assumed that it would operate as an arm of the Willapa Alliance, but all the benefits of having a large board of stakeholders became liabilities in a lending context, and the board members of the Willapa Alliance did not even have the professional positions of loan officer or bank staff to mitigate the difficulties of making loans to their neighbors, or to make it marginally more comfortable for potential loan clients to request loans from them. For these reasons, although the concept for ShoreTrust Trading Group was reviewed and further developed with the assistance of a Willapa-based economic

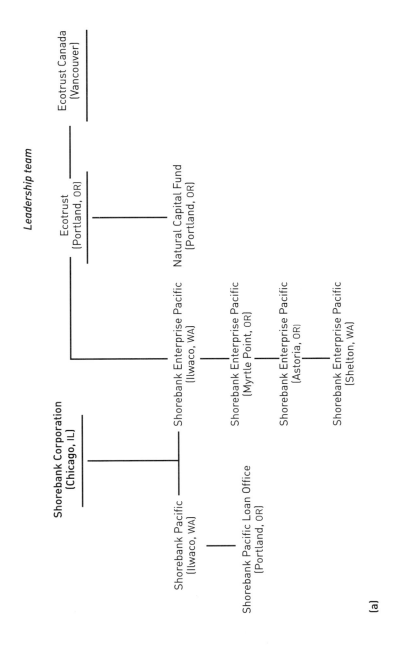

Figure 10.2 **Shorebank Enterprise Pacific: (a) organization of the leadership team and (b) internal organization** (continued over)

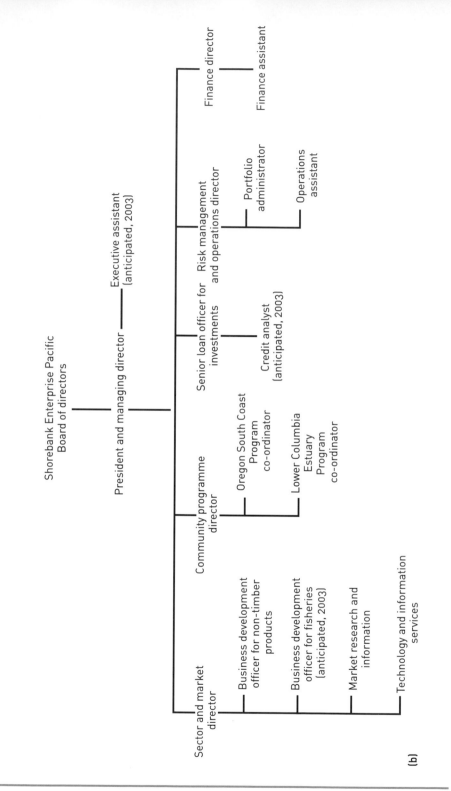

Shorebank Enterprise Pacific
Board of directors

President and managing director —— Executive assistant (anticipated, 2003)

Sector and market director

Business development officer for non-timber products

Business development officer for fisheries (anticipated, 2003)

Market research and information

Technology and information services

Community programme director

Oregon South Coast Program co-ordinator

Lower Columbia Estuary Program co-ordinator

Senior loan officer for investments

Credit analyst (anticipated, 2003)

Risk management and operations director

Portfolio administrator

Operations assistant

Finance director

Finance assistant

(b)

Figure 10.2 (continued)

million grant for start-up capitalization from a private philanthropic foundation, the Meyer Memorial Trust.[28] In addition, Enterprise Pacific would provide rural entrepreneurs with basic technical assistance and with market and product development information that would assist them in reaching regional and national "green" markets. The original business plan outlined Enterprise Pacific's organizational goal as: "to capture significant market demand for Willapa 'green' products and to grow the number of local firms that can supply that demand" (Shorebank Corporation and Ecotrust 1996: 68). The business plan described how staff would reach their goal by using the revolving loan fund and their marketing expertise to build "improved access to distribution networks, increased sales, an expanded workforce, and improved operating margins for locally-owned businesses" (1996: 68).

Enterprise Pacific's founders believed that not only could a healthy economy based on natural-resource-based industries encourage positive changes in environmental stewardship, and even restoration, but it could also provide residents in isolated coastal communities with high-wage jobs. When the new institution opened its doors, income from traditional resource-based industry was on the decline all along the coastal range, and commercial banks, wary of the boom–bust cycles of resource production, had limited their lending to resource-based business.[29] In addition, Ecotrust and the Shorebank Corporation believed that conventional banks were unlikely to lend to resource industries for risky business innovations such as third-party certification for socially or environmentally responsible production.[30] Enterprise Pacific was imagined not only as a source of high-risk credit, providing capital to individual entrepreneurs in resource-based industries,

development task force that was organized at the behest of the Economic Development Committee of the Willapa Alliance, ShoreTrust was organized to be completely independent of the influence of the Willapa Alliance. Many Willapa Alliance members found this frustrating as creative economic development was originally intended as the centerpiece of Willapa Alliance activities.

28   In fact, there was such substantial overlap in funding, staffing, and organizational operations between Ecotrust, the Willapa Alliance, and ShoreTrust that the funds from the Meyer Memorial Trust were actually granted to Ecotrust for the ShoreTrust project (Ecotrust 1994). ShoreTrust also received early capital investments from the Northwest Area Foundation and the Engelhard Foundation.

29   Community banks on the coast were typically still willing to lend in industries that had been hit hard by boom–bust cycles, particularly to individuals they knew well and had worked with over many years, but even they tended to try not to provide all the financing in any resource loan. A branch manager at the Bank of the Pacific, a community bank in southwest Washington, explained that, in struggling industries such as fishing and cranberries, they preferred to provide 50% or less of the total financing (personal communication, June 28th, 2000). In those cases, Enterprise Pacific provides an important service by sharing the risk.

30   However, it should be noted that Ecotrust and the Shorebank Corporation decided on the Willapa because it was there that Ecotrust and The Nature Conservancy had built the Willapa Alliance and because of what they saw as the ecological importance of the Willapa. In terms of available credit, they had already determined by 1992 that banks serving the Willapa were "aggressive, flexible, and responsive in terms of commercial lending. Consequently, credit gaps [were] narrower than customarily seen in smaller, rural areas" (Shorebank Corporation and Ecotrust. 1992a: 1).

but also as a source of business and product brokering services. The organization was expected to work with individual entrepreneurs, who had the experience to think in creative ways about how their industries might develop, to take advantage of increasing consumer interest in sustainability in order to develop new products, and to sell those products to metropolitan markets.

The structuring of sustainability lending, and other Shorebank Enterprise Pacific programs

Shorebank Enterprise Pacific has now been in business for more than seven years. It continues to provide three primary services:

- A revolving loan fund
- Assistance with market development and new "green" market connections
- Community economic development

The organization also remains mission-driven, focusing its energy on lending aimed at improving the local environment and economy and, concurrently, reaching a more equitable distribution of local resources. This trinity of economic, ecological, and social issues reflects the sustainability-focused and "triple-bottom-line" approach of Enterprise Pacific.

The revolving loan fund is Enterprise Pacific's central organizing feature. Even a cursory glance at the institution's offices and files reveals that making and managing loans is the staff's primary focus. The importance of loans is also depicted in the statistics that Enterprise Pacific uses to assess its organizational development over time (see Table 10.1).

The revolving loan fund provided more than US$12 million dollars in loans between 1995, when it formally opened its doors, and the beginning of 2002. Some 54% of those loans were to clients in the Willapa/Lower Columbia, within 65–70 miles of the office. Within this easy driving radius, the Enterprise Pacific staff has had the opportunity to become familiar to the rural communities it serves. The remaining loans were spread throughout the entire region, referred to as the coastal temperate rainforest. A total of 59% of Enterprise Pacific loans have gone to businesses in natural-resource-based industries, with the largest percentage of resource-based industry loans in the seafood sector.[31] The other 41% of Enterprise Pacific's total loans have been in community development, real estate and local services. Although resource-based industries might intuitively seem to provide the most comprehensive opportunity to integrate the economic, ecological, and social aspects of sustainability, the combination of commitment to community revitalization and the limited rural loan market has led Enterprise Pacific to locate a range

---

31 In the accounting system Enterprise Pacific employed prior to 2002, this was more evident. In the 2002 numbers, fish and shellfish loans (16%) are separated from aquaculture loans (9.25%). If the two are combined, the total amount of capital in loans to the seafood industry is 25.25%, which is still greater than that for the forest and wood products sector, at 22.71%. Nevertheless, the 2002 data does indicate that Enterprise Pacific lending is becoming more evenly weighted between sectors.

	Year							
	1995	**1996**	**1997**	**1998**	**1999**	**2000**	**2001**	**2002**
Number of employees	2	3	4	7	9	11	16	14
Fiscal year operating expenses[a]	N.A.	440	579	736	725	915	1,169	1,200
Earned income ratio (%)	N.A.	31	35	52	65	58	55	55
Value of loans outstanding[a, b]	350	787	1,189	2,291	3,725	4,250	4,750	4,000
Number of loans	4	15	23	16	26	33	27	26
Total revolving loan fund capital[a]	1,500	1,500	2,450	3,500	4,500	6,500	7,665	7,850
Net worth[a]	0	178	611	1,877	2,504	3,415	3,650	3,850

[a] In thousands of US dollars
[b] As at December 31st

Table 10.1 The evolution of Shorebank Enterprise Pacific, 1995–2002

Source: Shorebank Enterprise Pacific

of creative lending opportunities. Overall, Enterprise Pacific is managing the loan fund at approximately 2% historic losses.

Enterprise Pacific loans vary significantly in purpose, size, and cost. The majority of the Enterprise Pacific portfolio, approximately 67% of all loans, has gone to business expansion. The loan portfolio is also primarily concentrated in fairly short-term loans. Although several loans have had extended terms of more than 180 months, most have had term lengths ranging between 12 and 60 months.[32] This working capital tends to aid entrepreneurs who need to cover upfront production costs or expenses between investment and harvest. Enterprise Pacific has also invested, at slightly lower rates, in business start-up, product development,

32 In 2001, 38% of the loans had had term lengths of 12 months or less, and an additional 18% have had term lengths between 12 and 48 months. My numbers are slightly more current than are those in the similar assessment made by Alan Okagaki (2001: 18). In his analysis, 40% of the loans were less than 12 months, and 19% were greater than 12 months but less than 48 months. However, data from 2002 indicate that term lengths are increasing. Only 2 of 26 loans closed in 2002 had terms of less than 12 months. The average term length appears to be shifting toward 48–60 months.

and subordinated debt. The size of Enterprise Pacific loans is highly variable, ranging from US$425 to US$375,000, with an average of US$82,836.[33] This pattern suggests that the organization is successfully serving both the high-end and low-end credit gaps identified in the founders' initial scoping of the target geography (Shorebank Corporation and Ecotrust 1992a: 1). The interest rates that Enterprise Pacific offers its clients fluctuate fairly widely, from 3.25% to 13.5%, but they tend to center around 10%. These rates are extremely important to the organization's operations. Although Enterprise Pacific is sustained partly by private philanthropic foundation grants, it also relies on the interest generated from its loan portfolio. Earned income constitutes an average of 50% of operating expenses and thus interest features prominently in ensuring Enterprise Pacific's own well-being over time.

In an effort to make the link between capital and positive environmental change more transparent in its lending practices, Enterprise Pacific instituted a loan scoring system in 1999 that grades its loans in terms of both credit risk and mission relevance.[34] Like any purveyor of credit, the institution makes an assessment of the likelihood that it will successfully retrieve its money. However, in addition, Enterprise Pacific aims to provide credit that offers businesses a profit incentive to produce or harvest their products in a more environmentally and socially sustainable manner, so it also evaluates whether or not loans are likely to advance its organizational mission. Mission scores are appraised for each loan's environmental, economic, and social equity impact and are averaged so that each loan receives a grade between a positive A and a negative F (for a key to how credit risk and mission relevance are graded, see Table 10.2; for an example of a credit and mission scoring sheet, see Table 10.3).[35]

This scoring system has shown that balancing lending with mission goals can be challenging. Almost 90% of the loans receive mission grades of B or C.[36] Although most loans in the portfolio are strong in one of the three aspects of sustainability, very few are strong in all three dimensions. For example, although the timber and wood product loans rate relatively highly in terms of economic and environmental mission, they typically rank relatively low in terms of social equity. Loans in community development, real estate, and human services tend to be graded quite high in social equity and relatively low in their rankings in terms of environment

---

33   Some borrowers, however, have received multiple loans, so there are a few companies that have borrowed more than US$600,000 from Enterprise Pacific.

34   When the system was established, only active loans (69 of Enterprise Pacific's total 101 investments, by the end of the first quarter of 2001) were graded. Loans that had already been repaid were not assessed.

35   Neither Alan Okagaki's (2001) assessment of the loan portfolio nor mine indicate any correlation between mission score and credit score, although Enterprise Pacific initially considered accepting higher credit risk on loans that seemed particularly likely to advance the mission of improving the local economy through increasingly sustainable management of local resource industries The specific data that support Okagaki's analysis can be found in Okagaki 2001: 72-74; documents that suggest such a correlation was intended or considered include Shorebank Corporation and Ecotrust 1992a, 1992b, 1992c, 1993.

36   A total of 39% of the loans have received a B grade; 49% of the loans have received C grades. These data are accurate through the first quarter of 2001.

Score	Grade
Credit risk	
<10	A
11–15	B
16–24	C
25–30	D
31–35	E
>35	F
Mission relevance	
<25	A
26–38	B
39–50	C
51–65	D
66–74	E
>75	F

Table 10.2 Shorebank Enterprise Pacific: key to the grading of credit risk and mission relevance

and economy. This dynamic suggests it is difficult for Enterprise Pacific to have an impact on social equity, economic development, and environmental quality in any one loan, making it necessary for the organization to maintain a broad and diverse collection of clients in order to influence all (economic, ecological, and social) aspects of its mission interest (Okagaki 2001: 74).[37]

This mission diffusion has been somewhat surprising as the institution's mission interests looked easily attainable when Enterprise Pacific was first established. In 1994, the burgeoning "green" marketplace seemed to offer enormous opportunity to reshape natural resource production, distribution, and sales.[38] Then,

37 Okagaki has also noted that the qualities that make up a potential loan's economic mission score are really more environmental than they are economic (Okagaki 2001: 75). Although Enterprise Pacific judges its own performance by fairly standard economic indicators (such as number of jobs created and funds leveraged), it invokes "economic" standards such as efficiency of resource use and reduced dependence on synthetic substances to measure its clients' mission performance.

38 Interestingly, market data on socially and environmentally responsible purchasing, although limited post-2001, do not predict a significant drop in consumer spending. For example, although total grocery food sales were down by 0.6% in 2001, sales of organic food products grew by 24%, and sales of all organic and/or natural products increased by 13% (SPINS/ACNielsen 2002: 10). Current assessments of the "green" marketplace still tend to promote its potential to influence production practices, but they tend to be more tempered by awareness of the difficulties of distributing and retailing new kinds of products and by a sense of the long-term time-line that this kind of change might

Officer:			
Borrower:			
Loan number:			
Date:			
Credit risk score:			
Grade:			
Mission risk score:			
Grade:			
	Score		
	Best	**Worst**	**Actual**
(a) Credit risk rating summary			
Management	1	5	
Operating margins and cash flow	1	5	
Competitive advantage	1	5	
Balance sheet	1	5	
Industry and market	1	5	
Credit history of the principals	1	5	
Collateral or secondary repayment source	1	5	
Combined numerical rating	7	35	
Grade	A	F	
(b) Mission rating summary			
Environment:			
Maintain and restore ecosystem health	2	10	
Promote compact cities and towns	2	10	
Preserve biological diversity	2	10	
Total	6	30	
Equity:			
Meet human needs and use economic opportunity	1	5	
Improve ability to respond to change	1	5	
Access to knowledge of place and nature, and preserve cultural diversity	1	5	
Diversify local economies	1	5	
Invest capital in women and minorities	1	5	
Promote accountability by business and government to communities	1	5	
Total	6	30	

Table 10.3 **Shorebank Enterprise Pacific: example of a scoresheet to determine (a) credit risk and (b) mission relevance** (continued opposite)

	Score		
	Best	**Worst**	**Actual**
(b) Mission rating summary (continued)			
Economy:			
Increase resource efficiency	1	5	
Reduce dependence on non-renewable resources	1	5	
Reduce dependence on synthetic substances	1	5	
Turn waste into a resource	1	5	
Choose products and suppliers consistent with other principles	1	5	
Assign actual social and ecological costs to goods and services	1	5	
Total	6	30	
Combined mission rating	18	90	
Grade	A	F	

Table 10.3 (continued)

natural products publications regularly estimated the market for products produced and harvested in an environmentally sensitive manner at over US$115 billion, and in the seafood sector alone sales in natural food stores in Oregon, Washington, and California were approximately US$10 million annually (e.g. see the 1994 issues of *The Natural Foods Merchandizer*; New Hope 1994). Nature's Northwest grocery stores in Portland sold US$750,000 of seafood every year and did not feature any oysters, a market niche that seemed perfect for a Willapa product (Shorebank Corporation and Ecotrust 1992a: 7). The Enterprise Pacific strategy was based on linking rural producers to this growing market and using credit and consultants to ensure that their products would appeal to a premium natural product consumer.

Not only has it been challenging to find individual loans that integrate the economic, ecological, and social aspects of the Enterprise Pacific mission but it has proven difficult to take full advantage of markets for socially and environmentally responsible goods. In general, the organization has been successful at generating market demand. However, owing partly to the vagaries of industries affected by seasons, weather, and environmental conditions and partly to the struggles of small-scale production, Enterprise Pacific has been less effective at corralling regular product supply to fill that demand.

require. In sustainable forestry, for example, the Forest Stewardship Council's sustainable production certification does appear to have given a few smaller companies access to market share (Sokolove 2003), but the relatively expensive certification process has yet to produce identifiable economic premiums for most of the landowners and processors who have invested in it.

Another Enterprise Pacific challenge relates to effecting more broad-based economic change, which was a component of the original thinking that shaped the organization. That is, Enterprise Pacific was structured not only to access urban "eco-markets" but also to develop coordinated strategies for driving sectoral change. Sectoral approaches offered a way to link producers in specific resource industries, creating economies of scale in production and distribution while also ensuring sufficient product quantities on a consistent basis to interest distributors and retailers in urban centers. In addition, Enterprise Pacific's founders and staff believed that disparate individual loans were unlikely to add up to major change in resource industries. That belief led them to combine individual small business loans with sector-wide product development, marketing, and distribution programs. These programs could serve the dual purpose of connecting entrepreneurs in resource-based industries, so that they could see the benefits of eco-innovation in their field, and of linking multiple producers into supply networks, driving down the cost of reaching target markets.

However, Enterprise Pacific's sectoral programs have had mixed success, revealing an important gap between theory and practice. Two examples can demonstrate the types of connections Enterprise Pacific attempts to build in natural-resource-based industry supply chains and the kinds of market complexities these programs confront.

First, in 1997, Enterprise Pacific started a sectoral program in the special forest products industry, working with a cooperative of small producers and processors. The goal of the program was to standardize sustainable harvest practices while ensuring a sufficient price premium in the floral greens marketplace so that processors could both earn, and pay harvesters, a living wage. RainKist, a company started and owned by Enterprise Pacific, bought products from processors. These processors, in turn, agreed to buy greens from harvesters certified through a new sustainable harvesting program.[39] RainKist developed coordinated product lines, marketing materials, and distribution systems in an attempt to capture high returns from environmentally and socially responsible consumers for those greens processors. In addition, it worked to negotiate long-term leases for non-timber forest product harvests on public and private forestlands in the Pacific Northwest.

RainKist did not survive because of difficulties in coordinating supply and demand and complications in the management of the production practices. However, the concept was a rare complete integration of environmental, economic, and equity goals. It addressed the resource base and harvest practices. It offered (largely) minority harvesters higher prices on the floral greens they gathered and aimed to provide them with a stewardship interest in specific pieces of land. It developed coordinated strategies for marketing value-added goods, combining the creativity of local processors and Enterprise Pacific's own market knowledge. Finally, it built a coordinated network of organizations working on different aspects of one large, shared problem.

---

39 Shorebank Enterprise Pacific, in partnership with the Northwest Natural Resources Group, was also responsible for developing the new set of guidelines for sustainable harvest of non-timber forest products, published as *The Specialty Forest Products Stewardship Field Guide for Selected Species of the North American Coastal Temperate Rain Forest* (Shorebank Enterprise Pacific and Northwest Natural Resources Group 1998).

The second sectoral program example focused on salmon fishing at the mouth of the Columbia River. Also in 1997, Enterprise Pacific began linking gillnetters working a terminal net pen fishery on Youngs Bay with a Clatsop County distributor who was hoping to develop a successful business in sustainably harvested salmon. A terminal net pen fishery, or a select area fishery, is a strategy for restoring fishable salmon populations to places where native runs no longer exist. In many areas of the Columbia River, fishers cannot work healthy salmon runs because, on a particular stretch of river, or in a specific bay, the viable runs commingle with endangered runs. In those places, fishers might accidentally catch members of the endangered population, further threatening its existence. A select area fishery attempts to develop new runs in locations known to be free of returning runs of wild, endangered salmon. One such place is Youngs Bay on the Columbia. On Youngs Bay, the Clatsop County Economic Development Council runs a program to raise catchable salmon. It acquires excess chinook and coho fingerlings from hatcheries in other watersheds and sets them out in net pens. The fish are raised in the pens long enough to imprint Youngs Bay onto their homing instinct. Then they are released to live out the ocean water portion of their life-cycle, returning to Youngs Bay two to four years later to spawn. Because these fish return to an area known to be free of endangered stocks, state fish and wildlife regulators are able to allow an open fishing season when the salmon return to Youngs Bay.

In order to support sectoral change related to salmon fishing, Enterprise Pacific financed the distributor and then aided him in locating premium markets in Portland and Seattle natural food stores. When it proved difficult to obtain a price premium solely on the complicated story of a sustainably managed fishery, Enterprise Pacific and the distributor built a market for quality local fish. The fishers received a guaranteed price premium if they followed specific harvest practices, such as icing and bleeding the salmon immediately after capture. With these core aspects of quality assured, Enterprise Pacific then developed marketing materials emphasizing the quality, the nutritional value of fresh salmon from the mouth of the Columbia, the stories of the fishers who caught them and their long history of gillnetting in the river, and the positive environmental impact consumers could make by purchasing the salmon. Eventually, Enterprise Pacific bowed out of the process, leaving the new supply chain to stand on its own.

Again, the project balanced economy, environment, and equity in its strategy and goals. But Youngs Bay salmon are no longer sold in urban markets. It was difficult for the distributor to buy a regular supply of select-area salmon, even when the season was open and he was offering a price premium. Many fishers have long-standing relationships with particular distributors that extend over multiple fishing seasons. It is not a simple matter to sell fish to someone else during one season, as that choice could jeopardize a fisher's market for all the other fish he or she brings in for the rest of the year. That fact, combined with the small overall size of the net pen program and the resultant small numbers of fish available for capture in Youngs Bay, ensured that the program produced only a modest supply of fish for the urban markets. The distributor's yearly supply ranged from 2,000 to 3,000 fish and was simply insufficient as the foundation for a financially sustainable business.

Implementing the sustainability vision: challenges and opportunities for Shorebank Enterprise Pacific

As these examples indicate, it has proven difficult to translate captivating visions of the positive potential of the market into practical solutions to social and environmental problems. Although Enterprise Pacific has had some notable success, particularly with its revolving loan fund, issues of scale, pace, and impact assessment have troubled the organization during its first seven years. Clearly, a revolving loan fund is fairly limited in the effect it can have on a US$10 trillion national economy. That said, however, the organization faces much more specific problems, even in the context of the rural coastal region where it has chosen to focus its attention.

In terms of scale, Enterprise Pacific has been confronted by three fundamental questions:

- At what scale does basic economic change occur?

- What are the most effective strategies for matching the scale of rural supply to the scale of market demand?

- How can Enterprise Pacific maintain its current strengths as it grows its operations from an essentially community level to a truly regional lending institution?

One major lesson that emerged from the organization's five-year review of operations was that economic development is not a singular process. Rather, economic development can occur on many different scales, so any effort to catalyze a particular kind of development, such as a conservation economy, must first determine which activities drive the particular targeted market. In Enterprise Pacific's case, two scales of economic development stand out—sectoral economic development and community economic development. Between 1995 and 2000, Enterprise Pacific made little conscious distinction between economic change that could drive an entire industry to adopt new practices, and place-based economic change that could revitalize the economy of a coastal community.[40]

In response, the strategic plan that will guide its next five years of work commits Enterprise Pacific to both a regional, sector-based economic development goal and a watershed-based, community economic development aim. The complementary strengths and weaknesses of these two approaches attempt to ensure that Enterprise Pacific will engage in comprehensive economic development. The sector approach will draw on the institution's market knowledge. The linking of multiple producers within the coastal region will open opportunities for industry innovation, coordinated research and development, and shared marketing arrangements. Industry networks will also be able to produce more reliable amounts at the larger scale necessary to participate in urban markets. In addition, the sector approach will present Enterprise Pacific with a geographically dispersed loan market,

40 Alan Okagaki has been particularly succinct on this point. See his 2001 report, *Shorebank Enterprise Pacific: A Five-Year Assessment*, for a clear analysis of Enterprise Pacific's history in both sector-based economic development and place-based community development and his recommendations for a balanced approach in the future.

increasing the number of potential clients. The community-based approach will emphasize Enterprise Pacific's strengths in building personal relationships and locally relevant industry knowledge, using those assets to manage credit risk. Community lending will focus on creating visible evidence of positive environmental and social change in particular places.

Enterprise Pacific has also recognized that Ecotrust and the Shorebank Corporation created significant obstacles by trying to transfer an organizational model developed for urban neighborhoods to the rural Pacific Northwest. In the Chicago South Shore neighborhood, Shorebank had an area with 65,000 people in one square mile. The population density in South Shore provided a correlated density of possible businesses to fund. In contrast, Enterprise Pacific operates across more than 1,000 miles of coastline, with a residential density that is often below 150 people per square mile. The modest coastal population leaves a far smaller pool of potential loan clients and creative entrepreneurs in any one community. In addition, many of the Shorebank Corporation's early loans in the South Shore were for real estate development and improvement. The resultant changes were quickly visible, altering the esthetic of a measurable number of city streets and offering shared visual spaces that demonstrated to residents that the neighborhood was changing. In rural coastal communities, changes in the practices of any individual business typically are not visible to other people. Finally, in urban areas the demand for real estate might exceed supply, but the market rarely disappears if that demand is not entirely satisfied. However, in rural resource-based industries, the difference in the scale of production and the scale of demand often prevents coastal businesses from maintaining market share in the kinds of "green" and socially responsible markets Enterprise Pacific hopes to reach.

A coordinated sector approach could provide one way to address all of these challenges. A successful sectoral strategy offers the organization an entire region of potential clients, maximizing the market for Enterprise Pacific loans. In addition, this strategy could increase the visible effects of Enterprise Pacific lending within particular industries. For example, a concentration of loans in sustainable fishing, organic dairies, or more efficient and effective septic systems might build a recognizable brand for the salmon or milk products, or result in a demonstrable improvement in local water quality. Simultaneously, a sector approach could generate sufficient consistent supply to satisfy the upscale urban markets that provide price premiums for responsible production. A region-wide industry-specific economic development model could address many of the frustrations of planning and production that have plagued Enterprise Pacific's first few years.

However, a few million dollars is a small amount of money in conventional capital markets. With limited financial power and a large geographic region—the entire coastal temperate rainforest—in which it hopes to promote more sustainable business practices, Enterprise Pacific cannot influence every industry equally. Another lesson of the institution's early experience is that the structure of a particular industry shapes whether or not it is likely to be affected by the tools available to Enterprise Pacific. Pacific Northwest forestry, for example, is primarily the provenance of large, industrial companies. Enterprise Pacific simply does not have the capital resources to use the lure of a loan to drive a large corporation to make major changes to its production or harvest practices. It is possible, however, that the institution's loans could make a great deal of difference in the fishing industry, where small-scale ownership and independent operations remain much more common. Fishers might be interested in the smaller loans Enterprise Pacific could offer them, and they generally have the authority to change their business practices if they can see the benefits of doing so. Institutions seeking to emulate Enterprise Pacific should analyze the scale of asset ownership and control of production practices as they choose industries with which to partner.

The importance of industry structure also extends to markets. Enterprise Pacific has often made its job more difficult by working in emerging "green" markets, forcing itself to "create green product differentiation and engineer the green retail channel rather than just connecting products into an existing green market" (Okagaki 2001: 59). Although most socially and environmentally responsible markets are fairly new, some have managed to establish certification practices or standards and reliable market niches, such as for organic foods. A strategic focus on industries characterized by small business and established "green" or socially responsible markets could allow Enterprise Pacific, and other organizations seeking to follow its model, to make the most effective use of resources, given mission goals.

Although the sector approach has the potential to yield multiple benefits, it is not the sole answer to successful sustainability-focused lending. A place-based community approach is a necessary complement. Much of Enterprise Pacific's success has relied on highly personalized relationships and customized business interaction that cannot be sustained at a regional level. The institution operates on a philosophy it refers to as "trust-based engagement."[41] Staff believe that taking the time to develop solid relationships based on trust and mutual respect in the communities where the institution works offers two benefits. First, it helps manage risk on the Enterprise Pacific loan portfolio. Specifically, trust brings struggling clients into the office to ask for help in working out how to make their payments, change their business plans or restructure their loans. Second, savvy combinations of trust and capital can help to create broader environmental and economic impacts. For example, if Enterprise Pacific has gained a position of trust in the oyster industry, a beleaguered grower might seek its help in developing a plan to take advantage of foreseeable market shifts or ecological changes. Similarly, if Enterprise Pacific is trusted in local politics, a mayor or city council might turn to the institution for new ideas about how to revitalize local industry. These types of communication, however, are possible only after sustained local interaction and conscious engagement with community concerns, both of which are difficult to pull off at the regional scale.

The sector approach also obscures the geography of place that bounds communities. In other words, although innovative practices in particular industries might help to revitalize the economies of coastal communities, they might also merely enrich a few early adopters of particularly creative sustainable business practices and marketing plans. There is no necessary association between community development and pioneering industry practices. Enterprise Pacific must actively

41   Personal communication with John Berdis, Managing Director, Shorebank Enterprise Pacific, December 27th, 2002.

construct these social connections if it aims to change the experience of life on the Pacific Northwest coast. In recognition of this issue, Enterprise Pacific plans to continue a place-based community development strategy that supplements its broader sector aims. Although one community may not provide a concentration of innovative entrepreneurs that can catalyze a sector-wide shift in business practices, concentrated mission-driven lending and support for local initiatives in one community may contribute to a more vibrant local economy.

Place-based lending also provides a more reasonable opportunity to monitor the impacts of the institution's programs on an observable scale. Although impact assessment, particularly in complex systems where causal relationships are extremely difficult to demonstrate, will always be a challenge, Enterprise Pacific judges its performance against a peer group of community development financial institutions. These groups use fairly well-accepted metrics—including job creation and retention and amount of capital leveraged—to assess their success or lack thereof. They often specify the creation and retention of jobs for minority groups and women in the interests of measuring impact on social equity concerns in addition to impact on economic return. Ratios of investment cost per job created, or cost of each dollar leveraged, can offer a rough sense of the efficiency of organizational processes. Although Enterprise Pacific tracks these metrics, it does not have a framework for monitoring its environmental impacts or any qualitative effects it might have in the communities in which it works. The concentration of lending in specific geographic locations has the potential to allow the organization to develop and monitor specific environmental outputs correlated with lending practices. The conventional assessment parameters could supplement the place-based approach to give Enterprise Pacific a methodology to track its impacts more comprehensively.

Conclusions

Enterprise Pacific's experience indicates that it is possible to build environmentally and socially aware sources of credit. The institution has invested more than US$13 million with a very low rate of loan loss.[42] It has found a market for its loans, and its clients have almost always managed to repay those loans. Its institutional growth has been steady and regular. Enterprise Pacific has originated approximately US$1.6 million annually—an amount approximately equal to the loan origination of its peer community development financial institutions. Even in a very limited rural market, Enterprise Pacific has been extremely effective at getting loans "out the door" and in building a respected local presence in community politics. The institution has not only matched the performance of other non-profit organizations engaged in community economic revitalization but also has also developed substantial knowledge of natural-resource-based industries, the complicated ecological systems on which those industries depend, and the markets in

---

42 US$13 million is Enterprise Pacific's total production, including non-debt investments.

which those products are sold. Finally, Enterprise Pacific has helped to alter the landscape of non-profit philanthropy, working to convince philanthropic foundations to merge programs that fund community development and conservation. New institutions seeking to replicate the Enterprise Pacific model, however, must be clear about their strategies for raising operational funding, the mode and pace of change they can realistically hope to encourage, and the loan markets they hope to reach.

It is noteworthy in the current economic context that Enterprise Pacific is supported in part by funds available only to non-profit organizations. Grant funding and low-cost capital are essential to its operations because they allow for an extraordinary amount of research to explore the possible outcomes of Enterprise Pacific lending and the structure of "green" markets. That financial support also ensures that Enterprise Pacific is able to devote significant staff time to building and maintaining relationships with clients, scientists, potential partner organizations and distributors, suppliers, retailers, and consultants operating in a vast range of commodity chains. Both of these attributes are fundamental to Enterprise Pacific's success. A for-profit bank would tend to have difficulty devoting comparable resources to these kinds of investments in organizational effectiveness. The Shorebank Corporation addressed this problem in South Shore by building mutually supportive for-profit and non-profit institutions linked by common goals and management, with some mixed success.[43] In rural areas, where it may be difficult to find enough loans to support even one institution, two institutions may not be an effective strategy. Efforts to design an institution such as Enterprise Pacific in another rural area must weigh the benefits offered by a commercial bank against the flexibility provided by non-profit capital.

Any institution interested in providing sustainability-focused credit will also struggle with the issue of pace. Enterprise Pacific's approach clearly reflects the theory of geographer David Harvey, who asserts that, "all proposals concerning 'the environment' are necessarily and simultaneously proposals for social change" (Harvey 1996: 119). So, although it eventually aims to produce changes that benefit the biophysical world in the places where it works, Enterprise Pacific recognizes that those changes will occur, or not occur, only as a result of human actions. The institution is also deeply aware that those changes are unlikely to occur quickly. As with any non-profit organization seriously confronting questions of social or environmental change, Enterprise Pacific must address a difference in the pace of change it actually expects to catalyze and the pace of change its funders hope to see. As a market-based organization, Enterprise Pacific must confront an additional distinction between expected return on capital investment in conventional markets and the longer-term cycles of many biophysical processes. Replication of Enterprise Pacific's successes will rely on financial management attuned to the realities of gradual social and environmental change.

---

43 In Shorebank's experience, banks and non-profit organizations, even when staff are hired with the express goal of working together toward a shared objective, tend to develop radically different styles and structures. These differences can lead to mutual frustration as often as they lead to mutual support (Ron Grzywinski, personal communication, January 12th, 2001).

Enterprise Pacific's own evolution suggests that it is also vital to understand the scope and nature of the market for sustainability-focused credit when designing an institution that will seek to access that market. The very nature of the communities that Enterprise Pacific tries to serve has been the core of one of the most significant difficulties it faces. Focused on small rural communities, with few residents relative to urban areas, Enterprise Pacific and its affiliate for-profit organization, Shorebank Pacific, have struggled to gain market share. Enterprise Pacific initially aimed to demonstrate the environmental effects of capital provision in one or two rural watersheds. It soon learned that, particularly in areas that already have good community banks, it can be difficult to generate loan volume large enough to result in any measurable effects. A wide regional base from which to draw clients, or a geography that includes urban areas with a higher population concentration, could potentially allow an organization that aspires to adapt the Enterprise Pacific model to a new region to grow its loan portfolio more quickly.

Enterprise Pacific has addressed these challenges with expansion plans that integrate sectoral economic development with community economic develop-ment. It will direct future place-based lending toward rural locations where it has determined those loans have a high probability of resulting in measurable improvement in local ecological conditions. That place-based strategy will com-plement a regional plan that will give the institution access to a wider loan market in addition to offering opportunities to catalyze sustainable sectoral development. A new organization seeking to mimic Enterprise Pacific's activities would have to choose its own balance between those imperatives.

A mission-driven credit provider must also be clear about who its loan clients might be and why they will come in the door. Enterprise Pacific has found loan clients not only in a population of innovative rural entrepreneurs whose new ideas are so risky that conventional banks refuse to fund them, as they initially expected, but also in a population of entrepreneurs whose businesses are struggling. These struggling entrepreneurs seek non-bank capital because they have no other option. To them, Enterprise Pacific's triple-bottom-line sustainability mission appears less important than the institution's basic willingness to furnish capital and its ability to envision their businesses as viable. These loans may not have been what Enterprise Pacific expected, but they have had other unintended conse-quences. In some cases they have given the institution the opportunity to make "character" loans, in which the organization supports prominent leaders in local industry, often gaining important familiarity with and recognition in that industry. In other cases, they have demonstrated Enterprise Pacific's commitment to community economic stability to local residents. Taken together, they have shown Enterprise Pacific that the kind of change it hopes to catalyze must "start where people are at."

"Starting where people are at" means taking context seriously, at both the individual and the community level. It means understanding that the process of receiving and repaying an Enterprise Pacific loan opens an opportunity for conversation, and that the conversation may well be the most effective route toward long-term change. "Starting where people are at" also means, however, that Enterprise Pacific's mission-driven business recommendations may play only a small role in any one transaction. These dynamics have taught Enterprise Pacific not to look for economic, ecological, and social sustainability in every loan. It is possible that Enterprise Pacific will fund one or two incredibly successful sustainable innovations in resource industries, and that those innovations will drive massive shifts in the regional economy. However, Enterprise Pacific's experience teaches that the conversations about production practices, harvest practices, and business choices that the institution opens through its loans often provide the best chance to catalyze meaningful social and environmental change through lending and banking practices. Those conversations are the critical link between the sustainability-focused mission that drives Enterprise Pacific and the communities and entrepreneurs with which it works.

Enterprise Pacific puts capital into the hands of the people it believes are most likely to use it in ways that help to revitalize rural coastal communities and natural-resource-based industries. Its success at attracting philanthropic and conventional bank capital to its cause and building a market for socially and environmentally aware credit suggests a growing interest in supporting sustainable business practices among investors and consumers. Shorebank Enterprise Pacific demonstrates that it is possible to harness that interest in combination with the productive power of capital and credit to promote positive social and environmental change.

Part 4
Reporting and accountability

The difference between what we do and what we are capable of
doing would suffice to solve most of the world's problems.

Mohandas K. Gandhi

If humanity is to progress, Gandhi is inescapable. He lived,
thought and acted, inspired by the vision of humanity evolving
toward a world of peace and harmony. We may ignore Gandhi at
our own risk.

Martin Luther King Jr[1]

New international standards for corporate "responsibility," accountability, and
reporting are shaping a new vision for business. This alternative approach incorporates equal concern for ecological, social, and financial issues. Through this unlikely
guise, the compassion that infused Gandhi's efforts is being integrated into visions of
a new future for 21st-century businesses and economies.

---

1   Quoted in J. Miller and A. Kenedi (eds.), *Revolution: Faces of Change* (New York: Thunder's
    Mouth Press, 2000).

11

Improving sustainability disclosure
The Global Reporting Initiative Guidelines

Allen L. White
Special Advisor to the Global Reporting Initiative, USA

Accountability—of government, civil society, and especially of corporations—is one of the defining imperatives of the modern global economy. Corporations now constitute half of the world's largest economies. They dominate international finance, vastly exceeding the resources of governments and multilateral institutions as drivers of development. Yet, with this steady increase in economic might, there has been no corresponding rise in generally accepted accountability mechanisms.

Accountability is used here in the broadest sense—internal accountability among boards, management, and shareowners, and external accountability between corporations and society. The disjuncture between corporate power and corporate accountability lies at the core of heated debates over the costs, benefits, and future of globalization. The challenge remains to create markets that are stable, inclusive, and transparent.

Sound corporate disclosure is a cornerstone of accountability. However, the lagging indicators that form the foundation of financial performance reporting and analysis are becoming inadequate for predicting future financial performance. The most powerful value drivers—brands, reputation, capacity to innovate, alliances, human capital, intellectual capital—are not systematically disclosed in company reports. In the absence of standards, metrics, and protocols for measuring such critically important intangible assets, investors, analysts, and activists are left to their own devices to compile such information on a case-by-case basis. The cost is high, the quality often low, and results unsatisfactory.

In the post-Enron era, pressures are mounting among investors, fund managers, consumers, and other groups to expand the coverage of corporate reporting. It is in this context that the Global Reporting Initiative (GRI) has emerged as the leading initiative in building a new reporting infrastructure, designed to complement rather than displace financial reporting. GRI is the steward of that infrastructure—reporting guidelines that address the non-financial aspects of the economic, environmental, and social performance of organizations.

GRI's rapid evolution in just a few years from a bold vision to a new independent global institution reflects the imperative and the value that various constituencies assign to such a disclosure framework. The GRI process, rooted in inclusiveness, transparency, neutrality, and continual enhancement, has enabled GRI to bring concrete expression to accountability.

This chapter introduces the GRI and the trends that are driving increased sustainability disclosure. In addition, it describes the benefits of such reporting. It concludes with considering a few of the challenges that lie ahead in elevating sustainability reporting to unprecedented levels of rigor, consistency, and comparability.

Bringing concrete expression to accountability: the Global Reporting Initiative

GRI is a long-term, multi-stakeholder, international process, the mission of which is to develop and disseminate globally applicable sustainability reporting guidelines (hereafter referred to as the Guidelines), most recently revised and released in mid-2002 (GRI 2002a). The aim of the Guidelines is to assist reporting organizations and their stakeholders in articulating and understanding contributions of the reporting organizations to sustainable development. The Guidelines are for use by organizations[1] for reporting on the economic, environmental, and social dimensions of their activities, products and services.

GRI was convened in 1997 by the Coalition for Environmentally Responsible Economies (CERES) in partnership with the United Nations Environment Program (UNEP). It was established to elevate sustainability reporting[2] practices to a level equivalent to those of financial reporting, while achieving comparability, credibility, rigor, timeliness, and verifiability of reported information. GRI has undertaken this work with the active participation of corporations, environmental and social non-governmental organizations (NGOs), accountancy organizations, trade unions, investors, and other stakeholders worldwide.

---

1 This includes corporate, governmental, and non-governmental organizations. All are included within GRI's mission. In its first phase, GRI has placed an emphasis on corporations with the expectation that governmental and non-governmental organizations will follow in due course.

2 GRI uses the term "sustainability reporting" as synonymous with citizenship reporting, social reporting, triple-bottom-line reporting, and other terms that encompass the economic, environmental, and social aspects of an organization's performance.

Trends

Since publication of the first Guidelines in June 2000, the trends that catalyzed the formation of GRI have continued unabated and, in most cases, have intensified. The issues—globalization and corporate governance, accountability and citizenship—have now moved to the mainstream of policy and management debates in many organizations and the countries in which they operate. Support for creating a new, generally accepted disclosure framework for sustainability reporting continues to grow among business, civil society, government, and labor stakeholders.

If we observe the current landscape of business, economic, and social trends worldwide, it is possible to discern some of the forces, concurrent and interdependent, that have fueled GRI's rapid progress; these are summarized in Box 11.1 and discussed in more detail below. Each of these factors is important to understand the changing context.

Worldwide, the landscape of business, economic, and social trends is characterized by:

- An expanding globalization
- A search for new forms of global governance
- The reform of corporate governance
- A global role for emerging economies
- The increasing visibility of and expectations for organizations
- The measurement of progress towards sustainable development
- Governmental interest in sustainability reporting
- Financial market interest in sustainability reporting
- The emergence of next-generation accounting

Box 11.1 The current landscape of business, economic, and social trends worldwide

An expanding globalization

Expansion of global capital markets and information technology continue to bring unprecedented opportunities for the creation of new wealth. At the same time, there is deep skepticism among the thousands of activists who protested in Seattle, Quebec City, and Genoa against globalization that such wealth will do anything to decrease social inequities. The civil-society backlash against globalization and associated campaigns against particular companies have the potential to redefine the corporate "license to operate." Although governmental and non-governmental entities are players in trying to manage the globalization process, it is corporate activity that remains its driving force. The result: all parties, including corporations, are seeking new forms of accountability that credibly describe the consequences of business activities wherever, whenever, and however they occur.

Far from being a reporting scheme that is imposed on companies by NGOs, the GRI has had extensive corporate involvement. More than 45 companies have participated in pilot tests of the Guidelines and, as of July 2003, more than 290 companies[3] had released sustainability reports based on the Guidelines.

A search for new forms of global governance

Globalization challenges the capacity of existing international and national institutions to govern corporate activity. One dramatic indication of this concern has been the efforts of Friends of the Earth International to achieve a binding international convention on corporate accountability.[4] The borderless global economy requires equally borderless governance structures to help direct private-sector activity towards outcomes that are socially and environmentally, as well as economically, beneficial. National governments cannot keep up with governing transnational issues and companies.

Several models of international governance, such as those listed in Table 11.1, exemplify a new generation of initiatives that align governance with the challenges of an increasingly complex and interconnected world. A key theme in all these emerging governance models is the demand for higher levels of transparency.

	Issue governed
Montreal Protocol www.unep.org/ozone/montreal.shtml	Ozone-depleting substances
Kyoto Protocol http://unfccc.int	Greenhouse gases
Forest Stewardship Council www.fscoax.org	Forestry practices
Marine Stewardship Council www.msc.org	Fishing practices
International Labor Organization www.ilo.org	Labor practices
International Accounting Standards Board www.iasc.org.uk/cmt/0001.asp	Accounting standards

Table 11.1 Models for international governance

3   For a list of reporters, see www.globalreporting.org/guidelines/reporters_all.asp.
4   For more information on the binding international convention on corporate accountability proposed by Friends of the Earth, see www.foei.org/corporates/towards.html.

The reform of corporate governance

Pressures on corporations to establish and maintain high standards of internal governance are increasing. As society witnesses the growing influence of corporations in driving economic, environmental, and social change, investors and other stakeholders expect high standards of ethics, transparency, sensitivity, and responsibility from corporate executives and managers. Governance systems are increasingly expected to extend beyond their traditional focus on investors to address diverse stakeholders. The independence of board members, executive participation in external partnerships, compensation and incentive schemes, and the integrity of auditors are under increasing scrutiny.

Effective corporate governance depends on access to relevant, high-quality information that enables performance tracking and invites new forms of stakeholder engagement. The proliferation of corporate governance initiatives—the Cadbury Commission (Cadbury Commission 1992) and the Turnbull Report in the United Kingdom,[5] the King Report in South Africa,[6] Brazil's innovative New Stock Exchange,[7] Guidelines for Multinational Enterprises[8] and Corporate Governance Principles[9] of the Organization for Economic Cooperation and Development (OECD), and the World Bank's Corporate Governance Forum[10]—attest to rising expectations for high standards of corporate behavior.

A global role for emerging economies

The same globalization, accountability, and governance trends evident in industrial nations are taking root in emerging economies. Nations such as Brazil, India, and South Africa are full participants in the globalization process. The King Commission Report in South Africa includes one of the most comprehensive codes of corporate governance in the world.[11]

The technology innovation and capital flows that powered globalization over the past decade now permeate these emerging nations, positioning them as regional and global players on the economic stage of the 21st century. At the same time, tightly linked global supply chains are spreading common management practices and increasing accountability pressures into all segments of the value chain. Similar to how Ford, IBM, and other multinationals request their suppliers to become ISO 14001-certified,[12] reporting companies are asking their suppliers for

---

5　www.icaew.co.uk/internalcontrol
6　www.iodsa.co.za
7　www.novomercadobovespa.com.br/english/nm_novomercado.htm
8　www.oecd.org/home/0,2605,en_2649_34889_1_1_1_1_1,00.html
9　*Ibid.*
10　www.gcgf.org/about.htm
11　For more information on the King Commission Report, see www.iodsa.co.za.
12　Ford at: www.ford.com.au/inside_ford/community/environment/View_Latest_News.asp?file=env004.htm;
and IBM at: www-1.ibm.com/procurement/proweb.nsf/ContentDocsByTitle/United+States~13+Apr+98:+ISO14001?OpenDocument&Parent=Supplier+letters.

indications of their sustainability performance.[13] Corporate accountability has expanded from its early association with multinational corporations into a broad-based movement that is affecting private-sector entities of all sizes around the world.

The rising visibility of and expectations for organizations

The spread of the Internet and communications technologies is accelerating the global transfer of information and amplifying the speed and force of feedback mechanisms. Consumers, supported by growing media coverage of sustainability issues, have ready access to information about organizations at an unprecedented level of detail. Companies are facing more clearly articulated expectations from customers, consumers, and advocacy groups regarding their contributions to sustainable development.

Several high-profile campaigns exemplify the risks to reputation associated with perceived unacceptable sustainability management (e.g. Nike labor practices in Asian sweatshops,[14] Monsanto's distribution of genetically modified seeds,[15] Shell and the disposal of the Brent Spar offshore drilling platform[16]). The ubiquity of global brands makes them easy targets for global campaigns. Proactive transparency on sustainability issues is one means of engaging stakeholders constructively with less confrontation.

The measurement of progress towards sustainable development

As sustainable development has become widely adopted as a foundation of public policy and organizational strategy, many organizations have turned their attention to the challenge of translating the concept into practice. The need to better assess an organization's status and align future goals with a complex range of external factors and partners has increased the urgency of defining broadly accepted sustainability performance indicators.

The International Institute for Sustainable Development documents no fewer than 500 initiatives aimed at identifying sustainable development indicators.[17] As

---

13 Examples of companies that request sustainability performance information from their suppliers include: BT (www.btplc.com/Betterworld/Environment/ Procurementandtheenvironment/Procurementandtheenvironment.htm), Nike (www. nike.com/nikebiz/nikebiz.jhtml?page=25&cat=compliance&subcat=monitoring), and Novo Nordisk (www.novonordisk.com/sustainability/soc_responsibility/supply_chain. asp).

14 E.g. Global Exchange (www.globalexchange.org/campaigns/sweatshops/nike/index. html).

15 www.vshiva.net/aticles/monsanto_trials.htm [*sic*]

16 http://archive.greenpeace.org/~odumping/oilinstall/monitorbs/index.html

17 For a compendium of sustainable development indicator initiatives, see www.iisd.org/ measure/compindex.asp.

companies increasingly are measuring[18] their sustainable development performance, a corresponding increase in external measurement activities has occurred. In addition to the specialty stock market indices developed to highlight best-in-industry sustainability performance, numerous benchmarking organizations, surveyors, and asset managers around the world measure and publicize company sustainability performance.[19]

Governmental interest in sustainability reporting

When GRI was conceived in 1997, governmental interest in integrated economic, environmental, and social reporting was scant. Today, voluntary, statutory, and regulatory initiatives abound. In Australia, Denmark, Japan, the Netherlands, Norway, Taiwan, the United Kingdom, and USA, programs and requirements to enlarge the scope of conventional corporate financial reporting to include non-financial information are rapidly unfolding.[20] The European Union has challenged all businesses with more than 500 staff to produce sustainability reports (see European Union 2001), and has strongly recommended triple-bottom-line reporting in their corporate social responsibility (CSR) Strategy (see European Union 2002). Large Canadian banks and insurance companies (those with more than CAD\$1 billion in equity) are now required to describe the social contributions they make.[21] France's Decree No. 2002-221 on new economic regulations mandates that Paris-listed companies include the social and environmental impacts of their activities in their annual reports.[22]

Some of these governmental actions are motivated by national environmental and social policy goals, others by investor pressures to obtain a clearer picture of corporate performance via the securities regulatory process. All indications point to continuing expansion of governmental reporting initiatives to new countries and regions over the next few years.

18 According to the KPMG *International Survey of Corporate Sustainability Reporting 2002* (KPMG 2002), 45% of the Global *Fortune* 250 now produce some type of social, environmental, corporate citizenship, or sustainability report. This figure is up from 35% in 1999.

19 Among the many organizations conducting corporate sustainability ratings are oekom research (www.oekom.de/index_english.html), Corporate Knights Inc. (www.corporateknights.ca/best50/index.asp), SustainAbility Ltd. (www.sustainability.com) and Sustainable Asset Management (www.sam-group.com/e/forum/forum.cfm).

20 For a summary of voluntary and mandatory sustainability reporting programs in numerous countries, see www.uneptie.org/outreach/reporting/docs/GRI_govtmeeting.pdf.

21 This requirement is described in the Canadian government Bill C-8 at www.parl.gc.ca/common/Bills_ls.asp?lang=E&Parl=37&Ses=1&ls=C8&source=Bills_House_Government #3.Public%20Accountability%20Statements(txt).

22 See translated text near bottom of page: www.eurosif.org/srilf.shtml.

Financial market interest in sustainability reporting

The financial industry slowly but steadily is embracing sustainability reporting as part of its analytical toolkit. Spurred in part by growing demand for social and ethical funds among institutional and individual investors, new "socially responsible" indices are appearing each year. The Dow Jones Sustainability Index and FTSE4Good Index are only two recent high-profile examples.[23]

At the same time, the exploration of the relationship between corporate sustainability activities and shareholder value is advancing. Linkages between sustainability performance and key value drivers such as brand image, reputation, and future asset valuation are awakening the mainstream financial markets to new tools for understanding and predicting value in capital markets. In April 2001, a leading British asset management firm (Morley Fund Management [MFM]) announced it would vote against the annual accounts of the nation's largest firms unless they provided an environmental report (MFM 2001).

The emergence of next-generation accounting

The late 20th century saw worldwide progress in harmonizing financial reporting. Indeed, the rich tradition of financial reporting, continually evolving to capture and communicate the financial condition of the organization, has inspired GRI's evolution. Yet, today, many observers—including accountants themselves—recognize that characterizing the "bricks and mortar" economy of the past will not suffice as a basis for characterizing today's information economy. The valuation of intangible assets—human capital, environmental capital, alliances and partnerships, brands and reputation—must complement the valuation of conventional tangible assets—factories, equipment, and inventory. Under the rubric of "business reporting," "intangible assets analysis," and "value reporting," a number of accounting groups have launched programs to explore how accounting standards should be updated to embrace such value drivers.[24]

The benefits of reporting

All these trends are familiar to managers seeking to sharpen their competitiveness in a globalizing world. The business justification for reporting is appreciated by the hundreds of companies worldwide that have published some type of non-financial performance reports (e.g. environmental, social, corporate citizenship).[25] Observers point to numerous benefits derived from serious sustainability reporting, including the following.

23 More information on these indexes can be found at www.sustainability-index.com and www.ftse4good.com, respectively; see also Chapter 9 in this book.

24 The International Accounting Standards Board (www.iasb.org.uk) has a project on intangible assets. PricewaterhouseCoopers recommends "value reporting" (http://valuereporting2.pwcglobal.com/pwcvr/index.jsp).

25 For statistics on non-financial reporting, see www.corporateregister.com.

- Effective management. In a global economy where information (reliable or unreliable) travels at Internet speed, successful managers must take a proactive approach. Measuring and reporting both past and anticipated performance is a critical management tool in today's high-speed, inter-connected, "24 hour news" world.

- Stakeholder engagement. Today's strategic and operational complexities require a continual dialog with investors, customers, advocates, suppliers, and employees. Reports are a key ingredient in this dialog. They can help communicate an organization's economic, environmental, and social opportunities and challenges in a way far superior to simply responding to stakeholder requests for information.

- External partnerships. Businesses need positive relationships with external parties, ranging from consumers to investors to community groups. Transparency and open dialog about performance, priorities, and future sustainability plans help to strengthen these partnerships and to build trust.

- Internal integration. Sustainability reporting is a vehicle for linking typically discrete and insular functions of the corporation—finance, marketing, and research and development—in a more strategic manner. The reporting process opens internal conversations where they would not otherwise occur.

- Problem identification. The process of developing a sustainability report provides a warning of trouble spots—and unanticipated opportunities—in supply chains, in communities, among regulators, and in reputation and brand management. These discoveries can help management evaluate potentially damaging developments before they develop into unwelcome surprises.

- Broader visioning. Sustainability reporting helps sharpen management's ability to assess the organization's contribution to natural, human, and social capital. This assessment enlarges the perspective provided by conventional financial accounts to create a more complete picture of long-term prospects. Articulation of a company's sustainability vision helps to highlight the societal and ecological contributions of the organization and the "sustainability value proposition" of its products and services. Such measurement is central to maintaining and strengthening the "license to operate."

- Reduction in share price volatility. Fuller and more regular information disclosure, including much of what analysts seek from managers on an ad hoc basis, can add stability to a company's financial condition by avoiding major swings in investor behavior caused by untimely or unexpected disclosures.

During 2000–2002, these trends, separately and synergistically, have reinforced interest in GRI and its core mission.

Confluence of need and opportunity

Yet much work remains. Inconsistent reporting approaches developed by business, government, and civil society continue to appear. At the same time, many other organizations wonder how best to engage in reporting. As diverse groups seek information, the multiplicity of information requests gives rise to redundancy, inefficiency, and frustration.

As was the case in June 2000, GRI's 2002 Guidelines (GRI 2002a) represent another step in addressing the challenge of responding to surging demands for information, emanating from competing reporting frameworks. By drawing thousands of partners and hundreds of organizations into a multi-stakeholder process, GRI continues to work toward harmonization of disclosure, thereby maximizing the value of reporting for the reporting organizations and the report users alike.

Many challenges lie ahead. GRI recognizes that the goal of reporting on the economic, environmental, and social dimensions of organization-level activity— let alone a fully integrated sustainability assessment—is in the earliest stages of a journey that will continue over many years.

Through ongoing dialog with various stakeholders, GRI realizes that it needs to continue learning and developing before it can fulfill its mission of making sustainability reporting as routine as financial reporting. Hundreds of individuals and organizations have provided input on where the Guidelines need improvement.[26] Although GRI has made significant strides in its formative years, it should be seen as in year 5 of a 30-year development.

Dissemination of the Guidelines to new audiences is critical to gaining a broader consensus. Expanded outreach in developing areas of the world is a prime objective for GRI.[27] Outreach to corporate audiences is fundamental to ensuring that the quality and quantity of sustainability reporting improve. To date, corporate input through pilot tests and feedback sessions has been instrumental in the design of the Guidelines.[28] Reporting should be beneficial to reporters themselves, not just to the stakeholders reading the reports. Perhaps this is why companies have engaged with GRI to help define the reporting landscape.

Although GRI continues to focus on updating and refining the core Guidelines, production of a range of sector supplements to the Guidelines is high on GRI's agenda.[29] Early work has included supplements for tour operators, financial services, the automobile industry, and the mining sector. In collaboration with multi-stakeholder working groups, the range of sectors in the product portfolio will be expanded over the coming years. Depth to the Guidelines will also be added with further work on indicator definitions and measurement protocols.

26 See www.globalreporting.org/feedback/pubcomments.asp and www.globalreporting. org/feedback/archives.asp for feedback on versions of the Guidelines.

27 See www.globalreporting.org/workgroup/regional.asp and text near bottom of www.globalreporting.org/about/myths.asp for information on GRI regional outreach.

28 See www.globalreporting.org/feedback/archives.asp and www.globalreporting.org/ guidelines/archives/March99/TestCompanies/pilottestcompanies.asp for corporate input on the Guidelines.

29 For more information on GRI sector supplements, see www.globalreporting.org/ guidelines/sectors.asp.

In the borderless world of corporate activity a further challenge for GRI lies in clarifying the boundaries of enterprises for reporting purposes. Significant questions remain as to how much of the chain (i.e. how far up the supply chain and down the product chain) should be included within the purview of the reporting entity. There appears to be general agreement that impacts over which the reporting entity has direct control should be measured and reported, while impacts over which the reporting entity has only indirect control may not always be appropriate for measurement and reporting. (An exploratory paper on boundary issues is available on the GRI website.[30])

The reliability of sustainability reports is critical to the degree of public trust and confidence placed in them. GRI has recognized from the beginning that a process of compliance monitoring, of independent verification or assurance, is essential for the credibility of the reporting process. In parallel to work on the Guidelines, the Verification Working Group has produced guidance for the assurance of reports.[31] This guidance will continue to be refined as experience is gained through application.

A continual learning process

Relative to financial reporting, which has been in practice for 75 years, sustainability reporting is in its infancy. The long-term objective of developing "generally accepted sustainability accounting principles" requires both a concrete product incorporating the best thinking and a stable process through which continuous learning can occur. GRI will provide both the product and process by developing a steady flow of stronger guidelines, technical protocols, and industry sector supplements. All these products, and GRI's underlying process, are built on a commitment to technical excellence, a multi-stakeholder process and transparency embodied in GRI's mission as a new global institution.

GRI is poised to play a pivotal role in advancing comprehensive organizational disclosure, but this will happen only if it continues to effectively engage business, civil society, governments, and labor in an inclusive, consensus-based learning process. These values permeate GRI's governance and operations, and form the basis for its legitimacy as the world's leading sustainability reporting initiative.

---

30   See www.globalreporting.org/workgroup/Boundary.pdf.
31   See www.globalreporting.org/guidelines/2002/dannex4.asp for guidance on report assurance.

Part 5
Pathways forward to organizational and societal change

They always say time changes things, but you actually have to
change them yourself.

Andy Warhol

From inspiration comes action. Yet ongoing action focused on fundamental change
calls for clear pathways forward and deep personal commitment. All of these
elements are intertwined in this final part on applying lessons learned and fostering
organizational and societal change. Overall, change will occur through a combination
of the Galileo type of genius in perceiving completely new possibilities, the collaborative efforts of many people and organizations as "ant colonies," and the Gandhi-
like determination and compassion in leadership and action.

12

Organizational change for sustainability

Sissel Waage
The Natural Step, California, USA

Juli Torok
Independent Consultant, Berkeley, California, USA

> **It is not the strongest of the species that survives, nor the most intelligent; it is the one most adaptable to change.**
>
> *Charles Darwin, 1859*[1]

Companies must continually adapt to change. In response, new products are developed, mergers or acquisitions planned, and internal change initiatives launched. However, at times, contextual shifts are so extreme that entire industries can be wiped out and others born. Technological revolutions and even regulatory changes have fundamentally altered entire industries.

The move towards sustainability has the same characteristics of a fundamental shift that will redefine entire industries and even broader economic systems. The reasons are simple. The ecological and social contexts in which businesses operate are changing in very basic ways. Access to resources is becoming more restricted. Water is being privatized globally. Ecosystems—from the Amazonian through the Pacific Northwestern forests—are being simplified in their species composition and structure. Weather patterns are becoming more extreme. Disparities in wealth are increasing as poverty grows globally. Power is being consolidated. Capital is more "footloose" than ever. Increasing economic interdependences mean that problems become highly "contagious." All these elements relate to different aspects of sustainability. And together these and many other factors are presenting an increasingly compelling rationale for sustainability-focused organizational change.

The insurance companies were some of the first to take note of sustainability-related factors and the resulting need for organizational change. Frank Annighofer,

---

1 Quoted in Augustine 1998: 159.

chairman of the board at Germany's Gerling Consulting, part of a major insurance group, asserts:

> Corporate boards have not seen insurers as sustainability campaigners, but many soon will. Insurers are no keener on losing money than the rest of us, and the potential issues they face because of environmental risks are getting even larger . . .
>
> The sharpest tool that an insurance company has . . . is its insurance products . . . If no insurance cover is available for certain technologies considered unsafe or likely to cause environmental damage, the chances of this technology surviving decrease (Annighofer 1997, quoted in Elkington 1997: 209-10).

For companies, the identification of changes will become easier as trends continue. Crafting responses and organizational change efforts will, however, become the new challenge facing modern industrial businesses in the 21st century.

Types of organizational change

Within the fields of organizational theory and organizational development, researchers have historically considered change as either incremental, resulting in small alterations, or fundamental, characterized by risky and transformational shifts (e.g. see Barczak *et al.* 1987; Beckhardt and Pritchard 1993; Goodstein and Burke 1991). However, it is perhaps most accurate to view the incremental–fundamental change dichotomy as more of a continuum—where fundamental changes are larger and more uncertain and incremental changes are smaller and more sure—with a range of variation in between (Anderson and Anderson 2001).

Along this continuum, analysts understand "developmental change" (Anderson and Anderson 2001) as focusing on the improvement of existing skills, approaches, or processes that are no longer effective for either present or future needs. This approach to change focuses on improving what already exists in the organization in order to achieve better results. Total quality management (TQM) and Six Sigma are perhaps the most widely known examples, with a focus on organization-wide efforts that continuously improve a firm's ability to offer products and services valued by customers (e.g. see Ciampa 1991). These developmental change initiatives are usually a response to relatively small shifts in the overall business context and marketplace. Such initiatives are associated with relatively little risk in relation to other change efforts.

In contrast, "transitional change" (Anderson and Anderson 2001) is applied in response to larger contextual shifts. Under these circumstances, the goal is to replace core processes and procedures with completely new ones. In moving toward these different operational elements, the organization must dismantle the old way of operating and move into a transitional stage. At the same time, the new "structure" is being put into place. Examples of transitional change include reorganization, simple mergers or consolidations, divestitures, certain types of information technology (IT), or the development of new products, services, systems, or policies (Anderson and Anderson 2001).

Finally, "transformational change" (Anderson and Anderson 2001) is the most complex and occurs when marketplace and business context changes are so profound that a real break from past behavior and organizations is required. In some cases, the new state is discovered through the change process itself. Usually, this process results in changes related to how the organization and its employees perceive their business and operations. For example, the shrinking of the defense industry in the 1980s and 1990s sparked the need for transformational change in a number of companies. Deregulation also led to significant changes, particularly in the telephone, banking, gas, and electric utility industries when the certainty of selling their products for a guaranteed rate of return disappeared. Researchers assert that these kinds of change initiatives are "multi-dimensional, multi-level, qualitative, discontinuous, radical . . . involving a paradigmatic shift" (Levy and Merry 1986).

These types of organizational change can be combined with the level of understanding of sustainability issues and their effects on the external business context, as shown in Table 12.1. The quadrant relevant to a high understanding of the

		Degree of organizational responsiveness	
		Low	**High**
Understanding of external or contextual change	**High**	*Efficient business:* ● Takes a developmental approach to change ● Has a narrow eco-efficiency focus ● Adds new product lines (e.g. electric vehicles) ● Implements programs to reduce, re-use, and recycle	*Revolutionary business:* ● Undertakes transformational change ● Has an integrated sustainability focus (financial, ecological, and social) ● Seeks to obtain closed loops regarding materials and products ● Works to develop lease-not-buy model ● Integrates social issues in core practices and policies ● Effects change at the corporate industrial and societal levels
	Low	*Business as usual:* ● Has a focus on compliance ● Makes adjustments to product prices ● Gradually expands into new markets	*Reinvented business:* ● Undergoes transitional change ● Undertakes mergers and acquisitions as a competitive response ● Responds to poor market performance by executive turnover and extensive lay-offs

Table 12.1 **Matrix of organizational and external or contextual change in response to sustainability issues**

relevance of sustainability factors to businesses is the upper right-hand corner in which there is a large degree of understanding of external change that necessitates a large response from the company. Such "revolutionary" business approaches will be based on fundamental and transformational organizational change.

Action within the upper quadrants, particularly the upper right-hand quadrant, offers opportunities, such as first-mover advantage, as well as risks. The dynamics are complex and challenging. However, the likelihood of success in making fundamental organizational changes can be increased by heeding the lessons of organizational development theory.

Dynamics of organizational change

Although change initiatives can be risky, there are a number of common reasons why efforts fail (Box 12.1). Perhaps most significant is the difficulty for organizations to shift their structures as rapidly as contextual changes may require, which results in "structural inertia" and the replacement of older organizational forms with new ones (e.g. see Hannan and Freeman 1984). For example:

> Even such a successful and well managed company as IBM moves
> ponderously to take advantage of new opportunities. Granted, IBM
> eventually moved into the market for minicomputers and micro-
> computers and appears poised to dominate them. Still, the pro-
> tracted period of assessing these markets, waiting for the technology
> to stabilize and re-organizing production and marketing operations
> created the opportunity for new firms to become established . . .
> [and] flourish (Hannan and Freeman 1984: 152).

Kotter (1998) has examined the mistakes that leaders, or a "guiding coalition," need to avoid. According to him, change efforts fail because leaders:

- Do not establish enough sense of urgency
- Do not create a sufficiently powerful guiding coalition
- Lack a clear vision
- Communicate the new vision inadequately
- Fail to remove structural obstacles to change (such as job categories and appraisal systems that focus employees on the wrong outcomes)
- Place insufficient focus on creating short-term wins
- Declare success too soon
- Fail to ground changes to the organization's culture

Box 12.1 Common mistakes within processes of organizational change

Source: Kotter 1998

This case highlights the importance of perceiving change and acting on it in a timely fashion.

However, there are very real reasons for "structural inertia," both internally and externally (Hannan and Freeman 1984). Internal barriers include sunk costs; difficulties in the gathering, analyzing, and communicating information relevant to a change initiative and employee resistance to altering the political and historical status quo.[2] In addition, external constraints have an effect on the success or failure of a change initiative (Hannan and Freeman 1984) and may involve legal and fiscal barriers to entry and exit from markets, the regulatory environment and a lack of change in the broader sets of relationships on which a business relies.

Since companies depend on a broad range of relationships to make products and provide services, this final issue is significant. Fundamentally changing a company requires support for change within a web of suppliers, customers, and partners. This entire business network is imbedded within institutionalized sets of understandings (both formal and informal) of how business is to be conducted. A radical departure from these sets of implicit agreements by one organization will necessitate changes within the larger sets of relationships.

All these realities underscore the importance of perceiving information quickly, acting decisively to address internal barriers, and integrating a broad set of players, including the supply chain. Success will require thinking on the appropriate scale of change from the start and setting a few "big hairy audacious goals" (Collins and Porras 1994).

Conditions that facilitate successful change

Once an organization has determined that it will move forward with a change initiative, several key factors emerge for ensuring success (Box 12.2). Many of these elements relate to the timing of a change and the details of managing the change process.

Initiating change before the threat becomes severe

First, rather than reacting to a severe shock and then attempting to change it, the company should initiate change before the threat becomes severe. To do so,

---

2 The role of employee resistance to change is significant enough that it is factored into the organizational development process (Cummings and Worley 1993). For example, one researcher describes the effect on employee morale of adding change efforts to employees' already full plates: "When change continues to be poured into an already full sponge, the consequences are threefold: (a) morale deteriorates; (b) the initiatives that are attempted result in only short-term, superficial applications of the intended goals; and (c) people stop listening to the leaders, who continue to announce changes that never materialize" (Connor 1998). Resistance to change on an individual level involves feelings of loss and anxiety and can be alleviated by intensive communication about the change effort and by encouraging participation by organization members in planning and executing the change (French and Bell 1999; Strebel 1998).

- Initiate change before the threat becomes severe.
- Allow sufficient time for implementation, particularly in relation to core changes.
- Ensure that sufficient resources are committed to the effort.
- Build a broad base of change agents within the company.
- Foster a culture that empowers employees.
- Alter work processes to establish changes.
- Build internal capacity in order to avoid long-term dependence on external entities.
- Seek to support and inform change initiatives through existing professional networks.
- Expand on established routines and competencies.
- Appeal to people's emotions.

Box 12.2 Guidelines for successful organizational change

Sources: Belasco 1990; Haunschild and Miner 1997; Haveman 1992; Kotter and Cohen 2002; Kouzes and Posner 1990; Krackhardt 1990; March 1988, 1991; Pfeffer 1981; Pfeffer and Salancik 1978; Quinn and Spreizter 1997; Thompson 1967

however, involves the continual collection and interpretation of information related to the context in which the company operates. Managers understand the need to scan the environment and interpret information. However, the questions are whether they will pick up on unusual new trends and whether this information will be used by the organization in time. Both elements are essential to stress on a regular basis within companies interested in remaining in the lead.

Allowing sufficient time for implementation

Second, if the change necessitated is a fundamental shift, then one must allow sufficient time for implementation. In addition, it is noteworthy that incremental change to a core organizational technology or structure is more likely to be successful. If the change requires a large deviation from current core competencies, then a gradual, step-by-step approach is most promising.

Ensuring that sufficient resources are committed to the effort

Third, if change initiatives are launched, one must ensure that sufficient resources are committed to the effort. Organizational change is much more likely to be effective if enough time, people, and money are committed to the process. If an organization has no "slack," and is very "lean," then it is unlikely that proposals for change will be accepted, let alone funded. However, if the change proposal is perceived as legitimate by external forces, particularly within broader society, these dynamics can improve the relevance of the effort and allocation of resources.

Building a broad base of change agents within the company

Fourth, one must build a broad base of change agents within the company. The difficulties that leaders may face in implementing change can be diminished by collaborating with a number of other power holders and opinion shapers in the organization. This process, of course, relies on identifying the true power holders in the organization[3] and securing their agreement to pursue the change initiative. This work creates a sound basis for action supported by a shared sense of ownership and greater employee commitment to change initiatives.

Fostering a culture that empowers employees

Fifth, one should foster a culture that empowers employees. Cultures that are rigid and top-down, or "mechanistic," tend to increase managerial control and reduce the ability to take risks and adapt. In contrast, cultures that are "organic," bottom-up and less controlling emphasize risk-taking and personal accountability and have a higher tolerance for mistakes. The more bottom-up cultural characteristics are more conducive to change initiatives (Belasco 1990; Kouzes and Posner 1990; Quinn and Spreizter 1997).

Gathering and applying new information to alter work processes and establish organizational changes

Sixth, altering work processes is a key factor in successful change. These shifts can occur as simply as through introduction of new information, sometimes by new people. As the "organization code" or store of knowledge and routines becomes different, actions are likely to change. However, it is essential to ensure the correct collection and interpretation of information (March 1988, 1991).

Building internal capacity in order to avoid long-term dependence on external entities

Seventh, one needs to build internal capacity so as to avoid long-term dependence on external units that may be eliminated (Pfeffer 1981). If a change requires ongoing input from an external and expensive consultant, the organization will probably view it as less necessary and choose not to retain the consultant. However, if a consultant is used to build internal capacity, the change effort is more likely to succeed. For change to continue, it will have to be deeply seeded internally.

---

3 This identification can be accomplished through basic observation of decision-making processes or even by asking a few questions or taking a small survey (for more information, see Krackhardt 1990).

Seeking to support and inform change initiatives through existing professional networks

Eighth, one should seek to support and inform change initiatives through existing professional networks. Networks, and particularly ties between directors, can be key in spreading change interorganizationally. One study showed how firm managers use the same investment banking firm and mimic the acquisition strategies of other firms to which they are tied through directorships (Haunschild and Miner 1997). The use of such diffusion mechanisms may enhance the probability of successful change. However, it is essential to note that great care must be taken to translate the information to the new context for successful implementation.

Expanding on established routines and competencies

Ninth, one should expand on established routines and competencies. A study of 313 California savings and loan institutions over a period of ten years confirmed that, if a company builds on its established routines and competencies in a core change, it is more likely to survive (Haveman 1992). This approach can be particularly effective when coupled with findings from studies of the strategies that organizations use to manage their environments (Pfeffer and Salancik 1978; Thompson 1967). Strategic tactics—such as first-mover advantage, mergers and acquisitions, and diversification—all increase the chances of organizational survival. This body of work offers evidence that it is possible for an organization to move strategically in response to contextual shifts and be successful.

Appealing to people's emotions

Last, it is essential to appeal to people's emotions (Kotter and Cohen 2002). As organizational change expert and Harvard Business School professor John Kotter and management consultant Dan Cohen explain, in effecting internal change:

> the central issue is never strategy, structure, culture, or systems. All of those elements and others are important. But the core of the matter is always about changing behavior of people, and behavior change happens in highly successful situations mostly by speaking to people's feelings. This is true even in organizations focused on analysis and quantitative measurement, even among people who think of themselves smart in an MBA sense. *In highly successful change efforts, people find ways to help others see the problems or solutions in ways that influence emotions, not just thought* (Kotter and Cohen 2002: x [emphasis added])

Sustainability-focused organizational change

Overall, sustainability concepts offer a new set of issues that have the potential to define, and differentiate, businesses in the coming years. Sustainability-focused organizational change initiatives offer a range of benefits (Box 12.3). The challenge is how to change existing companies and organizations.

Integration of sustainability frameworks, such as The Natural Step, into initiatives aimed at bringing about organizational change offers a number of advantages, including:

- The promotion of cost savings through elimination of waste and increased efficiency in materials and energy use

- The encouragement of innovative thinking about product cycles and new markets

- The establishment of an action-oriented, goal-setting process

- The alignment of the company around changed institutional sets of understanding regarding sustainability

- The fostering of a systems view of the company (i.e. widening the focus from traditional bottom-line concerns)

- Increased morale and motivation, and the enabling of the preliminary attainment of easy and rewarding goals, creating buy-in for continued movements along the path to change

Box 12.3 Benefits of initiatives to bring about sustainability-focused organizational change

The changes that sustainability requires are quite possibly risky as they ultimately will affect the core mission and technology of a company. However, these issues can be mitigated, in the ways suggested above, to facilitate successful organizational change. And not taking action may be the largest risk.

13

Catalyzing action and organizational change

The role of personal and group (re)vitalization in sustainability initiatives

Hilary Bradbury
Case Western Reserve University, Ohio, USA

> The outward work will never be puny if the inner work is great. And the outward work can never be great or even good if the inward one is puny and of little worth.
>
> *Meister Eckhart*[1]

Acting on, and integrating, sustainability concepts into organizations requires attention both to technological issues and to social (or "people") issues. Moving towards sustainability will require significant shifts in technology and organizational coordination. Often, however, considerably more emphasis has been placed on the technological aspects of sustainability. The changes required sometimes sound as if an incomprehensible language must be learned about how to close "technical nutrient loops" or to increase "EER while maintaining BTU."[2] These technical terms can blind us to the even more important issues of human change that lie at the heart of sustainable development.

This chapter reminds those involved in sustainable development that all change must be implemented by people—as individuals, groups, organizations, or societies. Making changes to behavior is rarely easy. Launching initiatives and maintaining momentum is a great challenge. This important "people" side of great breakthroughs is described in the following pages, beginning with the Swedes who

---

1 Quoted in Fox 1994.
2 This translates roughly to mean "How does efficiency increase with energy output staying stable?" (EER is an abbreviation for energy efficiency rating; a BTU is a British thermal unit).

launched The Natural Step and then looking at a US corporate case with many of the same social attributes. Both cases highlight the connections between what sustains people internally and personally with their professional work on sustaining the external, "natural" environment. In addition, both cases vividly illustrate that it is not enough to develop a "right solution" to our sustainability challenges; we must also work out how our individual and organizational cultural behavior can be brought—in a participatory way—into alignment with sustainable development. The chapter shows that there are a range of ways in which this interplay between the internal and external, or personal and professional, can occur and deliver results.

In the next section I describe the work of The Natural Step in Sweden as a particularly powerful approach to integrating sustainability into organizations. The Natural Step combines explicit attention to technical issues with implicit attention to human–social concerns and places. Personal engagement and interpersonal dialog are central to the process. In the second section I focus on a brand-name corporation in the US that changed industry standards by designing a "zero to landfill" manufacturing process. In spite of differences, both cases offer examples of the same phenomenon which establish a strong and explicit connection between internal engagement and engagement in the work of sustainable development. In both cases, personal catalytic events reawakened personal priorities, allowing deep motivation in professional work to be maintained. In the subsequent section I offer some insights for business leaders regarding the crafting of successful change efforts in pursuit of sustainability. Some conclusions are drawn in the final section.

Overview of the early days of The Natural Step in Sweden

The Natural Step in Sweden—more correctly Det Naturliga Steget (DNS)—was founded in 1988 as a non-profit educational network. By 1996, it included approximately 10,000 network members. Founded by Karl-Henrik Robèrt, a leading cancer researcher, efforts initially focused on producing a scientific consensus statement about the most pressing environmental issues in Sweden. Approximately 50 of Sweden's senior scientists were involved, offering input and reading the draft statements. Business leaders agreed to underwrite the costs of disseminating the resulting consensus statement, which was produced as a colorful booklet. The booklet was sent to the entire Swedish population of eight million people in a direct mailing to schools and households. Its reception was celebrated with a televised gala attended by the Swedish King. After its launch, DNS was headquartered in Stockholm with about 20 staffers whose main work consisted of meeting the requests that poured in from all sectors of society for DNS educational presentations.

Robèrt's collaboration with fellow scientists John Holmberg and Karl Erik Eriksson, of Gothenburg University, further honed the scientific underpinnings of DNS. In this collaboration the four system conditions for sustainability were articulated (see Box 13.1), and DNS provided a framework to understand the complex phenomenon of sustainability through attention to human–social issues as well as to environmental issues. Once developed, the four system conditions took center stage as the primary contribution of DNS in helping business and other social institutions to strategize about moving toward greater sustainability.

Building on the original scientific consensus statement, the four system conditions for sustainability of The Natural Step (Det Naturliga Steget [DNS]) were articulated by Karl-Henrik Robèrt and John Holmberg. Working with these conditions, DNS appeared to tackle the complex phenomenon of **sustainability** that requires attention to environmental issues (see conditions 1–3) *as well as* human–social issues (see condition 4). The four system conditions are as follows:

1. In a sustainable society, Nature is not subject to systematically increasing concentrations of substances extracted from the Earth's crust.

2. In a sustainable society, Nature is not subject to systematically increasing concentrations of substances produced by society.

3. In a sustainable society, Nature is not subject to systematically increasing degradation by physical means.

4. In a sustainable society, human needs are met worldwide.

An organization's sustainability objectives are easily linked to these conditions; for example, its ultimate sustainability objectives may be stated as to:

- Eliminate our contribution to systematic increases in concentrations of substances from the Earth's crust

- Eliminate our contribution to systematic increases in concentrations of substances produced by society

- Eliminate our contribution to systematic physical degradation of Nature through over-harvesting, introductions, and other forms of modification

- Contribute as much as we can to the meeting of human needs in our society and worldwide, over and above all the substitution and dematerialization measures taken in meeting the first three objectives.

Finally, guidance is offered on how to put each of the sustainability objectives into practice:

- This means substituting certain minerals that are scarce in Nature with others that are more abundant, using all mined materials efficiently and systematically reducing dependence on fossil fuels.

- This means systematically substituting certain persistent and unnatural compounds with ones that are normally abundant or break down more easily in Nature, and using all substances produced by society efficiently.

- This means drawing resources only from well-managed ecosystems, systematically pursuing the most productive and efficient use both of those resources and land and exercising caution in all kinds of modification of Nature.

- This means using all of our resources efficiently, fairly, and responsibly so that the needs of all people on whom we have an impact, and the future needs of people who are not yet born, stand the best chance of being met.

Box 13.1 The Natural Step: the four system conditions

The clarity and simplicity of the Framework, with its four system conditions, and the way in which to apply them to decision-making, had great appeal. Government and professional networks—such as doctors, engineers, agronomists, and teachers for DNS—formed to see how the Framework might apply to their own professional domain. In turn, these networks enriched the insights and application of the DNS framework through the development of professionally anchored consensus statements. Today, a majority of the Swedish "states" use the framework to inform their governance. In addition, a number of business networks have been established to apply the system conditions. The multinational furniture manufacturer, IKEA, was the first to have all 30,000 employees exposed to the message of DNS. Scandic Hotels, Electrolux, and Swedish McDonald's followed suit. Each company, along with many more to follow, began to use DNS education to shape strategy and help design new products and processes (Bradbury and Clair 1999a; Nattrass and Altomare 1999). Independent studies (Meima 1996) have since shown the influence of these networks and their role in effecting change.

DNS also went global. Autonomous DNS organizations now exist in all continents. A group of respected North American scientists was convened in February 1997 at the Johnson Foundation's Wingspread facilities to examine the validity of the science behind DNS, in general, and the four system conditions, in particular. After two days of conversation, all those present—some of whom are Nobel Laureates known for their work on environmental issues—summarized their findings in a signed statement, agreeing that the principles are based on sound science and provide a "valid approach for addressing the problems [of environmental unsustainability]."[3] They further agreed that the principles are especially useful for the education of non-scientists, because of the accessible formulation. Robèrt has since been awarded the prestigious Blue Planet Prize, a type of environmental Nobel Prize, for his efforts to catalyze this momentum.[4]

Revitalizing personal aspirations for making a difference

In 1996 I conducted interviews with more than 20 DNS founder–leaders. Robèrt, a highly respected cell scientist and practicing cancer physician, expressed his compunction to break with the technical focus of his field and ask bigger questions. He says that he was not just passionate but "obsessed" with educating Swedes about environmental issues:

> When I studied environmental medicine, I was surrounded by scientists who got happy every time they discovered a new toxic pollutant. And later in my career, when I practiced medicine, too many

3   The Natural Step website at www.naturalstep.org.
4   The evolution of DNS has been, of course, much more difficult than a short overview can communicate. It has included Robèrt's personal and DNS organizational embarrassment over a well-publicized scandal in Sweden in which Robèrt was accused (then later acquitted) of embezzling funds. Similarly, the evolution of global momentum has run at different paces as the leaders in various countries have explored different organizational models. Today, organizational learning and DNS organizations continue to flourish in every continent.

colleagues were more interested in marginal improvements to medicines rather than in helping people avoid diseases. This was reflected in funding made available for prevention versus medicine improvement—the ratio was 1:10. I became more and more uninterested in designing ever more elegant medicines. There was a driving force in me, a power and urgency to do something more fundamental.

Robèrt's wife, Rigmor—as famous as her husband, for her work in analytical (Jungian) psychology—offered the following insight about his level of personal engagement:

> I started to understand that something was going on with Kalle [Karl-Henrik] as I listened to the dreams he was recounting. He was having amazing, quite elaborate dreams. When men are becoming creative they often have such dreams.

DNS had a founder with a public face, one internally driven to discover and do "the right thing." He communicated his sincerity and passion both explicitly and implicitly. Many others signed on to the issues and cause to which he directed attention. His engagement was infectious. He demonstrated the importance of "emotional intelligence," a capacity to resonate energy and enthusiasm by connecting with people by means of empathy and self-awareness (Goleman *et al.* 2002).

Hans Dahlberg, then leader of a large insurance company, stepped up as a leading financial sponsor. He pledged a considerable amount of money after his first meeting with Robèrt to be used for promoting DNS's approach to sustainable development. Dahlberg himself had long been concerned with environmental issues. He also wanted his company to regain a leadership position with regard to the environmental agenda given its commitment to customer well-being, which the company defined holistically. Dahlberg was mildly impressed that Robèrt had gone through his secretary for a meeting and was even more impressed with his scientific credentials and his support for scientific colleagues (who are trained to disagree rather than to reach consensus). Most of all, perhaps, he was impressed by Robèrt's capacity for articulating the issues clearly and with passion. Given his strategy to define concern for customer well-being broadly, he was happy to find someone as credible as Robèrt to help sell his message. He told me simply, "I was determined that Kalle should succeed."

In supporting Robèrt's work with DNS, Dahlberg was, in effect, revitalizing his own passion for environmental issues along with revitalizing the reputation and purview of his company. On Dahlberg's request, Robèrt was to meet Per Uno Alm (known as PUA) for help with the business and organizational aspects of DNS development.

PUA had worked his way through mainstream Swedish business from a working-class background to become a very successful organizational consultant. His practice was oriented to advising large companies, with their paralyzing bureaucratic style, to move beyond the inertia that their structure engendered. At first, PUA had no particular interest in issues of environmental sustainability and no real desire to meet Robèrt. He explains how he overcame his initial lack of interest during his first meeting with Robèrt:

> I found myself surprised at how articulate, inspirational, and sincere
> Kalle was. I saw that with Kalle in the public eye there was at least a
> chance of overcoming the perennial problem of the environmental
> movement, full as it is with so many well-meaning people who just
> instill such doom and gloom that the ordinary person is just para-
> lyzed. My reluctance lessened, but I would have stipulations. Kalle
> would have to be the public face of this movement. In effect, he
> would have to give up his private life for quite some time.

PUA brought his theory of organizational flexibility to DNS and pushed to drive
DNS to serve its mission rather than to grow itself as an organization. He explained
his strategy:

> I was willing to work if DNS would set to appealing to large but diverse
> portions of society. I was willing to see if we could get people to
> support us, not directly but by themselves getting the idea of what
> needed to be done inside themselves. From there comes so much
> energy. There is no limit to it really.

With PUA's commitment to having only a small staff and a flat, flexible
infrastructure he set the scene for a decentralized network. The network was ener-
gized by people internally driven to make a contribution within their own domain
of influence and motivated by a personal sense of connection to the issue of
sustainability. With PUA, a board of business advisors was created. These business
leaders were willing to offer their business acumen to help DNS develop strategy.
Over and over in interviews I was surprised by the depth, breadth, and commitment evident in the founding leaders' lives. All were extraordinary in their demonstration of "walking the talk." There was the former executive, who had acted as
chief executive officer (CEO) of a number of Sweden's largest businesses, who
traveled by bus rather than pollute the air with unnecessary car emissions. A short
time before our interview he had been diagnosed with cancer and explained that
he was now more determined than ever to fully commit his remaining time to the
cause of environmental sustainability.

Stories such as these are numerous and compelling. They vividly demonstrated
that what was sown in DNS was a personal commitment to issues of sustainability
that revitalized people. The individuals who were organizational leaders, in turn,
revitalized their organizations. This revitalization found expression in supporting
DNS learning-oriented networks. Rather than following a charismatic leader,
people were following their own deepest commitment, grateful for the direction of
resources that Robèrt inspired and fostered.

Revitalizing the capacity of groups to think together

DNS is based on a particular set of normative methods. Specifically, DNS methods
are grounded in a belief that the best way to achieve sustainability—as indicated
by the four system conditions—is through consensus-building and dialog, which
in turn helps to attain one's partners' commitment to creating a sustainable
society. The approach seeks to avoid "cookie-cutter" approaches to implementation by facilitating DNS and partners to think together by using the same frame of

reference. In turn, this method leads to an open system of change efforts designed by partners and elaborated through network-building across many sectors of society.

Together, these methods allow for a reawakening of an organization's and/or a group's capacity to think together. This process expands the group's behavior repertoire, freeing people from getting stuck in a debate and discussion mode in which new ideas are met with criticism and dismissal before adequate exploration.

Consensus-building: the "yes–and" approach

In the business arena specifically,[5] DNS methods seek to affirm a businessperson's experiences and concerns through a process of consensus-building and dialog. Those trained in the science that underpins the work of DNS seek points of agreement between the views of business partners and those expressed in the principles of sustainability. This method of conversing is called the "yes–and" approach. Robèrt himself, after what he explains were many false starts as a younger, less "agreeable" man, helped foster the approach. For example, a concerned business executive might say:

> My organization is totally dependent on fossil fuels for energy, so the system conditions are useless to me.

A DNS trainer, using the "yes–and" approach, might reply:

> Yes, you are currently dependent on fossil fuels, which are in finite supply and perhaps liable to be regulated because of concerns over global climate change. And, yes, this dependence may even make your organization economically unviable over time. Perhaps you might seek alternatives now while there is still time to get an advantage over those who are not concerned with sustainable development.

Including a partner's knowledge and creativity in strategizing

Consensus-seeking as it is practiced by DNS has a goal of promoting the discovery of common ground. When it works well, radical breakthroughs in thinking become possible and allow for new conceptualizations of business to be perceived. One of many examples of how this can help organizations transform themselves is the DNS effect on OK Petroleum. OK (pronounced "o-ko") was a Swedish oil company which has since merged with another firm. In the late 1980s Robèrt was invited to speak to the management team. Reportedly, an OK participant suggested it would be wise to remove lead from petrol, as it is violating system condition number 1. Another replied that the entire extractive business violates system condition number 1. The first person clarified his point:

---

5   Because I am a scholar of management I focused on the reciprocal influence of DNS and businesspeople. This is but one perspective on DNS. DNS influence on governance and on the development of eco-communities is equally profound.

> We are not supposed to do everything overnight. It would be a smart move [to remove lead from petrol] now as it is a "low-hanging fruit" and there is the possibility and already the market demand. If the market does shift, we are poised for other changes.

OK proceeded to produce what was reported to be the world's cleanest gasoline, "New Optima." Profit from New Optima—and from the positive public relations on its introduction—was reinvested in biofuel production. According to corporate officials, after executives became conversant with DNS framework they were able to reconceive their organization as an energy provider rather than simply as an oil supplier. The company even turned to the government and successfully convinced policy-makers to add an extra tax on its competitors' more-polluting fossil fuels.

Professional networks: not a "cookie-cutter" approach

As DNS flourished in Sweden, professional networks sought to apply DNS principles. In keeping with PUA's paradoxical vision of combining a strong public persona as leader with a decentralized organization of energetic people seeking to do "good work," these networks experienced the challenge of bringing motivated people together to develop consensus. Once motivated people are gathered together, however, there is no guarantee that they can work or take part in dialog that well.

I interviewed one of the network leaders who facilitated a consensus-building process. She illustrated to me the learning that took place about the dialog process itself:

> I slowly realized I was in a group of (well-known) scientists who had been in disagreement for decades. No one was taking the role of discussion leader. Two people chose to leave the group after our first meeting: one because as a researcher he didn't believe scientists should seek consensus. He thought we should always debate. The other believed that biotechnology would solve all our problems, so why discuss.

This opening meeting of a professional group suggested the typical approach to sustainability that exists in many arenas of life. It can be very challenging to actually have a conversation that builds on each other's ideas and generates completely new perspectives on old problems. Some people look to purely technical solutions "out there" to fix everything. Generally, capacity for conversation and thinking together, rather than mere debate, is low even among (or perhaps especially among?) the most highly educated.

The facilitator of the agronomy consensus-building process, for example, decided to hold a number of smaller meetings among individuals who disagreed on specific issues, rather than to continue convening large sessions. As a result, over nine months, better-quality dialog emerged. This agronomy consensus facilitator asserted:

> Some people were transformed by the process. The frequent meetings and the feeling of having a common task made it possible. The best outcome was unimaginable at the start. A well-known conven-

tional agronomist [i.e. one who promotes use of chemical fertilizers] went to a well-known organic agronomist [i.e. one willing to work only with the natural processes of pest resistance] and asked for a recommendation to work on an organic farm! It helped that the organic scientist had been very diplomatic in her style within the group.

In retrospect, her recommendations for consensus-building differ a little from Robèrt's. She suggests the importance of taking disagreements seriously and making them clear, but not focusing on the differences. Moreover, all people involved with DNS process agree on the importance of respectful interaction or, as Robèrt puts it, of "not violating the other person's sense of dignity." The revitalization of groups is in large part the revitalization of our capacity to speak with each other in a civil way, in spite of our possibly huge philosophical differences.

Reborn in the USA: a different context for personal and group revitalization

The work and principles of DNS informed, in part,[6] an electronics design initiative focused on "zero to landfill" principles within a US-based brand-name corporation, OCC.[7] In the 1990s, OCC launched a new line of fully digitalized office machines reported to be its largest "clean-sheet" project ever undertaken, at a cost of US$500 million dollars. Insiders referred to the development of these new items as the Streamline project. Today, these machines are 98% recyclable and over 90% remanufacturable. The product design involved many innovations inspired by concern for conservation of habitat and followed the maxim: "zero to landfill." The motto referred to the elimination of waste not only among the components and machines themselves but also among all the systems involved in the operation and servicing of the family of new machines. Wanting to hear what the project members' experience of the project was, I arranged to interview 30 participants drawn from a cross-section of everyone involved in the project. The interviews averaged around 90 minutes and included a brief survey instrument asking people to note their level of engagement in the project using a scale of 1–4.

The redesign project lasted about seven years and involved over 400 engineers. On the whole, project members reported being "reawakened," "rebalanced," "released," and "refreshed" by their work on Streamline. By means of the four-point-scale survey instrument, the average degree of engagement was 3.62 in the early stages and 3.48 at the finishing stages of the seven-year project. One engineer captured the sense of contribution as she explained the relief that comes from

6   As perhaps in all complex organizations there is a mix of approaches, ideas, and tentative solutions when starting a new project. In this case the leaders were informed by the work of DNS but did not undertake to formally train the employees in the system conditions. Nor indeed did it undertake to educate the project teams within any particular environmental or sustainability decision-making frameworks.

7   Pseudonyms have been used to protect the identity of the corporation and the project.

working on a project such as Streamline that allowed her to feel that her work could be as important as she had imagined as a younger woman:

> Before I started on the Streamline project I had been saying to my husband, "I went to school to do this: make these stinking machines!!" It felt like a big let-down from when I was starting out after college and had so wanted to make a great contribution to the world. But then, once on Streamline, there was a shift for me, not just on a work level, but on a personal level. I finally came to a conclusion about what I could do to make a difference here. I would have an impact on industry standards and on the world my kids would inherit. I began to feel very committed, responsible, engaged.

Vision quest: opportunity for rediscovering personal priorities

The experience of deep engagement that I came to uncover in my interviews and survey was catalyzed by the opportunity to partake of a "vision quest," which is a Native American practice of spending at least 24 hours alone, fasting, in a wilderness area. People's experiences are then shared immediately afterwards with a group of other "questers." The vision quest is only one, albeit powerful, method for getting in touch with personal priorities, much as the leaders of DNS had reconnected with their internal drive during their efforts to make a difference.

The decision to offer a vision quest was somewhat accidental and certainly unusual. The chief engineer's daughter—an environmentalist, who was working with environmental educators in New Mexico—had inspired the choice. The chief engineer knew it was a controversial proposition because the budget was tight. He also realized that he was offering an experience that was, as others succinctly expressed, "downright weird." On some deeper level, though, he also knew that they needed to break away from the typical practices associated with team-building, such as ropes courses. He wanted to allow for some "out of the box" experience in the hopes of catalyzing this new initiative. The decision to push for the vision quest reflected the same fresh way of thinking or seeing that PUA had stressed as he named the importance of "always being able to see new possibilities." The vision quest along with other efforts to inspire people to contribute their best are innovations in creating new contexts within which people can be creative.

Of the approximately two-thirds of the team that chose to participate, a striking number—a large majority—reported being profoundly changed. For almost all who went, this event was the first opportunity to hear their own voice in an area where "distractions" were elemental. It became an experience of personal rediscovery. A marketing manager remarked:

> I had simply never been alone a whole 24 hours like that, ever. You start hearing your inner voice, which you don't hear when you're totally wrapped in everything, consumed and bombarded by stimulation. By about five in the morning I was writing like crazy in my journal. That was the most refreshing experience. Perhaps secondary to the purpose they sent us!

A senior engineer, who was in his fifties, describes the profound change that has permeated his life ever since:

> I went on the vision quest very left-brained and came out right-brained . . . It's because I looked at me and saw how much of the world I had been missing with my logical engineer mind.[8]

Of course not everyone embraced the unusual experience. Two of the 22 interviewees did not find it to be so positive an experience. No one, however, found that the overall trip away had been a waste. As one of the two men, also in his fifties, explained:

> This vision quest, I just didn't get it. No food; I had to sleep outside; I come back and people are crying, telling personal stories that really I don't want to hear grown men tell. Yea, sorry, no buy-in from me on that one.
>
> The days weren't a complete waste, though. I did like the time of learning about the ecology. I took a lot from that, seeing all the connections of the plants . . . I am pretty conscientious about recycling since then and it influenced my work on Streamline quite a bit.

About a third of the team members decided not to go on the vision quest. Most explained that they were too busy with "real work;" some had family obligations. A small group found the idea of a vision quest somehow repugnant, as one who had refused to go on the vision quest explained:

> That vision quest stuff was a bunch of crap. If you [spoken to me, the interviewer] are so impressionable like the ones who went on it, you'll believe it made a big difference. [The trainers] were a bunch of old hippies who made a lot of money off that crap.

Nonetheless, for the majority of the two-thirds who did go, the vision quest offered refreshment. People's recollections even after five years were surprisingly vital. An engineer said:

> What stands out for me overall as personally fulfilling was the vision quest. It was a time to think about the right thing to do, when normally we rush so quickly to get things done, we forget. It was an opportunity to think about who you are and where you want to go. I felt like a million bucks when I came back. I had let go of some internal problems; really they were gone.

Team-building among workers of different pay or status levels was also facilitated. This cross-functional, flat, team effort adds a participatory approach to

---

8   He continued with a reference to "Native American things" he recalled from his childhood. He'd been educated as a child in classrooms that were composed of a majority of Native Americans—a fact he had forgotten until the vision quest: "And we ate vegetarian food, which I still seek out. And the other Native American things I have come back to now. I'm weird now you see! No doubt about it, my wife says I am a goddamned idiot. I could tell the chief engineer I love him, cause it's true, though he'd run the other way."

sustainability challenges that appears both to be necessary and appropriate.[9] Sustainable development presents us with a systemic and messy challenge because so many elements of sustainability are connected and interdependent; therefore, the input from all parts of a system may be particularly important. The cross-fertilization at OCC, made possible by the unusual circumstances of the vision quest, allowed for new conversations to happen, as described by a female part-time clerk:

> It was a unique experience. I really bonded with people I would never have spent time with. We still have lunch, myself and the five [senior] guys I met there.

Following the vision quest, participants relayed that they formed "an oasis" for each other, so that they could revitalize the transformative experience when back in the ordinary world of design and manufacturing. This group grew over the early years, when as many as two-thirds of the Streamline project staff went on vision quests and a number of practices from the vision quest experience were brought back to project headquarters to keep the spirit alive. For example, the use of a "talking stick" was recalled as significant during team meetings, so that more of a dialogic atmosphere could replace debates and grandstanding.

Committing to "zero to landfill"

On all vision-quest experiences the employees were escorted to a landfill as part of the environmental education. Although the four system conditions of DNS informed the Streamline process—through being incorporated into the engineering specifications for material acquisition decisions—the Streamline project community came up with its own central articulation of how loops should be closed. It became encapsulated in their maxim, "zero to landfill," which was articulated on the very first trip to which the small band of managers had gone. A reportedly serendipitous event had occurred at that first meeting. A machine from the previous major project line of OCC was seen sitting in the pile of rubbish. It was in this milieu that the slogan "zero to landfill" had been coined as an aspiration by the team. This motto was later revised to read "zero to landfill for our children."

The chief engineer explained that though he was very happy with this logo, he had not been an instigator, stating he "needed people to get on board the environmental cause of their own accord, or it would never happen." Most responded well, often with a variation that suggested the project was a "win–win" situation. One person summarized many people's sentiments, stating, "I realized that Streamline would be good for people, the culture, and for Nature." The top executive, to whom the chief engineer reported, explained: "people have got to internalize environmental leadership, it's got to be in the bones; you can't legislate it. People have to feel it and know they want it." After the vision quest, concern with environmental

---

9   For example, Scandic Hotels, a Scandinavian Hotel chain, first learned about DNS in the late 1980s and was inspired to pioneer the "green hotel room." The company found that many of its most effective cost-saving ideas came from the chambermaids, who saw what unnecessary costs are incurred with laundering barely used linens and replacing barely used bathroom toiletries.

issues seemed to be "in the bones." Or, as PUA once said, the employees had "got the idea of what needs to be done inside themselves."

Seeing personal sacrifice as worthwhile

Interviews with OCC staff revealed that people saw personal sacrifices related to their sustainability work as part of a higher purpose, as did the leaders of DNS. Thus commitment to purpose overrode, even negated, personal sacrifice while at the same time clarifying what was truly important.

Many of the engineers involved with the project reported working without overtime and losing vacations. A story that explains one person's sense of priorities on Streamline was shared relating to (re)considering priorities. The interviewee worked on the Streamline factory floor:

> Streamline caused my divorce. My wife divorced me and said it was because of the time I spent here. Now that I am off the project she has remarried me. I got my family back [. . . and] yes, I would do it again. [Interviewer: Really?!] Yes, I would, but I would come in at 3 am and not take the time away from my family like I did.
>
> Yes, it was worth the time I devoted to it. I could say that because I met my objectives, but it's really about self-satisfaction. My take is you don't work for anybody but yourself. I don't care if somebody else is paying you or not.

Indeed, there is not a clear split between life and work and so perhaps the need for balance falls into abeyance. When asked about the impact on family life and sacrifices beyond just what one was willing to accept personally, another person reported:

> I sacrificed a lot of family time, but in a funny way I am better now as a family man; more there when I am there. Before I was burned out going home; on Streamline I was awake and alive.

Enhancement of stakeholder relationships

The quality of relationships and capacity for dialog among the project team members and broader stakeholder groups, such as suppliers, became generally richer. The vision quest also helped support those with the unenviable task of explaining the radical redesign to suppliers, internal and external, all of whom were used to a more traditional, environmentally polluting process.

One participant recalled internal suppliers (inside OCC but outside Streamline) who simply laughed at the notion of zero waste and replied to the request for new supplies with "Yea, right; beam me up Scotty!" Demonstrating success with the new innovations (in an engineering "show me" culture) did much, over time, to quell these initial doubts.

Sensitivity to a broader environment

It was agreed by all, including the most unengaged, that sustainability objectives remained central throughout the project. A small number of interviewees complained that the focus on sustainability objectives was a waste of "precious resources"—by which they meant money—and that cutting corners or being less purist would have been better—by which they meant "immediately profitable." The majority, however, strongly felt that the sustainability objectives were a very good idea because sustainability not only addressed the environment but also actually became a driver of employee engagement.

Most importantly, it was clear that individual predilections were not the final arbiters of whether or not sustainability objectives were taken seriously. Rather, sustainability was written into all product and process specifications and therefore simply had to be met. This integration into the specifications was described as an expression of the will of the group, especially since the vision-quest experience:

> [The sustainability objective] drove a lot of our creative juices, knowing the impact this product would have on the environment.
>
> The environmental stuff is all over the specs, and the ability to make money at it. It's throughout design specs because it relates to the equation I put together based on environmentally friendly indices [from the 1992 output of the United Nations Conference on Environment and Development, on Agenda 21]. We have environmentally friendly indices and you can change the weighting factors. See, the recyclability of this little [machine] you can use at home is different than the big machine like I am working on now. That's where you can do remanufacturing. That little one you must dispose of; recyclability is more important and so I must change the factors and look at the material choices because you would make different material choices.
>
> I can show you product specs where we put the environmental issues into the specs and that had never been done before. The environmental side of it *must* go into the specs, into the goals. By getting the management to sign so we can say "you signed that!".

Drawing the connections

The OCC case illustrates important phenomena that are also present within the dynamics among DNS leaders. Both cases revealed personal reawakening within a context of concern for the natural environment and an increase in awareness of how natural systems work and one's own place within these systems. In addition, a sense of community with like-minded people emerged in both contexts and combined with a commitment to make a difference. Even in this commitment to make a difference, the cases are similar in their effort to develop and share common language within a group.

Sustained and passionate engagement in difficult organizational undertakings is a relatively rare thing.[10] This chapter has nonetheless offered two cases of deep engagement in transformational work of organizational change aimed at sustainable development. Hearing Karl-Henrik Robèrt speak is to experience passionate engagement in action. Over the years a group of equally committed and engaged people has been galvanized to take DNS work and apply it more broadly. There was a similar sustained passionate engagement in the Streamline project that lasted over seven years. The chief engineer empowered his staff to find their point of personal engagement and bring their creativity to the design of a completely new product system. For other companies engaged with change processes, the question is simple: how can such engagement be replicated in other contexts?

The premise of this chapter is that sustainability initiatives must be recognized as a process that is as equally about people as it is about scientific or technological issues. The cases highlight the importance of:

- Activating personal engagement

- Fostering systems thinking through the establishment of concrete human pathways through complex technological systems

- Creating a capacity for dialog within the team

Of course, any general insights about employee engagement with sustainability must be naturalized within a particular corporate or organizational culture. In highlighting these three issues (personal engagement, human systems thinking, and team dialog) this chapter stresses the need to connect the internal and external worlds of sustainability. Together these linkages operate as the core ingredients for coordinating the cultural change needed to achieve the necessary breakthroughs to allow for sustained organizational change. Such change is, in turn, necessary for sustainable development.

To have an impact, systems thinking must quickly be made meaningful on a human and a personal level. Team dialog, if it is to continue over time, must be made up of truly engaged personnel. Similarly, the foundation of a better external world always resides with engaged individuals. Although these issues are inseparable in practice, the following implementation pointers separate them to allow for adaptations that permit the "naturalization" of a company-specific approach.

In launching efforts to bring about sustainability-oriented change in an organization, a leader can examine current practices to build on what works. The practical implications include the need to:

- Allow people to find a specifically personal pathway that engages them fully in the work of sustainable development

- Facilitate the development of a community of like-minded people anchored in a capacity for team dialog

10 Regular national surveys suggest that a large majority of people are really not that engaged in their daily work: only 26% of employees report themselves as being "engaged;" 55% report themselves as "not engaged;" and 19% as "disengaged" (Tritch 2001).

● Increase the awareness of how natural systems work and help people understand linkages within those systems; systems thinking tools, such as the four system conditions, are especially helpful here

These guidelines, further developed below, are summarized in Tables 13.1[a]–13[c]

Helping others find a personal pathway through a change

Allowing people to find a specifically personal pathway that engages them fully in the work of sustainable development requires that a leader pay ongoing attention to the human–organizational aspects of sustainability (see Table 13.1[a]). Examination of current management practices may serve to clarify which practices support the change management required for innovations in support of sustainable development.

Allowing people to find a specifically personal pathway that engages them fully in the work of sustainable development means allowing people to become conscious of what sustains their internal personal engagement with their work. Leaders are therefore encouraged to create an opportunity, such as a vision quest, in which employees can consider what deeply engages them. Allowing employees to articulate the connection between what is important in sustaining their lives and what is important for sustaining the company over the long haul generates a "win–win" situation in which employees and their company can flourish.

Creating a community of like-minded people

Facilitating the development of a community of like-minded people anchored in a capacity for team dialog implies a need for team building and assistance through facilitation (see Table 13.1[b]). Team building is certainly not a novel practice in business. In this era of self-managed teams, the work to facilitate the emotional intelligence and so-called "soft skills" that teams need is worth the investment. Focusing on how to be in dialog with each other is crucial. Moreover, stretching beyond the known to "out of the box" preparation for team members is likely to be required if one truly values a break with the past, which is so often essential in integrating sustainability concepts within company practices. Again, examination of current practices may serve to clarify what can be built on and what needs to be created from scratch. Here, the future design in Table 13.1[b] contains blank space in keeping with the admonition that a "one size fits all" approach must be replaced with an "indigenous" sense of what can work in distinct companies.

Increasing people's awareness of how natural systems work

Increasing the awareness of how natural systems work, especially in a way that allows people to understand linkages within those systems, is very important. Systems thinking tools, such as the four system conditions, are especially helpful (see Table 13.1[c]). However, as we have seen above in the Streamline case, the simpler motto of "zero to landfill for our children" is a homemade application of the same fundamental insight that closed-loop, system thinking is required to allow

Examining current practices	*Designing future practices*
[a] Helping others to find a personal pathway	
Examine the "soundbites" you most often use to describe the sustainability issues on which you want people to focus. For example, do you talk a lot about "increasing EER while maintaining BTU"?	Introduce the problem by describing a human pathway through the technical problems. For example, tell a real story about technology that features people getting the desired results, or talk about legacy issues, such as the wish to create a better world for your employees' children.
Reflect on who is in your "inner circle:" that is, who do you regularly consult with in your day-to-day operations?	If you are not already doing so, talk more with the "people people" in your company—not only those trained in organizational development and human resources but also the opinion leaders whose actions people emulate. Accept that *people* make change happen (or slow down or prevent that change). Keep up a dialog with all involved.
List the stakeholder groups with which you regularly keep in touch. Complete a "back of the envelope" stakeholder map to notice who you systematically forget.	Convene employee groups—remember that employees often represent many stakeholder groups. In addition to being employees, these people are often community members, relatives of customers and suppliers, parents of the future generation, and so on.
What personal preparation is afforded those employees who are mandated to tackle sustainability issues? Is it just another project?	Assume that sustainability touches people more deeply than, for example, a TQM program. Use this insight as a win–win strategy to allow employees to align their personal and work lives more deeply.
What team-building exercises do you use? Would it be effective to use new methods to reflect an expectation of new insights and breakthroughs?	Embrace anxiety and fears about constraints, ignore the overly rational voices on your team and invite the use of some "out of the box" approach to employee preparation for this work.

BTU: British thermal unit   EER: energy efficiency rating   TQM: total quality management

Table 13.1 Guidelines for facilitating organizational change towards sustainability: examining current practices and designing practices for the future in order to [a] help others to find a personal pathway, [b] create a community of like-minded people, and [c] increase people's awareness of how natural systems work (continued over)

Examining current practices	Designing future practices
[b] Creating a community of like-minded people	
Jot down ten words to describe the chemistry of the participants in the last three meetings you attended. How much fun was there? How much did people build on each others' ideas? How much did you want to get away from the meeting because of frustrations or other negative feelings?	
What kind of conversational skills get rewarded (or trampled) in your company culture?	
Time how long a new idea lasts in a conversation before someone says how impossible it is. A few seconds? A few minutes? How many good ideas survive in your meetings?	
[c] Increasing people's awareness of how natural systems work	
Invite employees to make a list of the materials they use every day that are products of mining the Earth's crust (e.g. metals, fuels, and other minerals).	Identify ways that your organization can systematically decrease its dependence on these materials.
Invite employees to make a list of the synthetic, toxic, persistent, and bioaccumulative substances on which your organization is dependent (e.g. human-made plastics and chemical compounds).	Identify ways that your organization can systematically decrease its dependence on toxic, persistent, and bioaccumulative substances.
Invite employees to make a list of organizational activities that encroach on natural systems that are productive (e.g. the asphalting of green spaces; over-fishing).	Identify ways that your organization can systematically decrease its economic dependence on those activities that encroach on productive parts of Nature.
Invite employees to make a list of how the organization depends on resources in ways that are out of proportion to their added (human) value (e.g. the sending of products that could be recycled to landfill; human resource policies that fail to sustain or help regeneration of human creativity).	Identify ways that your organization can systematically decrease use of resources that decrease rather than add human value.

Note: the blank spaces in part [b] are a reminder that a "one size fits all" approach must be replaced with an "indigenous" sense of what can work in distinct companies; the four sets of suggestions in part [c] are based on the four system conditions of The Natural Step (see Box 13.1).

Table 13.1 (continued)

the average employee (engineer or not) to sustain a systems approach. Applying the principles of sustainability can also be a way to align employee motivation.

Systems thinking using the system conditions articulated by DNS is perhaps best when it allows people to articulate criteria to which all can contribute for designing the future. The suggestions in Table 3.1[c] are intended to help make the system conditions meaningful at a human level.

Conclusions

In this chapter I have focused on putting the people back into our thinking about sustainable development and sustainability-oriented organizational change. This focus is important, perhaps crucial, to complement an overly technological consideration of the issues associated with sustainable development. It is the people and the human–organizational elements of a business that are more likely to make or break the success of sustainability projects. Getting the technology issues right is itself daunting, but leaders must be careful not to ignore the messier and possibly more daunting issues associated with allowing people in an organization to generate the necessary innovations. The issues highlighted are all efforts to "put the people back in the system."

Both case studies suggest a correlation between these people factors and the success of processes on the path to sustainable development, including:

- The necessity of drawing human pathways through all abstract systems, thereby making these systems real enough for people to be able to locate the arena in which they can make a personal contribution to sustainable development

- Allowing people to connect internal and external worlds so that the personal energy reserved for what people really care about can be used, in "win–win" fashion, to energize a company's or organization's work

- Facilitating better teamwork and more generally realizing the importance of emotional intelligence if people are to work well together

- Fostering a workplace that reflects an understanding that the foundation of all innovation and breakthroughs is engaged individuals

The medieval poet Meister Eckhart reminds us that our outer and inner work is interconnected. To state again his words quoted at the top of this chapter:

> the outward work will never be puny if the inner work is great. And the outward work can never be great or even good if the inward one is puny and of little worth (quoted in Fox 1994).

The work of sustainable development requires vital men and women making their best contributions, fueled by an inner drive. Certainly, the future of our children's children depends on these efforts.

14
Conclusion
A shift towards sustainability within companies and the financial services sector

Sissel Waage
The Natural Step, California, USA

> Surprise is always relative, which explains why whenever something unexpected befalls us, there is always someone who "saw it coming."
>
> *Michael Thompson*[1]

It is no longer unusual to hear assertions that ecological and social factors affect business and the bottom line. Clear testaments to this reality include insurance companies' mounting claims as a result of natural disasters and retail companies' problems following workers' rights violations or severe ecological impacts. The growing awareness of how sustainability issues impact corporate revenues is enabling businesspeople to see that ecological and social factors affect their enterprises and the economy. The question is no longer *if* sustainability is relevant to business, but *when* recognition will translate into action and *how* fundamental changes will occur within companies' core strategies and operations.

Together, the cases in this book illustrate that sustainability is permeating many economic sectors and a wide range of businesses. Ecological and social issues are no longer being explored only when a firm is faced with PR debacles or rapid regulatory change. Now, sustainability-focused action is occurring within the private sector for a range of reasons as diverse as the players.

For Hewlett Packard, dematerialization is an essential step in saving costs, improving products, and exploring alternative business models. For Norm Thompson, changing the entire corporate culture is an effort to introduce "seamlessness" in who they are as people and what they do in their work (Senge and Carstedt

---

1 Quoted in Janssen 2002: 241.

2001). For the small, rural businesses in the Pacific Northwest, creating a collaborative marketing model—based on integrating ecological, social, and economic concerns and practices—offers a clear way to build viable businesses. For Verdant Power, developing a new sustainability-focused enterprise is simply intelligent entrepreneurship, particularly given the growing need for energy and the increasing concern about climate change. For the Dow Jones Sustainability Index, valuing sustainability is critical to more accurately analysing and recognizing risks and opportunities within existing business models. For Shorebank Enterprise Pacific, establishing a new kind of bank and offering credit enables the sustainability-focused enterprise approach to spread. And, finally, for the Global Reporting Initiative, forming a new set of conversations about corporate accountability and reporting is an essential element of defining new practices within the private sector.

None of these cases shows that action has to emerge from duress attributable to regulatory change or activist pressure. Sustainability-informed action simply makes sense.

Innovation is becoming a key driver of this shift. It is being spurred by visionary goals about what business can become and how it is tightly linked to ecological dynamics and social relations. As others have noted, the fusion of sustainability concepts into business offers an opportunity for the "creative destruction" of current models in response to human needs and desires (e.g. see Hart and Milstein 1999). Former General Electric chief executive officer (CEO) Jack Welch explained this level of innovation and the need for "stretch targets:"

> If you *do* know how to get there, it's not a stretch target . . . The CEO of Yokogawa, our Japanese partner in the medical-systems business, calls this concept "bullet-train thinking." That is, if you want a 10-mile-per-hour increase in train speed, you tinker with horsepower, but if you want to *double* its speed, you have to break out of both conventional thinking *and* conventional performance expectations (Welch 1993, quoted in Gupta and Govindarajan 2000: 78).

In this sense, sustainability inspires, and requires, innovation of new proportions within business. It demands a *new* kind of sustainability-oriented "bullet train thinking."

This type of thinking and innovating is based on the non-synchronous leaps of the "Galileos" of the world. It necessitates the collaborative systems-based work of "ant colonies" and leadership infused with the compassion and vision that characterized the efforts of Gandhi.

All these attributes are essential for establishing new, sustainable businesses and economies. The exact pace of the changes are unknown and the specific actions of companies are still emerging. The ability, or inability, to fully "retrofit" large, modern corporations to reflect principles of sustainability has yet to be proven. What is clear, however, is that shifts are occurring and early movers are exploring and defining this new business landscape.

Bibliography

Abramovitz, J. (2001) *Unnatural Disasters* (Washington, DC: Worldwatch Institute, www. worldwatch.org/pubs/paper/158facts.html).

AEI (Alliance for Environmental Innovation) (1999) *Greener Catalogs* (Boston, MA: AEI, Environmental Defense).

Albion, M. (1996) *The Future of Socially Responsible Business: MBA Students Speak Out* (San Francisco: Students for Responsible Business).

Allenby, B., and D. Richards (eds.) (1994) *The Greening of Industrial Ecosystems* (Washington, DC: National Academy of Engineering, National Academy Press).

—— and W. Cooper (1994) "Understanding Industrial Ecology from a Biological Systems Perspective," *Total Quality Environmental Management*, Spring 1994: 343-54.

Alsop, R. (2001) "Corporations Still Put Profits First, But Social Concerns Gain Ground," *Wall Street Journal*, October 20th, 2001: B12.

Ameer, P., S. Feldman, and P. Soyka (1996) *Does Improving a Firm's Environmental Management System and Environmental Performance Result in a Higher Stock Price?* (report on behalf of IFC Kaiser, November 1996).

Anderson, D., and L. Anderson (2001) *Beyond Change Management: Advanced Strategies for Today's Transformational Leaders* (San Francisco: Jossey-Bass).

Anderson, R. (1999) *Mid-course Correction. Toward a Sustainable Enterprise: The Interface Model* (White River Junction, VT: Chelsea Green).

Annighofer, F. (1997) "Insurers and Sustainable Development," *Environmental Strategy Europe* (London: Campden Publishing).

Arrow, K., B. Bolin, R. Costanza, P. Dasgupta, *et al.* (1995) "Economic Growth, Carrying Capacity, and the Environment," *Science* 268: 520-21.

ASTO (Australian Senate Table Office) (2001) *Senate Bills List 2001*: 40.

AtKisson, A. (1999) *Believing Cassandra* (White River Junction, VT: Chelsea Green).

Augustine, N. (1998) "Reshaping an Industry," *Harvard Business Review on Change* (Boston, MA: Harvard Business School Press): 159-87.

Ayres, R.U. (1989) "Industrial Metabolism," in *Technology and Environment* (Washington, DC: National Academy Press): 23-49.

Azar, C., J. Holmberg, and K. Lindgren (1995) "Socio-ecological Indicators for Sustainability," *Ecological Economics* 18: 89-112.

Baker Fox, A. (1995) "Environment and Trade: The NAFTA Case," *Political Science Quarterly* 110.1: 49-68.

Barczak, G., C. Smith, and D. Wilemon (1987) "Managing Large-scale Organization Change," *Organizational Dynamics* 23-35.

Bayne, N. (2000) "Why Did Seattle Fail? Globalization and the Politics of Trade," *Government and Opposition* 35.2: 131-51.

Beckhard, R., and W. Pritchard (1993) *Changing the Essence* (San Francisco: Jossey-Bass).

Belasco, J. (1990) *Teaching the Elephant to Dance: The Manager's Guide to Empowering Change* (New York: Plume).

Benyus, J. (1998) *Biomimicry: Innovation Inspired by Nature* (New York: William Morrow).

Bradbury, H. (1998) *Learning with The Natural Step: Cooperative Ecological Inquiry through Cases, Theory and Practice for Sustainable Development* (doctoral dissertation, Boston College; Ann Arbor, MI: UMI Dissertation Service).

—— and J. Clair (1999a) "The Natural Step: A Partnership between Business and Environmentalists for Sustainable Development," *Academy of Management Executive* 11.5 (November 1999): 551-64.

—— and —— (1999b) "Promoting Sustainable Organizations with Sweden's Natural Step," *Academy of Management Executive* 18.4: 63-74.

Brown, L.R. (2001) *Eco-economy: Building an Economy for the Earth* (New York: W.W. Norton).

Burros, M. (1999) "Plastic Wraps and Health: Studies Raise Questions," *New York Times*, January 13th, 1999: F5.

Burrows, P., and H. Green (2001) "Less-is-more Computing," *Business Week*, June 18th, 2001: 104-105.

Cadbury Commission (1992) *Report of the Committee on the Financial Aspects of Corporate Governance* (London: Cadbury Commission, December 1992).

Capra, B. (Dir.) (1991) *Mind Walk* (distributed by Malofilm).

Capra, F. (1988) *The Turning Point* (New York: Bantam Books).

Ciampa, D. (1991) *Total Quality Management* (Seabrook, MD: Ducochon Press).

Clean Air Act (Amendment) (1990) 42 USC, secs. 7511a(d)(1)(B) (Washington, DC: US Government Printing Office).

Collins, J., and J. Porras (1994) *Built to Last: Successful Habits of Visionary Companies* (New York: HarperBusiness).

Community Reinvestment Act (1977) 12 USC 2901 (Washington, DC: US Government Printing Office).

—— (1995) 12 USC 2901, see Regulations 12CFR 25, 228, 345 and 563c (Washington, DC: US Government Printing Office).

Connor, D. (1998) *Leading at the Edge of Chaos: How to Create the Nimble Organization* (New York: John Wiley).

Consumer Reports (1998) "Hormone Mimics Hit Home: Tests of Plastic Wraps, Baby Foods," *Consumer Reports* 63.6: 53.

Cook, D., J. Oldmark, P. Willis, and K.-H. Robèrt (2002) "Strategic Planning for Social Sustainability," paper presented at the Global Intelligence Network Conference 2002, Corporate Social Responsibility: Governance for Sustainability, Gothenburg, Sweden, June 23–26th, 2002.

Cowe, R., and S. Williams (2000) *Who Are the Ethical Consumers?* (Manchester, UK: The Co-operative Bank, December 15th, 2000, www.co-operativebank.co.uk).

Creyer, E., and W. Ross (1997) "The Influence of Firm Behavior on Purchase Intention: Do Consumers Really Care About Business Ethics?," *The Journal of Consumer Marketing* 14.6.

Cummings, T., and C. Worley (1993) *Organization Development and Change* (Reading, MA: Addison-Wesley).

Daily, G.C., T. Söderqvist, K. Arrow, P. Dasgupta, P.R. Ehrlich, C. Folke, A.-M. Jansson, B.-O. Jansson, S. Levin, J. Lubchenco, K.-G. Mäler, D. Starrett, D. Tilman, and B. Walker (2000) "The Value of Nature and the Nature of Value," *Science* 289: 395-96.

Dalaker, J. (2001) *Poverty in the United States: 2001* (Washington, DC: US Department of Commerce, US Bureau of the Census, www.census.gov/prod/2001pubs/p60-214.pdf).

Darwin, C. (1859) *On the Origin of the Species* (New York: Gramercy [2003]).

DeSimone, L., F. Popoff, and WBCSD (World Business Council for Sustainable Development) (1997) *Eco-efficiency: The Business Link to Sustainable Development* (Cambridge, MA: The MIT Press).

Deutsch, C.H. (2001) "Together at Last: Cutting Pollution and Making Money," *New York Times*, September 9th, 2001.

Dillard, A. (1992) *The Living* (New York: Harper Collins).

Donnelly, J. (2003) "Lives Lost," *The Boston Globe*, January 29th, 2003.

E/TEM (*E/The Environmental Magazine*) (2002) "Insured Destruction: Global Climate Change Threatens the Insurance Industry," *E/TEM*, August 27th, 2002 (www.emagazine.com/july-august_2002/0702curr_insured.html).

Ecotrust (1994) "ShoreTrust Trading Group Combines Jobs and Environment: Innovative Business Assistance Group opens in Ilwaco, Washington," press release, September 6th, 1994, Ecotrust, Portland, OR.

—— (2001) *Natural Sense: The Conservation Economy Emerges, 1991–2001* (Portland, OR: Ecotrust).

—— and Conservation International (1991) *Coastal Temperate Rain Forests: Ecological Characteristics, Status and Distribution* (Portland, OR: Ecotrust and Conservation International).

Electrolux (1994) *Electrolux Annual Report* (Stockholm: Electrolux).

Elkington, J. (1997) *Cannibals with Forks: The Triple Bottom Line of 21st Century Business* (Oxford, UK: Capstone Publishing); Gabriola Island, BC, Canada: New Society Publishers).

Ernst & Young (1997) *Measures that Matter* (Boston, MA: Ernst & Young).

European Union (2001) "European Union Sustainable Development Strategy," http://europa.eu.int/eur-lex/en/com/cnc/2001/com2001_0264en01.pdf.

—— (2002) "Communication from the Commission Concerning Corporate Social Responsibility: A Business Contribution to Sustainable Development," http://europa.eu.int/comm/employment_social/soc-dial/csr/csr2002_en.pdf.

FLG (*Federal Law Gazette*) (2001) *Gesetz zur Reform der gesetzlichen Altersversicherung und zur Förderung eines kapitalgedeckten Altersvorsorgevermögens (Altersvermögensgesetz AvmG)*, Bundesgesetzblatt Volume I, June 29th, 2001: 1,310.

Fox, M. (1994) *The Reinvention of Work: A New Vision of Livelihood for Our Time* (San Francisco: HarperSanFrancisco).

French, W., and C. Bell (1999) *Organization Development* (Upper Saddle River, NJ: Prentice-Hall).

Frost, R. (1979) *The Poetry of Robert Frost* (ed. Edward Connery Latham; New York: Henry Holt).

Funk, K. (2001) *Sustainability and Performance: Uncovering Opportunities for Value Creation* (London: Cap Gemini Ernst & Young Center for Business Innovation).

Geiser, K. (2001) *Materials Matter: Toward a Sustainable Materials Policy* (Cambridge, MA: The MIT Press).

GEMI (Global Environmental Management Initiative) (2001) *New Paths to Business Value: Strategic Sourcing—Environment, Health and Safety* (Washington, DC: GEMI).

Goleman, D., R. Boyatzis, and A. McKee (2002) *Primal Leadership: Realizing the Power of Emotional Intelligence* (Cambridge, MA: Harvard Business School Press).

Goodstein, L., and W. Burke (1991) "Creating Successful Organization Change," *Organizational Dynamics* 19L: 5-17.

Gordon, P. (2001) *Lean and Green: Profit for your Workplace and the Environment* (San Francisco, CA: Berrett-Koehler).

Gottlieb, R. (1993) *Forcing the Spring: The Transformation of the American Environmental Movement* (Washington, DC: Island Press).

Graedel, T., and B. Allenby (1995) *Industrial Ecology* (Englewood Cliffs, NJ: Prentice Hall).

GRI (Global Reporting Initiative) (2002a) *Sustainable Reporting Guidelines*, www.globalreporting.org/guidelines/2002.asp.

—— (2002b) "Final Report of the Measurement Working Group," January 2002, www.globalreporting.org.

Gupta, A., and V. Govindarajan (2000) "Knowledge Management's Social Dimension: Lessons from Nucor Steel," *MIT Sloan Management Review* 42.1 (Fall 2000): 77-80.

Hannan, M., and M. Freeman (1984) "Structural Inertia and Organizational Change," *American Sociological Review* 49: 149-64.

Hart, S., and M. Milstein. (1999) "Global Sustainability and the Creative Destruction of Industries," *MIT Sloan Management Review* 41.1 (Fall 1999): 23-33.

Harvey, D. (1996) *Justice, Nature and the Geography of Difference* (Oxford, UK: Basil Blackwell).

Haunschild, P., and A. Miner (1997) "Modes of Interorganizational Imitation," *Administrative Science Quarterly* 42: 472-500.

Haveman, H. (1992) "Between a Rock and a Hard Place: Organizational Change and Performance under Conditions of Fundamental Environmental Transformation," *Administrative Science Quarterly* 37: 48-76.

Hawken, P. (1993) *The Ecology of Commerce: A Declaration of Sustainability* (New York: HarperBusiness).

——, A. Lovins, and L.H. Lovins (1999) *Natural Capitalism: Creating the Next Industrial Revolution* (New York: Little, Brown).

Heal, G. (2000a) "Valuing Ecosystem Services," *Ecosystems* 3: 24-30.

—— (2000b) *Nature and the Marketplace* (Washington, DC: Island Press).

Hillel, D. (1991) *Out of the Earth: Civilization and the Life of the Soil* (New York: The Free Press).

Hilty, L., T. Ruddy, and D. Schulthess (2000) *Resource Intensity and Dematerialization Potential of Information Society Technologies* (Series A: Discussion Paper 2000-01; Solothurn, Switzerland: Solothurn University of Applied Sciences Northwestern Switzerland).

Holliday, C. (2001) "Sustainable Growth, the DuPont Way," *Harvard Business Review*, September 2001: 129-34.

——, S. Schmidheiny, and P. Watts. (2002) *Walking the Talk: The Business Case for Sustainable Development* (Sheffield, UK: Greenleaf Publishing).

Holmberg, J., and K.-H. Robèrt (2000a) "Backcasting: A Framework for Strategic Planning," *International Journal for Sustainable Development and World Ecology* 7.4: 291-308.

—— and —— (2000b) "Backcasting from Non-overlapping Sustainability Principles: A Framework for Strategic Planning," *International Journal of Sustainable Development and World Ecology* 7: 1-18.

Huselid, M. (1995) "The Impact of Human Resource Management Practices on Turnover, Productivity, and Corporate Financial Performance," *Academy of Management Journal* 38.3.

IDG News Service (2002) "PC Sales Surpass One Billion," 1 July 2002, www.pcworld.com/news/article/0,aid,102386,00.asp.

ILO (International Labor Office) (1991) *Tripartite Declaration of Principles Concerning Multinational Enterprises and Social Policy* (Geneva, Switzerland: ILO).

Jacobs, J. (2000) *The Nature of Economies* (New York: Modern Library Press).

Janssen, M. (2002) "A Future of Surprises," in L. Gunderson and C.S. Holling (eds.), *Panarchy: Understanding Transformations in Human and Natural Systems* (Washington, DC: Island Press): 241-60.

Kiuchi, T., and B. Shireman (2002) *What We Learned in the Rainforest: Business Lessons from Nature* (San Francisco, CA: Berrett-Koehler).

Kotter, J. (1998) "Leading Change," in *Harvard Business Review on Change* (Boston, MA: Harvard Business School Press): 1-20.

—— and D. Cohen (2002) *The Heart of Change: Real-life Stories of How People Change their Organizations* (Cambridge, MA: Harvard Business School Press).

Kouzes, J., and B. Posner (1990) *The Leadership Challenge* (San Francisco: Jossey-Bass).

KPMG (2002) *International Survey of Corporate Sustainability Reporting 2002* (London: KPMG).

Krackhardt, D. (1990) "Assessing the Political Landscape: Structure, Cognition and Power in Organizations," *Administrative Science Quarterly* 35: 342-69.

Kuhn, T.S. (1962) *The Structure of Scientific Revolutions* (Chicago: University of Chicago Press, repr. 1970).

Laszewski, L., and T. Carey (2002) "Integrating Environmental Product Design into Inkjet Printing Supplies," *IEEE* (Institute of Electrical and Electronic Engineers) Conference, May 6–9th, 2002.

Lenhi, M. (2000) "Measuring Corporate Eco-efficiency: A Guide for Companies to Measure their Economic and Environmental Excellence," *Corporate Environmental Strategy* 7.3: 256-66.

Levy, A., and U. Merry (1986) *Organizational Transformation* (New York: Praeger).

March, J. (1988) *Decisions and Organizations* (Oxford, UK: Basil Blackwell).

—— (1991) "Exploration and Exploitation in Organizational Learning," *Organization Science* 2: 71-87.

Marsh, G.P. (1864) *Man and Nature* (New York: Charles Scribner [1965]).

Maslow, A. (1987) *Motivation and Personality* (Reading, MA: Addison-Wesley).

McDonough, W., and M. Braungart (1998) "The Next Industrial Revolution," *The Atlantic* (www.theatlantic.com/issues/98oct/industry.htm).

—— and —— (2001) "Five Steps towards Reinventing the World: An Excerpt from an Article in April/May *Green@Work Magazine*," www.mbdc.com/feature_ may2001.htm.

—— and —— (2002) *Cradle to Cradle: Remaking the Way We Make Things* (New York: North Point Press).

McKinley, G. (2002) *Good Examples* (Ashland, OR: Jefferson Sustainable Development Initiative).

Meima, R. (1996) "The Alpha Case: A Grounded Theory of Corporate Environmental Management in an IT Company," in J.P. Ulhøi and H. Madsen (eds.), *Industry and the Environment: Practical Applications of Environmental Management Approaches in Business* (Aarhus, Denmark: Aarhus School of Business).

MFM (Morley Fund Management) (2001) "Morley Fund Management introduces environmental reporting requirement to voting policy," press release, at www.morleyfm.com/news_frm.htm → 10 April 2001.

Nattrass, B., and M. Altomare (1999) *The Natural Step for Business: Wealth, Ecology and the Evolutionary Corporation* (Gabriola Island, BC, Canada: New Society Publishers).

—— and —— (2002) *Dancing with the Tiger: Learning Sustainability Step by Natural Step* (Gabriola Island, BC, Canada: New Society Publishers).

Natural Step (1997) "US Scientists Sign on to Principles," *Wingspread Journal* (Racine, WI: The Johnson Foundation, Inc.).

New Hope (1994) *The Natural Foods Merchandizer* (1994 issues, volume 16; Boulder, CO: New Hope Communications Inc.).

O'Brien, C. (1999) "Sustainable Production: A New Paradigm for a New Millennium," *International Journal of Production Economics* 60-61: 1-7.

O'Meara, M. (2000) "Harnessing Information Technologies for the Environment," in *State of the World 2000* (Washington, DC: Worldwatch Institute).

OECD (Organization for Economic Development and Cooperation) (1994) *Guidelines for Multinational Enterprises* (Paris: OECD).

Okagaki, A. (2001) *Shorebank Enterprise Pacific: A Five-Year Assessment* (final report; Missoula, MT: Alan Okagaki and Associates, and Shorebank Enterprise Pacific).

Oxley, H., T.-T. Dang, and P. Antolín (2000) *Poverty Dynamics in Six OECD Countries* (OECD Economic Studies Number 30; Paris: OECD, www.oecd.org/pdf/M00023000/M00023916. pdf).

Packard, D. (1996) *The HP Way: How Bill Hewlett and I Built Our Company* (New York: Harper Business).

Peet, R., and M. Watts (eds.) (1996) *Liberation Ecologies: Environment, Development, Social Movements* (London: Routledge).

Pensions Act (Child Support, Pensions and Social Security Act) (2000) *Public General Acts: Elizabeth II* (Chapter 19; London: The Stationery Office).

Pfeffer, J. (1981) "Management as Symbolic Action: The Creation and Maintenance of Organizational Paradigms," in L.L. Cummings and B.M. Staw (eds.), *Research in Organizational Behavior, Volume 3* (Greenwich, CT: JAI Press): 1-52.

—— and G. Salancik (1978) *The External Control of Organizations* (New York: Harper & Row).

Pralahad, C.K., and S.L. Hart (2002) "The Fortune at the Bottom of the Pyramid," *Strategy and Business* 1st quarter 2002, www.strategy-business.com.

Prudham, S. (1999) *Knock on Wood: Nature and the Fictitious Commodity in Oregon's Douglas Fir Region* (PhD dissertation; Berkeley, CA: University of California at Berkeley, Energy Resources Group).

PwC (PricewaterhouseCoopers) (2000) *Creating Business Value through Corporate Responsibility* (London: PwC).

—— (2001) Audit letter, 31 August 2001, www.sustainability-index.com.

Quinn, D. (1992) *Ishmael: An Adventure of the Mind and Spirit* (New York: Bantam Books).

Quinn, R., and G. Spreitzer (1997) "The Road to Empowerment: Seven Questions Every Leader Should Consider," *Organizational Dynamics* 26.2: 37-49.

Radtke, H., and S. Davis (1999) *Economic Description of Selected Coastal Oregon and Washington Counties* (Pacific Northwest Coastal Ecosystems Regional Study; Seattle, WA: University of Washington Sea Grant Program).

Rees, W.E., and M. Wackernagel (1994) "Ecological Footprints and Appropriated Carrying Capacity: Measuring the Natural Capital Requirement of the Human Economy," in A.-M. Jansson, M. Hammer, C. Folke and R. Costanza (eds.), *Investing in Natural Capital: The Ecological Economics Approach to Sustainability* (Washington, DC: Island Press).

Reilly, F.K., and K.C. Brown (1997) *Investment Analysis and Portfolio Management* (Fort Worth, TX: Dryden Press).

Renner, M. (2001) "Overview: The Triple Health Challenge," excerpted from *Vital Signs 2001: The Trends that are Shaping our Future* (Washington, DC: Worldwatch Institute, www.worldwatch.org/pubs/vs/vs01/VSexcerpt.html).

Richards, D. (1999) "Harnessing Ingenuity for Sustainable Outcomes," *The Bridge* 29.1 (www.nae.edu/nae/naehome.nsf/weblinks/NAEW-4NHMK4?opendocument).

Robbins, W. (ed.) (1983) *Regionalism and the Pacific Northwest* (Corvallis, OR: Oregon State University Press).

—— (ed.) (2001) *The Great Northwest: The Search for Regional Identity* (Corvallis, OR: Oregon State University Press).

Robèrt, K.-H. (1994) *Den Naturliga Utmaningen* (*The Natural Challenge*) (Stockholm: Ekerlids, Swedish language).

—— (1997) "ICA/Electrolux: A Case Report from 1992," paper presented to the 40th CIES Annual Executive Congress, Boston, MA, June 5-7th, 1997.

—— (2000) "Tools and Concepts for Sustainable Development: How do They Relate to a Framework for Sustainable Development, and to Each Other?," *Journal of Cleaner Production* 8.3: 243-54.

——, B. Schmidt-Bleek, J. Aloisi de Larderel, G. Basile, J.L. Jansen, R. Kuehr, P. Price Thomas, M. Suzuki, P. Hawken, and M. Wackernagel (2002) "Strategic Sustainable Development: Selection, Design and Synergies of Applied Tools," *Journal of Cleaner Production* 10.3: 197-214.

Robinson, J.B. (1990) "Futures under Glass: A Recipe for People who Hate to Predict," *Futures* 22.8: 820-42.

Rolnick, J. (2001) "A Passion for Raising Beef the 'Grazewell' Way," *Business Viewpoint* 41.4 (July/August 2001): 12-13, 26-27.

Romm, J., and D.T. Sy (1996) "Red Books, Green Hills," in L.T. Cruc, A.T. Rambo, K. Fahrney, T.D. Vien, J. Romm and D.T. Sy (eds.) *The Impact of Economic Reform on Restoration Ecology in the Midlands of North Vietnam* (Honolulu, HI: East–West Center).

Russell, P. (1995) *The Global Brain Awakens* (Palo Alto, CA: Global Brain Inc.).

Schaltegger, S., and R. Burritt (2000) *Contemporary Environmental Accounting: Issues, Concepts and Practice* (Sheffield, UK: Greenleaf Publishing).

Schmidheiny, S., and BCSD (Business Council for Sustainable Development) (1991) *Changing Course: A Global Business Perspective on Development and the Environment* (Cambridge, MA: The MIT Press).

Schmidt-Bleek, F. (1994) "Revolution in Resource Productivity for a Sustainable Economy: A New Research Agenda," *Fresenius Environmental Bulletin* 2: 245-490.

—— (1997) *MIPS and Factor 10 for a Sustainable and Profitable Economy* (Wuppertal, Germany: Wuppertal Institute).

Schwantes, C. (1996) *The Pacific Northwest: An Interpretive History* (Lincoln, NE: University of Nebraska Press).

Senge, P., and G. Carstedt (2001) "Innovating Our Way to the Next Industrial Revolution," *MIT Sloan Management Review* 42.2 (Winter 2001): 24-37.

Shorebank Corporation and Ecotrust (1992a) *Interim Report on the Ecotrust/Shorebank Development Project in the Willapa Bay* (internal draft report; Ilwaco, WA: Shorebank Corporation and Ecotrust, November 1992).

—— and —— (1992b) *Interim Report on the Ecotrust/Shorebank Development Project in the Willapa Bay* (internal draft report; Ilwaco, WA: Shorebank Corporation and Ecotrust, December 1992).

—— and —— (1992c) *Interim Report 2: Proposed Design for a Willapa Development Institution* (internal report; Ilwaco, WA: Shorebank Corporation, and Ecotrust, December 1992).

—— and —— (1993) *First Environmental Bancorporation: A Regional Development Strategy* (presented to the Willapa Alliance EcoDevelopment Committee; Ilwaco, WA: Shorebank Corporation and Ecotrust, August 11th, 1993).

—— and —— (1996) *ShoreTrust: The First Environmental Bancorporation* (Portland, OR: Ecotrust).

—— and Northwest Natural Resources Group (1998) *The Specialty Forest Products Stewardship Field Guide for Selected Species of the North American Coastal Temperate Rain Forest* (Ilwaco, WA: Shorebank Enterprise Pacific, 1st edn, August 1998).

SJMN (San Jose Mercury News) (2002) "Utilities Face New Requirements," *SJMN*, September 1st, 2002: 27A.

Socolow, R., C. Andrew, F. Berkhout, and V. Thomas (eds.) (1994) *Industrial Ecology and Global Change* (Cambridge, UK: Cambridge University Press).

Sokolove, J. (2003) "Doing Good by Doing Well: Entrepreneurial Environmentalism in the American West" (PhD dissertation; Berkeley, CA: University of California at Berkeley Department of Environmental Science, Policy and Management).

SPINS/ACNielsen (2002) *A SPINS Brief on the Organic Marketplace and the New National Organic Program Standards* (San Francisco, CA: SPINS/ACNielsen).

SsgA (State Street Global Advisors) (2001) "State Street Global Advisors Announces CHF 500 Million SRI Mandate Win from Swiss Federal Social Security Fund," press release, May 21st, 2001.

Strebel, P. (1998) "Why Do Employees Resist Change?," in *Harvard Business Review on Change* (Boston, MA: Harvard Business School Press): 139-57.

SustainAbility (2001) *Buried Treasure: Uncovering the Business Case for Corporate Sustainability* (London: SustainAbility).

Sustainable Northwest (1997) "Oregon Country Beef," in *Founders of a New Northwest* (Portland, OR: Sustainable Northwest): 85-86.

—— (1998) *Founders of a New Northwest 1998* (Portland, OR: Sustainable Northwest, www.sustainablenorthwest.org).

Swan, J. (1972) *The Northwest Coast: Or, Three Years Residence in Washington Territory* (Seattle, WA: University of Washington Press [1857]).

Taub, R. (1994) *Community Capitalism* (Boston, MA: Harvard Business School Press [1988]).

Thompson, J. (1967) *Organizations in Action* (New York: McGraw–Hill).

Tritch, T. (2001) "Talk of Ages," *Gallup Management Journal,* Winter 2001: 32.

UNDP (United Nations Development Program) (2002) *Human Development Report* (New York: UNDP, http://hdr.undp.org/reports/global/2002/en/statements/lead_author.cfm).

UNICEF/UNEP/WHO (United Nations Children's Fund/United Nations Environment Program/World Health Organization) (2002) "Children in the New Millennium: Environmental Impact on Health," www.who.int/mediacentre/releases/release36/en.

US EPA (US Environmental Protection Agency) (1997) *Emerging Global Environmental Issues* (EPA 160-K-97-001; Washington, DC: US EPA Office of International Activities).

Van Daalen, C. (2000) *Sustainable Agriculture . . . Continuing to Grow* (Portland, OR: Sustainable Northwest).

Verschoor, C. (1998) "A Study of the Link between a Corporation's Financial Performance and Its Ethics," *Business and Society.*

Vitousek, P.M., H.A. Mooney, J. Lubchenco, and J.M. Melillo (1997) "Human Domination of Earth's Ecosystems," *Science* 277: 494-99.

Von Weizsäcker, E.U., A. Lovins, and L.H. Lovins. (1997) *Factor Four: Doubling Wealth, Halving Resources* (London: Earthscan Publications).

Wackernagel, M., and W. Rees (1996) *Our Ecological Footprint* (Gabriola Island, BC, Canada: New Society Publishers).

Wagner, M. (2001) *A Review of Empirical Studies Concerning the Relationship between Environmental and Economic Performance: What does the Evidence Tell Us?* (Lüneburg, Germany: Center for Sustainability Management, www.environmental-performance.org/outputs/Wagner.PDF).

WBCSD (World Business Council for Sustainable Development) (2000a) *Building a Better Future: Innovation, Technology and Sustainable Development* (Paris: WBCSD).

—— (2000b) *Eco-efficiency: Creating More Value with Less Impact* (Conches, France; Geneva: WBCSD, www.wbcsd.org).

WCED (World Commission on Environment and Development) (1987) *Our Common Future* (Oxford, UK: Oxford University Press).

Weaver, P., L. Jansen, G. van Grootveld, E. van Spiegel, and P. Vergragt (2000) *Sustainable Technology Development* (Sheffield, UK: Greenleaf Publishing).

Wilsdon, J. (2001) *Digital Futures: Living in a Dot-com World* (London: Earthscan Publications).

—— and P. Miller (2001) "Mind over Matter: Greening the New Economy," in J. Wilsdon (ed.), *Digital Futures: Living in a Dot-com World* (London: Earthscan Publications).

Wilson, A. (2001) "Building Materials: What Makes a Product Green?," *Environmental Building News* 9.1.

Wilson, E.O. (2002) *The Future of Life* (New York: Alfred A. Knopf).

Worldwatch Institute (2001) *Vital Signs 2001: The Trends that are Shaping our Future* (Washington, DC: Worldwatch Institute, http://secure.worldwatch.org).

Further reading

Amburgey, T., D. Kelley, and W. Barnett (1993) "Resetting the Clock: The Dynamics of Organizational Change and Failure," *Administrative Science Quarterly* 38: 51-73.

Astley, W.G., and A.H. Van de Ven (1983) "Central Perspectives and Debates in Organizational Theory," *Administrative Science Quarterly* 28: 245-74.

Barley, S.A., and G. Kunda (1992) "Design and Devotion: Surges of Rational and Normative Ideologies of Control in Managerial Discourse," *Administrative Science Quarterly* 37: 363-99.

——, G.W. Meyer, and D.C. Gash (1988) "Cultures of Culture: Academics, Practitioners and the Pragmatics of Normative Control," *Administrative Science Quarterly* 33: 24-60.

Barnett, W., and G. Carroll (1995) "Modeling Internal Organizational Change," *Annual Review of Sociology* 21: 217-36.

—— and M. Hansen (1996) "The Red Queen in Organizational Evolution," *Strategic Management Journal* 17: 139-57.

Baron, J., F. Dobbin, and P. Jennings (1986) "War and Peace: The Evolution of the Modern Personnel Administration in US Industry," *American Journal of Sociology* 92: 350-83.

——, M. Hannan, and D. Burton (1999) *Labor Pains: Organizational Change and Employee Turnover in Young High-tech Firms* (working paper; Stanford, CA: Stanford Graduate School of Business).

——, B. Mittman, and A. Newman (1991) "Targets of Opportunity: Organizational and Environmental Determinants of Gender Integration within the California Civil Service," *American Journal of Sociology* 96: 1,362-401.

Beckhard, R. (1993) "Choosing and Leading a Fundamental Change," *Academy of Management Newsletter*, Summer 1993: 6-8.

Beer, M., R. Eisenstat, and B. Spector (1990) *The Critical Path to Corporate Renewal* (Boston, MA: Harvard Business School Press).

Blau, P., and W. Scott (1962) *Formal Organizations: A Comparative Approach* (San Francisco: Chandler).

Bradbury, H. (1999) "Learning with The Natural Step: Cooperative Ecological Inquiry through Cases, Theory and Practice for Sustainable Development" (doctoral dissertation, Boston College; Ann Arbor, MI: UMI Dissertation Services).

Brown, V., and G. Jackson (1999) "Stitching the Pieces Together: Sustainable Community Case Studies from the Pacific Northwest," a project of the Pacific Northwest Regional Council of the President's Council on Sustainable Development.

Burt, R. (1980) "Models of Network Structure," *Annual Review of Sociology* 6: 79-141.

Cannella, A., and R. Paetzold (1994) "Pfeffer's Barriers to the Advance of Organizational Science: A Rejoinder," *Academy of Management Review* 19: 331-41.

Carroll, G., and M. Hannan (2000) *The Demography of Corporations and Industries* (Princeton, NJ: Princeton University Press).

—— and A. Teo (1996) "On the Social Networks of Managers," *Academy of Management Journal* 39: 421-40.

Cestero, B. (1999) *Beyond the Hundredth Meeting: A Field Guide to Collaborative Conservation of the West's Public Lands* (Bozeman, MT: Sonoran Institute).

Chandler, A. (1977) *The Visible Hand: The Managerial Revolution in American Business* (Boston, MA: Harvard University Press).

Cyert, R., and J. March (1992) *A Behavioral Theory of the Firm* (Englewood Cliffs, NJ: Prentice Hall).

Davis, G. (1990) "Agents without Principles? The Spread of the Poison Pill through the Intercorporate Network," *Administrative Science Quarterly* 36: 583-613.

Defenders of Wildlife (1999) *Incentives for Conservation: An Oregon Biodiversity Partnership Report* (Lake Oswego, OR: Defenders of Wildlife).

Delacroix, J., and A. Swaminathan (1991) "Cosmetic, Speculative and Adaptive Organizational Change in the Wine Industry: A Longitudinal Study," *Administrative Science Quarterly* 36: 631-62.

Durning, A.T. (1999) *Green-collar Jobs: Working in the New Northwest* (Seattle, WA: Northwest Environment Watch).

Freedman, L. (2002) "Successes and Lessons Learned in the Pacific Northwest," speech prepared for the National Leadership Team, US Forest Service, Welches, OR, 19 March 2002.

Galaskiewicz, J., and R. Burt (1991) "Interorganizational Contagion in Corporate Philanthropy," *Administrative Science Quarterly* 36: 88-106.

Gersick, C. (1991) "Time and Transition in Work Teams: Toward a New Model of Growth," *Academy of Management Journal* 31: 9-42.

Golembiewski, R. (1989) *Organization Development: Ideas and Issues* (New Brunswick, NJ: Transaction Publishers).

Granovetter, M. (1985) "Economic Action and Social Structure: The Problem of Embeddedness," *American Journal of Sociology* 91: 481-510.

Gray, G., M.J. Enzer, and J. Kusel (eds.) (2001) *Understanding Community-Based Forest and Ecosystem Management* (Binghamton, NY: Food Products Press).

Greiner, L. (1972) "Evolution and Revolution as Organizations Grow," *Harvard Business Review* 50: 37.

Greve, H. (1996) "Patterns of Competition: The Diffusion of a Market Position in Radio Broadcasting," *Administrative Science Quarterly* 41: 29-61.

—— (1998a) "Managerial Cognition and the Mimetic Adoption of Market Positions: What You See is What You Do," *Strategic Management Journal* 19: 967-69.

—— (1998b) "Performance, Aspirations and Risky Organizational Change," *Administrative Science Quarterly* 43: 58-87.

—— (1999) "The Effect of Core Change on Performance: Inertia and Regression to the Mean," *Administrative Science Quarterly* 44: 590-614.

Guillen, M.F. (1994) *Models of Management: Work, Authority and Organization in Comparative Perspective* (Chicago: University of Chicago Press).

Halliday, A. (1993) "Product Change: The Perils of Moving too Fast," *Harvard Business Review* 71: 10.

Imhoff, D. (1999) "Wild Farms: Seeking a Watershed Approach to Agriculture," *Orion Afield*, Spring 1999: 34-36.

Johnson, K. (1997) *Toward a Sustainable Region: Evolving Strategies for Reconciling Community and the Environment* (Seattle, WA: Northwest Policy Centre).

Katz, R. (1982) "The Effects of Group Longevity on Project Communication and Performance," *Administrative Science Quarterly* 27: 81-105.

Kaufman, H. (1971) *The Limits to Organizational Change* (Tuscaloosa, AL: The University of Alabama Press).

Kelly, D., and T. Amburgey (1991) "Organizational Inertia and Momentum: A Dynamic Model of Strategic Change," *Academy of Management Journal* 34: 591-613.

Kodama, F. (1992) "Technology Fusion and the New R&D," *Harvard Business Review*, July/ August 1992: 70-77.

Lant, T., and S. Mezias (1992a) "An Organizational Model of Convenience and Reorientation," *Organization Science* 3: 47-71.

—— and —— (1992b) "Managing Discontinuous Change: A Simulation Study of Organizational Learning and Entrepreneurship," *Strategic Management Journal* 11: 147-79.

Lawrence, P., and J. Lorsch (1967) *Organization and Environment: Managing Differentiation and Integration* (Boston, MA: Graduate School of Business Administration, Harvard University).

LCAOF (Liz Claiborne Art Ortenberg Foundation) (2001) "Case Studies," in *Collaborative Resource Management in the Interior West: A Workshop Held at Red Lodge, Montana, October 18–22, 2001* (New York: LCAOF).

Leiberson, S., and J.F. O'Connor (1972) "Leadership and Organizational Performance: A Study of Large Corporations," *American Sociological Review* 37: 117-30.

Levitt, B., and J. March (1988) "Organizational Learning," *Annual Review of Sociology* 14: 319-40.

March, J. (1997) "Organizational Performance as a Dependent Variable," *Organization Science* 8: 698-707.

—— and J. Olsen (1975) *Ambiguity and Choice in Organizations* (Bergen, Norway: Universitetsforlaget).

—— and H. Simon (1958) *Organizations* (New York: John Wiley).

Mauer, R. (1996) *Beyond the Wall of Resistance: Unconventional Strategies that Build Support for Change* (Austin, TX: Bard Books).

Meindl, J.R., S.B. Erlich and J.M. Dukerich (1985) "The Romance of Leadership," *Administrative Science Quarterly* 30: 78-102.

Meyer, J., and B. Rowan (1983) "Institutionalized Organizations: Formal Structure as Myth and Ceremony," *American Journal of Sociology* 83: 340-63.

Miller, D., and M. Chen (1994) "Competitive Attack, Retaliation and Performance: An Expectancy Model," *Strategic Management Journal* 15: 85-103.

Miner A. (1990) "Seeking Adaptive Advantage: Evolutionary Theory and Managerial Action," in J.A.C. Baum and J.V. Singh (eds.), *Evolutionary Dynamics in Organizations* (New York: Oxford University Press): 76-89.

Palmer, D., P. Jennings and X. Zhou (1992) "Late Adoption of the Multidivisional Form by Large US Corporations," *Administrative Science Quarterly* 38: 100-31.

Pfeffer, J. (1975) "Beyond Management and the Worker: The Institutional Function of Management," *Academy of Management Review* 1: 36-46.

—— (1976) "The Ambiguity of Leadership," *Academy of Management Review* 2: 104-12.

—— (1982) *Organizations and Organization Theory* (Boston, MA: Pitman).

—— (1993) "Barriers to the Advance of Organization Science: Paradigm Development as a Dependent Variable," *Academy of Management Review* 18: 599-620.

—— (1995) "Mortality, Reproducibility and the Persistence of Styles of Theory," *Organization Science* 6: 681-86.

Porter, M., and C. van der Linde (1995) "Green and Competitive: Ending the Stalemate," *Harvard Business Review*, September/October 1995: 120-34.

Reynolds, A. (2000) "Community Awareness: The Next Wave of Environmental Information," *Environmental Perspectives* 16 (Boston, MA: The Tellus Institute, April 2000).

Robbins, H., and M. Finley (1996) *Why Change Doesn't Work* (Princeton, NJ: Peterson's).

Romm, J. (1999) *The Internet Economy and Global Warming* (Washington, DC: Center for Energy and Climate Solutions).

Salancik, G., and J. Pfeffer (1978) "A Social Information Processing Approach to Job Attitudes and Task Design," *Administrative Science Quarterly* 23: 224.

Satarug, S., J.R. Baker, P.E.B. Reilly, M.R. Moore, and D.J. Williams (2002) "Cadmium Levels in the Lung, Liver, Kidney Cortex and Urine Samples from Australians without Occupational Exposure to Metals," *Archives of Environmental Health* 57.1: 69-77.

Schmidt, C. (2002) "Antibiotic Resistance in Livestock: More at Stake than Steak," *Environmental Health Perspectives* 110.7: 396-402.

Schoonmaker, P., B. Von Hagen, and E. Wolf (eds.) (1997) *The Rain Forests of Home: Profile of a North American Bioregion* (produced by Ecotrust and Interrain Pacific; Washington, DC: Island Press).

Scott, W.R. (1998) *Organizations: Rational, Natural and Open Systems* (Upper Saddle River, NJ: Prentice Hall).

Sjodin, A., D. Patterson and A. Bergman (2001) "Brominated Flame Retardants in Serum from US Blood Donors," *Environmental Science and Technology* 35.19: 3,830-33.

Suzuki, D., and H. Dressel (2002) *Good News for a Change: Hope for a Troubled Planet* (Toronto: Stoddart).

Tushman, M., and P. Anderson (1986) "Technological Discontinuities and Organizational Environments," *Administrative Science Quarterly* 31: 439-65.

Uzzi, B. (1996) "The Sources and Consequences of Embeddedness for the Economic Performance of Organizations," *American Sociological Review* 61: 674-98.

Van Maanen, J. (1995) "Fear and Loathing in Organization Studies," *Organization Science* 6: 687-93.

Vastag, B. (2002) " 'Cipromania' and 'Superclean' Homes are Now Increasing Antibiotic Resistance," *Journal of the American Medical Association* 288.8: 947-48.

Vickerman, S. (1997) *Stewardship Incentives: Conservation Strategies for Oregon's Working Landscape* (Washington, DC: Defenders of Wildlife).

WBCSD (World Business Council for Sustainable Development) (1996) *Eco-efficient Leadership for Improved Economic and Environmental Performance* (Conches, France; Geneva: WBCSD).

Wegner, M. (1987) "Creating New Jobs in the Service Sector," *Annals of the American Academy of Political and Social Science* 492: 136-50.

Williamson, O. (1975) *Markets and Hierarchies: Analysis and Antitrust Implications* (New York: The Free Press).

Abbreviations

3P	Pollution Prevention Pays (3M)
AEI	Alliance for Environmental Innovation
AIDS	acquired immune deficiency syndrome
AiO	all-in-one
ASTO	Australian Senate Table Office
BCSD	Business Council for Sustainable Development
bps	basis points
BTU	British thermal unit
CD-ROM	compact disc read-only memory
CEO	chief executive officer
CERES	Coalition of Environmentally Responsible Economies
CFC	chlorofluorocarbon
CO_2	carbon dioxide
CSR	corporate social responsibility
DAX	Deutscher Aktienindex
DDT	dichlorodiphenyltrichloroethane
DJ	Dow Jones
DJSI	Dow Jones Sustainability Index
DNS	Det Naturliga Steget (The Natural Step)
E/TEM	*E/The Environmental Magazine*
EBITDA	earnings before interest, taxes, depreciation, and amortization
EDF	Environmental Defense Fund
EER	energy efficiency rating
EPA	Environmental Protection Agency
ERT	Environmental Resources Trust
FLG	*Federal Law Gazette*
FSC	Forest Stewardship Council
FTSE	Financial Times Stock Exchange
GDP	gross domestic product
GEMI	Global Environmental Management Initiative
GNP	gross national product
GRI	Global Reporting Initiative
HCFC	hydrochlorofluorocarbon

HFHC	Healthy Forests, Healthy Communities
HIV	human immunodeficiency virus
ILO	International Labor Organization
IPO	initial public offering
ISO	International Organization for Standardization
IT	information technology
IUCN	International Union for the Conservation of Nature
JSFP	Jefferson State Forest Products
KLD	KinderLydenbergDomini
kWp	peak kilowatt
LCA	life-cycle assessment
MFM	Morley Fund Management
MIPS	material input per unit of service
MPS	managed print services (Hewlett Packard)
MSCI	Morgan Stanley Capital International
NASDAQ	National Association of Securities Dealers Automated Quotations (USA)
NCCA	National Community Capital Association (USA)
NGO	non-governmental organization
NYSE	New York Stock Exchange
NYSERDA	New York State Energy Research and Development Authority
OCB	Oregon Country Beef
OECD	Organization for Economic Cooperation and Development
PC	personal computer
PCB	polychlorinated biphenyl
PEM	proton-exchange membrane
PR	public relations
PRI	program-related investment
PUA	Per Uno Alm
PVC	polyvinyl chloride
PwC	PricewaterhouseCoopers
QUEST	quality, utilizing employee suggestions and teamwork (Interface, Inc.)
R&D	research and development
RMI	Rocky Mountain Institute
ROE	return on equity
RRR	required rate of return
SAM	Sustainable Asset Management,
SJMN	*San Jose Mercury News*
SRI	socially responsible investment
TQM	total quality management
TR	total return
UDHR	Universal Declaration of Human Rights (United Nations)
UNCED	United Nations Conference on Environment and Development
UNDP	United Nations Development Program
UNEP	United Nations Environment Program
UNICEF	United Nations Children's Fund
WBCSD	World Business Council for Sustainable Development
WCED	World Commission on Environment and Development
WEEE	Waste Electrical and Electronic Equipment
WHO	World Health Organization
WRI	World Resources Institute
WWF	World Wide Fund for Nature

Biographies

Ray Anderson graduated from Georgia Institute of Technology in 1956 with highest honors and a bachelor's degree in industrial engineering. He learned the carpet and the textile businesses through more than 14 years holding various positions at Deering-Milliken and Callaway Mills. In 1973 he set about founding a company to produce the first free-lay carpet tiles in the USA—Interface, Inc. He developed a partnership with Britain's Carpets International plc that year and set up operations in LaGrange, GA. Some ten years later, Interface took over Carpets International and today Mr. Anderson is chairman of the world's largest producer of commercial floor coverings. After founding Interface in 1973, Mr. Anderson and his company revolutionized the commercial floor covering industry. More recently, Mr. Anderson has embarked on a mission to make Interface a sustainable corporation by leading a worldwide effort to pioneer the processes of sustainable development. Named one of the USA's "100 Best Companies to Work For" in 1997 and 1998 by *Fortune* magazine, Interface has diversified and globalized its businesses, with sales in 110 countries and manufacturing facilities on four continents. Mr. Anderson received the inaugural Millennium Award from Global Green, presented by Mikhail Gorbachev, in 1996, and was named co-chairman of the President's Council on Sustainable Development in 1997. He was also recognized in 1996 as the Ernst & Young Entrepreneur of Year for the Southeast Region, and as the Georgia Conservancy's Conservationist of the Year in 1997. In January 2001, the National Academy of Sciences selected Mr. Anderson to receive the prestigious George and Cynthia Mitchell International Prize for Sustainable Development, the first corporate chief executive officer to be so honored. In September 2001, the SAM-SPG Award Jury presented the Sustainability Leadership Award to him in Zurich, Switzerland. Mr. Anderson's book, *Mid-course Correction* (Chelsea Green, 1998) describes Interface's transformation to environmental responsibility as well as his own personal journey as a leader in the field of sustainable development.
ray.anderson@us.interfaceinc.com

Hilary Bradbury is an assistant professor of organizational behavior at the Weatherhead School of Management at Case Western Reserve University in Cleveland. Her research and practice interests coalesce around two areas: action research, which is doing research *with* rather than *on* people, and sustainable development. These two areas of interest come together in her research on organizations where engagement with sustainability often

requires the management of deep organizational change. Dr. Bradbury has published in *Organization Science, Academy of Management Executive* and *The Journal of Management Inquiry*, and co-edited the *Handbook of Action Research* (Sage Publications, 2001) with Peter Reason. She has also been closely associated with the work of the Society for Organizational Learning (SoL) and enjoys the colleagueship of Peter Senge, John Carroll, and John Ehrenfeld of SoL on an NSF grant supporting study of corporate efforts to develop sustainability-oriented practices. Overall, Dr. Bradbury's recent work explores the intersection of personal and global sustainability.
www.weatherhead.cwru.edu/bradbury

Gretchen C. Daily is an interdisciplinary research scientist in the Department of Biological Sciences at Stanford University, USA. An ecologist by training, Dr. Daily is working to develop a scientific basis—and political and institutional support—for managing Earth's life-support systems. Her efforts span basic science, environmental policy analysis, teaching, and public education. Dr. Daily works extensively with economists, lawyers, businesspeople, and government agencies to incorporate environmental issues into business practice and government policy. She has served on a subcommittee of the Presidential Committee of Advisors on Science and Technology (1997-98) and on numerous other panels and committees for the United Nations, the World Bank, private foundations, and scientific institutions. She was elected Fellow of the American Academy of Arts and Sciences in 2003 and in 2000 was recipient of the 21st Century Scientist Award. Dr. Daily received her PhD in biological sciences from Stanford University.

Cecilia Danks is an assistant professor in the School of Natural Resources at the University of Vermont, USA, where she teaches classes in certification, community forestry, and environmental studies. Her research focuses on comparative policies for community forestry and socioeconomic issues in the Northern Forest. Previously, Dr. Danks was the director of socioeconomic research for the Watershed and Research Training Center, in Hayfork, CA, which conducts training, research, and economic development activities to promote forest and community health.
cdanks@uvm.edu

Katherine Ellison is an investigative journalist and veteran foreign correspondent for Knight Ridder Newspapers who has reported from Asia, Africa, and Latin America. The recipient of many journalism honors, including the George Polk Award and the Overseas Press Club Award, she won the Pulitzer Prize for International Reporting for a series of articles in *The San Jose Mercury News* concerning the plundering of the Philippine treasury by Ferdinand and Imelda Marcos. The articles later became the basis for *Imelda: Steel Butterfly of the Philippines* (McGraw-Hill, 1998). Since April 2000, Ms. Ellison has been working as a consulting writer for the Center for Conservation Biology, writing articles about the economics of conservation, published in media including *Time* magazine, *Fortune, Worth*, and *The Washington Post*. She received her BA in international relations and communication from Stanford University, USA.

Alois Flatz is head of research at the Sustainable Asset Management (SAM) Group. Before joining SAM, he was permanent advisor to the Austrian Minister of Environment. He has also worked for the Federation of Austrian Industry, where he led several projects, including work on the Austrian Packaging Ordinance. Dr. Flatz graduated from the Vienna University of Economics, Austria, with a master's in business administration. He earned his PhD from the Institute of Management at the University of St. Gallen, Switzerland.

Martin Goebel is the founding president of Sustainable Northwest, USA. He has worked for a wide range of public and non-profit organizations, including the Mexican forest service, as a community forestry specialist, as well as in several international conservation organiza-

tions—The Nature Conservancy, Conservation International (which he helped found), and the World Wild Fund for Nature. Mr. Goebel serves on the Sustainable Oregon Working Group of John Kitzhaber (Governor of Oregon) and the Intelligent Consumption Project of Mike Dombeck (Chief of the US Forest Service). He is also a member of the advisory council of the Ecosystem Workforce Program, the International Sustainable Development Foundation, the Institute for the Northwest, the San Diego Museum of Natural History, the Mexico Nature Conservation Fund (Mexico City), and Proesteros (Ensenada, Baja California Norte). Mr. Goebel received a bachelor's degree in forestry at Oregon State University and a master's degree at Texas A&M University, in natural resource conservation and development.
mgoebel@sustainablenorthwest.org

Thilo Goodall is responsible for investment decisions and risk management for institutional mandates, and for quantitative and macroeconomic analysis. After receiving his high-school diploma, Thilo joined a local Bank in Minden (Germany) for 2 ½ years. He then studied Economics at the Universities of Freiburg (Germany) and Madison/Wisconsin, with an emphasis on macroeconomics and econometrics. After receiving his master's degree, Thilo became an assistant to the professor at the Institute for Economic Studies, before joining SBC Brinson, the Asset Management division of Swiss Bank Corporation. He developed long-term global risk-and-return scenarios and valuation and risk models. He also set asset allocation and equity market strategies as a member of regional and global investment committees. Thilo holds a PhD in economics and earned the charter to use the Chartered Financial Analyst (CFA).

David Hudson is an independent consultant focusing on environmental strategy and impact analysis. In addition to his work on dematerialization at Hewlett Packard, Mr. Hudson is currently designing an environmental performance tracking system for the company's global operations. Previously, he worked with several start-up technology companies and served as IT Director at Business for Social Responsibility (BSR). He received his MBA from the University of California at Berkeley
david@hudson-consulting.com

Matt Klein was a principal at Montgomery Securities (now Bank of America Securities) and at Robertson Stephens. He co-founded and serves as managing member of a successful private equity partnership and also co-founded a growth equity limited partnership. Mr. Klein also founded, and serves as the executive director of, a small charitable foundation focused on social and environmental sustainability. Mr. Klein's primary occupation is as the chief executive officer of Verdant Power, a sustainable energy company that produces electrical and mechanical energy in an environmentally benign way from free-flowing water currents (i.e. without use of dams or impoundments). His personal and professional interests are directed towards a broad definition of sustainability, and his efforts are focused on supporting the most efficacious organizations in this field. Mr. Klein has a bachelor's degree in economics from Duke University and he has earned the designation of Chartered Financial Analyst.
mklein@verdantpower.com

Colin le Duc is Head of Research Operations for SAM Research, a member of the SAM Group. He is responsible for the research process covering large-cap companies for both the Dow Jones Sustainability Index as well as SAM's actively managed funds. He started his career with TotalFina in Paris and London, working in corporate strategy and natural gas marketing functions. Subsequently, he moved into corporate strategy consulting with Arthur D. Little Ltd. in London, with particular focus on sustainability in the energy sector. As a member of ADL's Global Energy Practice, he gained extensive experience with blue-chip clients around the world. Plus, he has spent time in venture capital, also in London. He holds a BSc dual honours degree in International Management and Modern Languages from the University of Bath, UK, and has completed the Corporate Finance Program at London Business School.

Frank Marquardt is a writer and editor. He partners with non-profit and for-profit organizations to help them communicate the value of sustainability. He founded Tralition Associates, a research organization dedicated to exploring best practices in sustainability and human performance and is a senior conservation fellow with the Bay Area Alliance for Sustainable Communities. Currently, Mr. Marquardt is investigating the connections between corporations, democracy, and sustainability. He holds a master's degree from Illinois State University and a bachelor's degree from Reed College.

George McKinley currently directs the Jefferson Sustainable Development Initiative, a regional non-profit initiative in southwest Oregon and northwest California that works to integrate community health with natural resource stewardship. Prior to this work, he taught on the subject of nature and culture for ten years at the Sierra Institute, a field studies program based at the University of California. From 1992 to 1998 he owned and operated Chinquapin Mountain Designs, a small-scale vertically integrated wood product and custom milling operation.

george@jeffnet.org

Lynelle Preston, as the Environmental Sustainability Manager at Hewlett Packard, is responsible for driving principles of sustainability throughout Hewlett Packard's core business functions. She manages strategic planning, partnership development, and new business opportunities for Hewlett Packard's Environmental Strategies and Sustainability Group. Ms. Preston has an MBA from University of California at Berkeley, an MS in environmental management from University of Michigan, and a BA in anthropology from Middlebury College. Before joining Hewlett Packard, Ms. Preston worked for more than seven years in the environmental non-profit sector. She worked with The Mountain Institute, which implements community-based conservation projects in the major mountain regions of the world, the World Wide Fund for Nature (WWF) in Washington, DC, NOLS (National Outdoor Leadership School), and the Jackson Hole Conservation Alliance. Ms. Preston is currently a board member for Net Impact, a network of 5,000 MBA students committed to sustainable business.

Karl-Henrik Robèrt, one of Sweden's foremost cancer scientists, founded The Natural Step in 1989. His research on damaged human cells provided a platform for his interest in environmental issues. With Dr. John Holmberg he developed the four "system conditions" for ecological sustainability, which later became known as the foundation for The Natural Step Framework. Today, a large number of business corporations and Swedish municipalities are working with The Natural Step Framework to approach sustainable development in a systematic and strategic way. Prior to working on sustainability issues, Dr. Robèrt received his MD in 1975 and his PhD in 1979. In 1982 he became a professor of internal medicine. In 1984 he won the Swedish Hematological Association Research Award. From 1985 to 1993 Robèrt headed the Division of Clinical Hematology and Oncology and the Department of Medicine at Huddinge Hospital. He was also the editor of *Reviews in Oncology* from 1987 to 1993 and has also authored numerous scientific publications concerning leukemia, lymphoma, lung cancer, and their clinical implications. More recently, Dr. Robèrt has focused on sustainability issues. In 1995 he was appointed professor of resource theory at the University of Gothenburg, Sweden. He has written many books and articles on the environment and sustainability that encourage an understanding of the linkage between ecology and economy, while also providing a structured methodology for planning systematically towards sustainability, and informing the selection and design of various tools and concepts for a systematic monitoring of sustainable development. In 1999 Dr. Robèrt was awarded the Green Cross Award for International Leadership, and in 2000 he was awarded the Blue Planet Prize, the Nobel Prize of Sustainability. For a review of this work, see Dr. Robèrt's publication *The Natural Step Story: Seeding a Quiet Revolution* (New Society Press, 2002).

Derek Smith serves as the Corporate Sustainability Manager at Norm Thompson Outfitters, in Portland, OR. His areas of focus include paper and forestry, product toxicity, climate change, packaging, human rights, and stakeholder engagement. In addition to his duties at Norm Thompson, Mr. Smith is a director of the Recycled Paper Coalition and the Oregon Business Association and is a member of the steering committee of the Fiber Council of the Organic Trade Association. Mr. Smith has an MBA from the University of Oregon and a BSc from San Jose State University. He hails from Sacramento, CA.
dsmith@nortom.com

Jennifer L. Sokolove holds a postdoctoral fellowship in the College of Natural Resources at the University of California at Berkeley, CA. Her research explores contemporary collisions between environment and economy, particularly the processes of marketing, consumption, and investment that link rural places and resource industries to urban economies. Her most recent project examines examines non-profit efforts to engage businesses and entrepreneurs in economic development integrated with environmental conservation. She has worked extensively with community-directed conservation and development efforts in a range of localities across the western United States. Jen completed her PhD in Environmental Science, Policy, and Management at the University of California at Berkeley, and received her BA from Stanford University, CA.
jensok@nature.berkeley.edu

Karen Steer is the program coordinator for the Healthy Forests, Healthy Communities Partnership. She has also held positions with the Wilderness Society, the National Park Service Social Science Program, the US Army Corps of Engineers' community impact assessment for the lower Snake River Juvenile Salmon Migration Recovery Feasibility Study, and the Peace Corps in Honduras, where she served for three years as a protected-areas consultant. Ms. Steer holds a bachelor's degree in environmental science from Allegheny College and a master's degree in social ecology from Yale School of Forestry and Environmental Studies.
ksteer@sustainablenorthwest.org

Juli Torok has worked as a strategy consultant in the financial services industry. She graduated from Stanford Business School with a master of arts in business research, where her focus was on organizational change and the effect of leadership training on performance. Prior to her graduate studies, Ms. Torok obtained a bachelor of arts in psychology from the University of California at Berkeley. Early affiliation with the United Nations Energy Resources Department led to her interest in, and continued engagement with, sustainability issues.

Erica Tucker-Bassin acts as a consultant to SAM (Sustainability Asset Management, Switzerland), and is currently completing market research in Canada for SAM. Prior to moving to Canada, Erica was responsible for SAM Research client services and communication. She was also an analyst for the entertainment, recreational products, and textile industries. Her previous work experience includes communication and knowledge management project work for Zurich Financial Services Group, as well as communication and environmental project work for the Swiss Organization for Facilitating Investments/KPMG. She also helped to establish and secure funding for the Environmental Management and Law Association in Budapest, Hungary. Erica received a master's degree in international economics from the University of Maastricht, Netherlands. She also holds a bachelor's degree in urban and regional studies from the College of Architecture, Art, and Planning at Cornell University, USA.

Sissel Waage is Director of the research program at The Natural Step's US office. She has been working on sustainability, conservation, and development issues for over ten years and has experience on three continents. Dr. Waage has conducted research on a range of topics, including natural-resource-based businesses and economies, community-based conservation, collaborative decision-making, and consensus-building processes. Prior to joining The Natural Step, she worked with Sustainable Northwest and facilitated the establishment of a new community conservation-based development organization in rural northeastern Oregon. Dr. Waage has also served as a program officer in the East and Southern Africa Program of the World Wide Fund for Nature (WWF), where she collaborated with public-sector and private-sector partners to design and manage conservation-based development projects. She has also worked at a forest research station and several other conservation and development organizations. Dr. Waage completed her PhD at the University of California, Berkeley, in the Department of Environmental Science, Policy, and Management, and received her bachelor of arts degree from Amherst College, in Massachusetts. She has also studied at the University of Oslo, in Norway, as a Fulbright Scholar, and at the National University of Singapore.

Allen L. White is Co-Founder and former Acting Chief Executive of the Global Reporting Initiative (GRI). He currently serves as Special Advisor to GRI, focusing on the North and Latin America. Dr. White is also Vice-President and Member of the Board of Tellus Institute, a Boston-based sustainability think-tank. He advises business, foundations, multilateral organisations, and governments on issues pertaining to sustainability accounting and reporting, corporate governance, and accountability practices.

Index